THE EVERYTHING.

Guide to Starting and Running a Catering Business

Dear Reader,

You picked up this book, in all likelihood, because you love cooking for others, and you dream about having your own business, perhaps leaving your current job. Everyone tells you that you should start your own catering business, but you're not quite sure what's involved and how you can make a living.

If this sounds about right, do yourself a favor and read on. This comprehensive guide for the beginning caterer who wants to gain a foothold and the established caterer who wants to grow, will let you know what's involved in starting and running a catering business. This book will tell you what skills you need, how to start a business, the biggest challenges you'll face, and new trends in catering.

One of the unique aspects of this book is that it not only contains practical information about catering, but also critical tips on how to position, sell, and market yourself, so that you actually find and retain paying clients. This book will take you step by step through the entire process of living your catering dream.

This guide is the first valuable tool you'll need to become a catering entrepreneur. It lists many important resources and includes the actual experiences of successful caterers, and it will help you create a unique, viable business.

Joyce Weinberg

The EVERYTHING® Series

Editorial

Innovation Director	Paula Munier
Editorial Director	Laura M. Daly
Executive Editor, Series Books	Brielle K. Matson
Associate Copy Chief	Sheila Zwiebel
Acquisitions Editor	Lisa Laing
Associate Development Editor	Elizabeth Kassab
Production Editor	Casey Ebert

Production

Director of Manufacturing	Susan Beale
Production Project Manager	Michelle Roy Kelly
Prepress	Matt LeBlanc Erick DaCosta
Interior Layout	Heather Barrett Brewster Brownville Colleen Cunningham Jennifer Oliveira
Cover Design	Erin Alexander Stephanie Chrusz Frank Rivera

Visit the entire Everything® Series at *www.everything.com*

THE

EVERYTHING®

GUIDE TO STARTING AND RUNNING A

CATERING BUSINESS

Insider advice on turning your
talent into a lucrative career

Joyce Weinberg

Aadams media

Avon, Massachusetts

*To my parents, my family, my son, Jonah, my friends and colleagues,
and to all the dedicated, hardworking caterers who
work to make their clients' events so special.*

An Everything® Series Book.
Everything® and everything.com® are registered
trademarks of F+W Publications, Inc.

Published by Adams Media, an F+W Publications Company
57 Littlefield Street, Avon, MA 02322 U.S.A.
www.adamsmedia.com

ISBN 10: 1-59869-384-0
ISBN 13: 978-1-59869-384-3

Printed in Canada.

J   I   H   G   F   E   D   C   B   A

Library of Congress Cataloging-in-Publication Data
Weinberg, Joyce.
Everything guide to starting and running a catering business / Joyce Weinberg.
p.   cm.
ISBN-13: 978-1-59869-384-3 (pbk.)
ISBN-10: 1-59869-384-0 (pbk.)
1. Caterers and catering. I. Title.
TX921.W44 2007
642'.4—dc22
2007015885

*This book is available at quantity discounts for bulk purchases.
For information, please call 1-800-289-0963.*

Contents

Acknowledgments

Caterers are very busy people, and I want to thank those who took the time to help me with this book. Special thanks to trade magazine publisher Gary Abeyta, caterer Jim Davis, food writer Deanne Moscowitz, and publicist Shelley Clark of Lou Hammond Associates. Bill Hansen was a tremendous help. Thanks also to Stephan Baroni of Hudson Yards Catering, Liz Neumark and Jo Herde of Great Performances, and Jeffrey Stillwell and Kimberly Sundt at Abigail Kirsch.

Thanks to Andrea Bass, Eric Gelb, and Robert Weinberg for reviewing some chapters.

Thanks to Joyce at NACE and Candy Wallace at AAPPC. Lancaster, Penn., caterer Sally Kramer helped me get started, and New York chef Janelle Palm helped keep me going with her encouragement. Thanks to Patsy Mohan for watching Jonah while I wrote the book. I'm grateful to my literary agent, Barb Doyen, for bringing me this opportunity and to my editor at Adams Media, Lisa Laing.

Top Ten Things You Need to Know about the Catering Business

1. Like all food businesses, catering is a business of pennies, so careful cost tracking and controls are needed to run a profitable business.

2. Catering requires a wide variety of skills in addition to excellent cooking; it involves everything from organization and logistics to finance and customer service.

3. To be a successful caterer, you need to love marketing and selling yourself and your services.

4. The catering business, if run efficiently, is generally more profitable than most restaurants, but less profitable than the nightclub business.

5. The biggest challenge in the catering business is finding and retaining enough good people to help you cook and serve.

6. There's always enough room in the industry for another creative and well-run business that serves delicious food.

7. Customers are looking to caterers to create an entertaining, restaurant-quality experience. Caterers do more than just cook and serve food: They create a whole environment, bringing their customers' dreams to life.

8. A catering business can be started with relatively little capital.

9. Running your own catering business will allow you to be as creative as you like.

10. Catering requires a tremendous amount of physical work, from transporting heavy items to standing on your feet cooking and serving for hours.

Introduction

The catering business is a dynamic, growing industry—and there will always be a demand for it. No one has figured out how to efficiently provide delicious food and drink in a festive atmosphere to hundreds—if not thousands—of guests without the old-fashioned hard work of a professional catering team.

Catering is here to stay, and the industry is continually attracting new talent with innovative ways of bringing great food and drink to clients. From new food station concepts to creative food display ideas, the catering business is constantly evolving. Today, celebrity chefs are starting their own catering enterprises because catering is *hot*! It's a high profile industry, filled with excitement and challenges.

Many people around the country depend on caterers to bring their special events to life. Caterers do it all, from serving the rich and famous in Los Angeles and New York to creating the wedding of a lifetime for a young couple in Atlanta or Milwaukee—and they never miss a beat. As a group, caterers are among the hardest working people in the country, especially during the holiday and wedding season.

All caterers have two things in common: passion and drive. Whether they run a small off-premise catering company in Idaho or a large catering business in Florida, all caterers are in the business because they love it. Few enter the catering business to make money. Making a living is great, but it's not what drives a caterer to wake up at 4 A.M. to prepare for a morning wedding. Seeing the smiling faces of guests enjoying a smoothly run event is what keeps caterers working so hard. Oh, and yes, getting paid for a job well done is very satisfying indeed.

Caterers have to be good at a lot of things—from cooking to selling to precise planning. They must have people skills in spades in order to fulfill their role of buyer, seller, employer, and planner.

Catering is an all-encompassing profession. It utilizes all of your abilities—both physical and mental. If you have a passion for food and for making people happy, you may well be suited to running your own catering business.

By reading this guide and by taking stock of your skills and abilities, you'll know by the end of Chapter 20 whether or not you're up to the challenge of the catering industry. By following the steps described in this book, you'll be well on your way to becoming a professional caterer or growing your existing business to the next level.

Only with the dedication, passion, and professionalism of creative food professionals like you will the industry continue to flourish and evolve. The future of the catering industry, dear reader, is up to you. May this guide inspire you, prepare you, and hasten you to launch your catering career. Best of luck!

Chapter 1

What Is Catering?

Caterers do everything from delivering sandwich trays for office lunch meetings to providing sumptuous beach lobster bakes for several thousand people. There are a variety of ways to gain the experience you need to become a successful caterer. Caterers come from all walks of life and work in cities and small towns across the country. Some operate independently, while others are sizeable corporate entities with dozens and even hundreds of employees. This chapter provides an introduction to the dreams and realities of the catering business.

What Does Catering Really Mean?

This book focuses on small and mid-sized independent caterers and discusses in detail how they operate, attract customers, and grow. The catering industry is a multibillion-dollar-a-year industry, involving tens of thousands of professionals and their staffs, serving millions of people a year.

Fact

According to *Webster's Dictionary*, *catering* means "to provide food and service for." It's a general definition, and it leaves a lot unexplained. For our purposes, caterers are men and women who work in licensed commercial kitchens, who are properly insured, and who are trained and skilled in preparing and serving a variety of foods to groups of guests.

While "providing food and service for" seems simple enough, there's a lot that goes into properly catering an event for a client. A successful caterer combines business savvy, culinary wisdom, and event planning expertise into one seamless enterprise.

A Moving Company with Perishables

One of the best ways to think about the catering business is to think of it in terms of a moving business with perishables. When you're transporting a five-tiered wedding cake from your commercial kitchen to a client's home twenty miles away, you're in the moving business. There's a lot of equipment lugging and ingredient schlepping, and there's no way to get around it.

Not only do you have to move many delicate objects from point A to point B without breaking them, you also have to maintain their temperature to keep the food safe. You'll be feeding a lot of people, and the last thing you want is to cause anybody to get sick.

☀ Alert

Perishable food must be kept at strict temperatures in order to be kept fresh and free from bacteria. You must keep foods out of the "danger zone" (40–140°F), where dangerous bacteria can grow. Take extra precautions when you are transporting food over long distances.

The Caterer as Juggler

Being a caterer involves mastering a multitude of skills and juggling many tasks at once. Merely being a great cook and having a flair for entertaining isn't enough. This is what makes the catering business such a tricky one. A good caterer is a good chef, a deft mover, a skilled planner, an adroit salesperson and marketer, an able business person, and a charming customer service representative all in one.

Catering combines the physicality of cooking, transporting, setting up, serving, and cleaning with the mental demands of planning and executing. Catering is a service business, and you're only as good as your next job. While having a good reputation is important, you can't ride on it for long. It's a fiercely competitive market, and businesses don't last without a lot of hard work and sweat.

Running Your Own Business

Becoming a caterer means starting and running your own business. You'll be responsible for everything from sales and marketing to procurement and staffing. Cooking is only one aspect of being a caterer.

E ssential

Running your own catering business means you're an entrepreneur, an innovator, and someone who recognizes opportunities and gathers resources to take advantage of them. You have to anticipate the market's needs, introduce new tastes and techniques, and separate yourself from your competition without making yourself too outlandish.

Having your own business has its positives and negatives. One thing is for sure: It's never dull or boring. Before you take the big leap and decide to start your own catering company, read this book carefully and evaluate your skill set. It will give you the tools to discover some of the most important skills required of successful caterers. You'll also have a chance to think about what you're good at, what you need to improve, and whether your skills are compatible with the business of catering.

Running your own business is a big responsibility. If you have an entrepreneurial flair and have always had a side interest in selling products or services, then you may enjoy the freedom that running your own business brings. However, think carefully before leaving a job with benefits, especially if you've never ventured off on your own in your professional life.

Fact

Catering is one of the most multidisciplinary careers you can have. It requires you to use several specialized skills at the same time. If you love cooking and multitasking and tend to get bored easily, catering might be the way to put your passions to work for you.

You may sit at your desk and daydream about having your own catering business, but the reality won't be as pretty. Having your own business means there's no safety net. At the beginning, you'll most likely be on your own. You may have a supportive spouse, great friends, and a helpful mentor, but the ultimate responsibility will be yours.

At your job there may be a billing department, a sales department, a marketing department, a product development lab, a manufacturing division, transportation and logistics departments, and a host of other departments from human resources to customer service. When you have your own catering business, you'll be all those departments—and you'll have to cook!

Running your own catering business gives you the freedom to do what you want without answering to a boss or manager. This is refreshing, but it's also daunting when you stop to consider what being your own boss entails. You'll have to breathe down your own neck, which is as tricky figuratively as it is physically. No one is going to check to make sure that you paid your vendor bills so that when you call to order next time, you'll still be a customer in good standing.

The variety of tasks can be both stimulating and overwhelming. Some people find the freedom of running their own business and controlling their own destiny exhilarating. Others find it scary and enjoy working as part of a large corporate team. By reading this book, you'll begin to understand what branching out on your own involves and whether it's the right move for you.

There are very fun parts of the business and less fun parts of the business, and this book explains them all. Overall, it's a fun business run by passionate professionals. Food is love to many people, so you'll be delivering a very powerful emotion.

E ssential

Consider the mundane when you plan how to run your business. Choose reliable Internet and telephone service providers so you can be sure the things you take for granted will work when you expect them to. Decide on a bank and familiarize yourself with all of its business options.

Fun Aspects of the Catering Business

One of the joys of the business is working with clients to design their special events. This process allows you to fulfill your client's vision for her occasion. Often, you'll be instrumental in fulfilling dreams for weddings, special anniversaries, or other once-in-a-lifetime events. While it's a big responsibility, having the chance to make people happy and show them what you can do is probably the main reason why you want to go into catering in the first place. You enjoy showing off your creative cooking skills and love to organize parties. You get tremendous satisfaction from seeing people enjoy themselves and devour your creations.

Working with Clients

Another perk of the catering business is meeting and working with a wide variety of people. This will add to the spontaneity of your daily life.

Clients come in all shapes and sizes. Some will have experience working with caterers, and others will not. Some will give you a budget and let you run free with all the details of the party. Other clients will have an exact vision for what they want and will specify everything from the color of the cocktail napkins to the size of the shrimp. Most clients are enjoyable to work with, and working with all types of clients has its rewards.

Getting Referrals and Repeat Business

Seeing repeat clients or being referred by former clients gives you a sublime sense of satisfaction. It means you are doing a good job and your clients trust you. This is the best way to get your business to grow and to establish a stellar reputation. All the public relations in the world can't accomplish what positive word of mouth from previous customers can do.

Getting Paid

There's no better feeling than doing a great job and getting paid for it. There's a great sense of accomplishment when you fill out the deposit slip and mail your check to the bank.

Cooking for the Event

You love to cook, and that's one of the main reasons you're pursuing a catering career. Being able to bring your culinary vision to reality is a lot of fun for you. It's not easy—the kitchen may be hot and you may be on your feet for hours—but it pays off when everything is done and ready to be served to the guests.

Dealing with Vendors and Staff

Working with professional suppliers and staff who like working with you is a great feeling. Unlike nine-to-five jobs, you may not work with the same people for forty hours a week, so working with your favorite business contacts is a treat.

Not-So-Fun Aspects of the Catering Business

Like any job, there's drudgery. There will be daily tasks associated with catering that you'd rather not do.

Hours of Ingredient Prep

One of the minuses of the catering business is the amount of time spent buying, washing, peeling, cutting, and measuring ingredients before you even cook them. Dream about the day that you'll be able to afford to hire someone to help you do this while you focus on selling and planning your catering jobs.

Cleanup

The kitchen cleanup and after-party cleanup involved with some of your jobs isn't the most fun, but it is part of the job. Often, you'll have to haul trash bags, restack rented tableware, and lug equipment after a long day. And remember, leaving a client's office or home neater than when you arrived is a sign of a quality caterer.

Paperwork and Invoicing

There's no way to escape it. You're operating a business, and that involves record keeping, paying your bills, and making sure clients pay you. Writing proposals, making adjustments, pricing jobs, billing clients, organizing deposits, arranging for food and other deliveries, paying taxes and local permit fees—it all requires discipline.

Working with Clients

Working with clients is generally an enjoyable process, but it's one of those unique factors that can be both positive and negative. Some clients will be more challenging than others. There will be clients who yell at you when they have a bad day and clients who ask for unreasonable changes at unreasonable hours, but it's important to learn to take a few deep breaths and think about your response before acting.

Transporting the Food

Whether you're carrying large platters of baked salmon from your truck to an outdoor tent or transporting a finished wedding cake and hundreds of hors d'oeuvres in a van, moving food is always an adventure. No matter what kind of catering you do, you'll have to transport food in various stages of preparation. This is especially challenging for two reasons: The food has to be kept at the proper temperature so it doesn't spoil or melt; and food, by nature, is delicate and doesn't like to be disturbed.

E Alert

Packing carefully and planning for the worst is always the best plan of attack. Experienced caterers know how to compensate for extra last-minute guests and food that gets ruined on the way to the event. Expect surprises and they won't seem so disastrous.

Knowing how to handle food that will be moved is a tricky and delicate operation. Experienced caterers know the tricks of the trade. They know what can be transported and what's best not included for that remote outdoor party, and they can tell you what should be assembled, finished, and decorated on-site and what can be done in the kitchen. Working for a caterer that handles large outdoor and off-site parties will help you learn the tricks of the trade.

While using a specially outfitted truck or van that has storage compartments, shelves, and other amenities is certainly helpful, mishaps happen to everyone. Bumps in the road, unexpected stops, even changes in humidity affect the food. The best caterers bring tools, edible glue, and an extra decorating medium to repair any last-minute emergencies.

Dealing with Vendors

Like clients, most vendors are pleasant enough to deal with. There are some, however, who are quite gruff and others who aren't exactly professional. Beware of the few who will try to take advantage of new business owners. Try to find vendors that you trust and can get along with. Hopefully you'll have relationships with them for years. They can provide you credit when you need it, they will talk about you to others in the industry, and they can also provide references and referrals.

Personal Chefs

Personal chefs are not recognized as caterers. They don't work in commercial kitchens, and they usually don't have experience cooking for and serving very large groups of people.

There is a great amount of variability in the skills that personal chefs have. Some personal chefs are self-taught and have never worked in professional kitchens; others have graduated from excellent culinary schools and have a lot of cooking experience.

✔**E**xpertise

Dave Lieberman is a self-taught cook who hosts a show targeted toward twenty-somethings on the Food Network, *Good Deal with Dave Lieberman*. In addition to his television show, he's a private chef and a cookbook author. Lieberman opened a catering business while he was still an undergraduate at Yale University.

In an effort to raise the level of qualifications in this growing and unregulated field, several trade organizations in the United States certify chefs. The U.S. Personal Chef Association (*www.uspca.com*) will certify personal chefs who meet the educational and experience guidelines it has established. Members need at least two years of eligible work experience, must have a current ServSafe certificate for food handling from the National Restaurant Association, and have to pass the USPCA written exam.

Should You Start as a Personal Chef?

If you've never been very entrepreneurial, feel restricted by limited resources, and aren't sure you're ready to leap into the catering profession, starting as an independent personal chef might be the right path to pursue. Here are some of the pros of being a personal chef:

- You're cooking.
- You'll have a set schedule and will be able to manage your time.
- It's often a good beginning for a catering business.
- It's easier than being a full-service caterer because there's no outsourcing.
- You'll be cooking mostly simple, casual meals for small numbers of people.
- There's less financial risk, and personal chefing requires less of a financial investment than a catering business.

Of course, there are cons as well:

- You won't really be your own boss—you'll be dependent on one or two clients.
- You're subject to the daily whims of your client.
- There's less variety than catering.
- You won't be as visible to potential clients.
- You'll be cooking mostly simple, casual meals for small numbers of people so make sure this type of cooking will keep you satisfied.

Personal chefing is a growing industry in the United States. Taking the personal chef route to explore your culinary passion is discussed in Chapter 7.

Chapter 2

Understanding the Catering Industry

The catering industry is a large, fractured industry with many players. Since caterers are usually located within an hour's drive from their party destination, the industry has tens of thousands of members, each with a small share of the entire market. The catering market is quite versatile, and it's easy to use your strengths to your advantage. Whether you specialize in casual picnics, corporate events, or black-tie weddings, there's something for everyone in catering.

Overview of Catering in the United States

There are more than 53,000 caterers listed in the U.S. yellow pages, not including hotel or restaurant caterers, and annual sales for the industry exceed $6 billion. Catering is a growing market for ambitious entrepreneurs. It is also a highly competitive industry, and you need to know about the market if you want to survive.

To give you a brief picture of the industry, take a look at the following survey completed by Catersource, a Chicago-based business that runs a large trade show for independent caterers and provides seminars for those in the industry. Catersource surveyed more than 300 independent caterers around the country. Most were well-established caterers in business for more than five years. Here are some of the results:

- Just over half of the businesses owned their production facility or kitchen; the remainder leased space. One percent had a different arrangement, and this seems to be growing with the rise of shared commercial kitchens.

- Two-thirds of the businesses said that their average party size was 100–250 guests.
- The average catering business owner works an average of 59 hours per week.
- All operators hired part-time staff during peak times.
- Nearly 80 percent focused on off-premise catering, while 20 percent were on-premise caterers, either operating in a stand-alone banquet facility or operating through a hotel, private club, restaurant, or other large venue.

Trade organizations are a valuable resource for a new caterer. They provide educational materials about starting your own catering business and offer opportunities for networking.

Ⓔ Fact

Two of the largest catering trade organizations are the National Association for Catering Executives (✐*www.nace.net*) and the International Caterers Organization (✐*www.icacater.org*). Both organizations host professional conferences, and they are an excellent source of industry information.

Joining a trade organization can save you time and money and provide you with new and creative ideas for growing your business. Have a business issue and don't know where to turn? A quick call to NACE or ICA will point you in the right direction. The contacts you meet through organization events can give you referrals for an accountant or lawyer in your area.

Catering Industry Segments

The catering business is divided into several areas. The easiest segment to track is the large-scale catering done by hotels and conference centers for corporate meetings, trade groups, and other similar events. Harder to measure are the tens of thousands of small catering businesses across the country run by individuals. This is generally good news for you because no one, not even your stiffest competition, will have much more knowledge of the industry than you do.

There is always room in the industry for another quality player to take a small share of business. It is relatively easy to get into the business since it doesn't require much special equipment, proprietary knowledge, or huge amounts of investment. If you can make it through the first few years and grow your client base, you can probably stay in business quite a long time, as long as you maintain your high quality of food and service.

The bad news is that with so many players, there's a lot of competition and you have to work hard to stand out from the crowd. The following sections introduce the different types of catering. Consider which types are best suited to your image of a catering business, which will complement your skills, and which will give you the most visibility.

Off-Premise-Only Caterers

A large segment of the business consists of off-premise caterers, and this is the segment that you will be operating in. These are companies that bring ingredients and staff to a home, office, or other location and take care of the food for the client's party, meeting, or other event. They may bring partially cooked or assembled ingredients to the location and finish the foods on-site. They will definitely bring prepped ingredients, enough for the number of guests agreed upon in the contract.

These firms bring cooks, servers, and other staff as needed, including bartenders and grillers. Off-premise firms vary in size and complexity. Some are small and rent tables, linens, and stemware for their clients. Others are sizeable entities, complete with a fleet of trucks; their own tables, linens, and tabletop items; and a full-time, year-round staff.

Restaurants

Most restaurants offer some type of catering service, since they already have a licensed kitchen and staff. It makes sense for most restaurants to sell catering items because it provides added revenue for the business. Restaurants already employ prep cooks and chefs and have to pay rent or a mortgage, so the more revenue they can generate to offset their overhead, the more profitable they'll be. Party platters, cakes, and other catering items can be prepared during slow times of the day in between meal services.

Since restaurant chefs are already adept at devising menus, creating a catering menu is a relatively easy process. They're already established and set up with food vendors and suppliers, so ordering food for catering jobs is simple. Little special equipment is needed for restaurants to turn out catered items. All that is required are some platters, special packing materials, and extra refrigerator space.

 Fact

Some restaurants say they cater but aren't really set up for it. Other restaurants get a substantial amount of their revenue from catering. When doing competitive research, make sure to ask the restaurant owner or manager how much catering they do and what kinds of events they cater.

If the restaurant doesn't have a separate party room for on-site parties, the owners may offer to rent out the entire restaurant for parties. Often they'll do this only during slow times of the week or year or they will charge the equivalent of a weekend night's business. If the restaurant has a separate space for parties, they're more likely to have a more sophisticated catering program and an in-house event person.

National restaurant chains are part of this segment of the business, and they can afford to advertise on television. Red Lobster, for example, sells platters of shrimp and other seafood that can be ordered by phone and picked up.

If a restaurant is known for its great gourmet sandwiches, fried chicken, salads, or brownies, it probably offers platters of these items for office and in-home parties. Sometimes the dishes that a restaurant is known for, however, don't travel well, so the restaurant can't offer its house specialties for off-site events. French fries, soufflés, and other delicate and intricate dishes that aren't designed for catering can't be sold for off-site enjoyment.

While this means that you'll count local restaurants as your competition, don't despair. Most restaurants don't have separate catering divisions, so their marketing and customer service for catered events isn't that evolved. Restaurants focus on the guests eating in their dining rooms. You, as an independent caterer, will focus exclusively on your guests and their needs, whatever they are. You will be totally focused on your customers and able to service them better than a restaurant where catering is just an added revenue stream.

Gourmet/Grocery Stores

Well-known gourmet store chains and upscale grocery chains like Whole Foods Markets and Food Emporium also offer catering services. Single-location gourmet havens like Zingerman's in Ann Arbor, Michigan, provide catering items in addition to their standard on-site fare.

Grocery and gourmet store catering allows customers to order a specific quantity of food and pick it up later, although delivery options are sometimes available. Many of these stores have full kitchens and staff to prepare food for their deli sections, and they sell catering items to bring in added sales. Many of the larger stores have glossy, full color brochures with professionally stylized shots of their menu items.

E ssential

Many gourmet stores display their extensive catering menus and offer copies for customers to take. Start a collection of these menus and use them for menu-writing ideas. Look at the item descriptions and study how the menus use words to convey the tastes of the dishes.

The biggest factor grocery store catering has going for it is convenience. It allows customers to take care of their weekly shopping and special party needs all in one stop. Particularly in more rural areas, where there are likely to be fewer caterers, grocery stores provide food for casual entertaining.

Gourmet stores usually offer fairly sophisticated catering menus and services. Sometimes they'll even be able to provide service staff. Dean & DeLuca caters many off-site parties and provides clients with trained service staff if needed.

Large Caterers

The largest catering companies have several divisions and specialize in several different types of catering. Brooklyn-based Smokin' Grill has a full-service division, an outdoor division, and a self-service division. Similar catering companies either have their own building or have contracts to operate out of certain locations.

Some large caterers do both on-premise catering and off-premise catering. Bill Hansen Catering, a large caterer in Southern Florida, has its own villa for on-premise catering in Coral Gables, Florida, and does off-premise catering at dozens of other venues in the area, from the Dauer Museum of Classic Cars to the Miami Metro Zoo.

On-Premise-Only Caterers

Some large caterers only serve food in their own catering halls. These firms do nothing but host large parties such as weddings, confirmations, bar and bat mitzvahs, and local award ceremonies. These are destination catering halls, which are designed to look good and to prepare and serve many people efficiently. On any given weekend day during the spring, summer, and fall, multiple weddings, bar mitzvahs, and anniversary parties may be happening on the same day. The kitchen might prepare food for three to five thousand people on a particular Saturday.

Catering halls are large buildings with spacious rooms for entertaining, commercial kitchens, special rooms for brides and bridal parties, bathroom facilities, and parking lots. They have no guest rooms for overnight guests.

Hotels and Conference Centers

Hotels and conference centers around the country specialize in hosting large groups for meetings, trade shows, and other big events. Many hotels have their own conference center with a large catering kitchen that can handle events for hundreds, if not thousands. The Marriott and Hyatt hotel chains have conference centers adjacent to their properties across the country.

Conference centers are often independent operations with special amenities and rooms for hosting large corporate and non-profit groups for sales meetings and other functions. They are often located in suburban and rural settings and offer guests peace and quiet. They can offer catering services, overnight accommodation, audiovisual equipment, and special activities for guests such as golf, boating, and hiking.

While you will not be competing with this segment of the industry directly, it's important to know what's going on in the industry. Also, smaller hotels and conference centers without large catering facilities may need the services of an independent caterer from time to time.

Outdoor Caterers

Some caterers specialize in catering outdoor picnics and events, including large tent parties. These caterers usually have a special truck outfitted with cooling bins, running water, and sometimes even an oven. These specialists might be a division of a large catering company or a separate company. Often these companies will bring large grills and rotisseries so that they can grill meats and vegetables right in front of guests for parties.

Outdoor catering is particularly tricky because it involves dealing with wind, insects, and geographical and meteorological challenges. The outdoor catering business is not recommended for the catering novice or the faint of heart. In the northern states, the outdoor catering business is highly seasonal, so owners must do all their business between April and October.

✓**E**xpertise

Specialty Caterers

Caterers are only limited by their own imaginations. For customers who want something unique, there is a legion of niche caterers that do one thing only and do it well.

There are also caterers that specialize in children's parties, dessert parties, and other specific types of occasions. Specialty catering is where you might be able to find a niche in your location. Use your imagination and come up with an original catering idea that can be a novelty at parties.

Kosher Caterers

Another segment of the catering business is represented by kosher caterers. While these caterers may differ in the type of kosher certification they have, they all specialize in either meat and fish dishes or in dairy dishes. The same caterer won't offer both types of dishes at the same event. All kosher caterers will use strictly kosher ingredients. They will not use nonkosher seafood (shrimp, lobster, scallops, mussels, and other shellfish), and they will not mix cheese and other dairy products with poultry, veal, beef, or lamb.

There are a wide variety of kosher caterers across the country. Many large kosher caterers have exclusive contracts with the catering halls at large synagogues and provide the food for all weddings, bar and bat mitzvahs, and other temple events.

Some kosher caterers have their own mobile kitchens in trucks, so that they don't have to use someone else's kitchen or one that may not be strictly kosher. Like other restaurants, many kosher restaurants and delis will prepare their food in platters and large portions for off-site parties. In general, kosher caterers charge a premium over nonkosher caterers because kosher meats and other kosher products are more costly than many non-kosher items. Kosher caterers follow Jewish tradition and laws and can't start cooking or serving food on Saturdays until an hour after sundown, when the Sabbath ends. This is the reason that during the summer, kosher affairs start late on Saturday night and guests often aren't served dinner until midnight.

E ssential

There are several different styles of kosher caterers. For the different Jewish groups in the United States—Ashkenazis (from Eastern Europe), Sephardis (from Spain) and Mizrahis (from Iran, Iraq, Turkey, etc.)—kosher caterers tend to specialize in either traditional Eastern European dishes, traditional Sephardic dishes, or traditional Arab dishes.

Of course, you don't have to be Jewish to be a kosher caterer. If there is a large, growing traditional Jewish population in your area, you may want to investigate this segment of the business.

Ethnic Caterers

There are caterers who specialize in serving their communities' particular cultural needs. Think about your local community and the holidays and events they celebrate. Italian communities pull out all the stops for the San Gennaro festival, and Russian communities celebrate Maslenitsa, the spring festival. Some caterers specialize in Sweet 15 parties for *la quinceañera* celebrations. Just like kosher catering, you do not need to celebrate these occasions yourself, but you do need to understand and respect them.

Twenty-First-Century Catering

Catering is a constantly evolving field. Market shifts introduce more clients to catering, and new trends in food sources and preparation affect your business.

Commitment Ceremonies

More than 2 million American couples wed every year. Almost half the total cost of an average wedding is spent on the reception and catering. One segment in particular is growing within the wedding catering arena—large celebrations for gay weddings and commitment ceremonies. Caterers and wedding planners who cater to the gay market in their areas are finding many new customers. With gay rights on the front burner of the American political landscape and many state legislatures taking up the issue of gay marriage, the size, intricacy, and number of large celebrations for gay unions is expanding.

Natural, Organic, and Local Ingredients

As recently as ten years ago, caterers could use ingredients from just about anywhere. Fish was fish, beef was beef, and milk was milk. Caterers didn't have to be concerned with where their produce, poultry, seafood, and cheeses were grown, caught, or made, since customers weren't particularly concerned. As long as the food was fresh and prepared well, customers were satisfied.

Today, the culinary landscape has changed, and customers demand to know exactly what type of beef you'll be using, where the fish is from, and where the tomatoes and corn were grown. There have been huge changes in the food industry over the last generation that have caused customers to be more concerned about where their food comes from and how it was grown and raised.

Organic dairy products and meat products are vastly different from their conventional counterparts. The animals are not given hormones or antibiotics. Many organically raised animals are grass-fed and therefore require more grazing land. Because of their grass diet they have a lower fat content. Organic milk is worth the premium, especially for children and for producing flavorful dairy products like artisanal cheeses and ice creams.

Demand for large amounts of quick, convenient foods spurred the use of pesticides, antibiotics, preservatives, and chemicals to increase crop yields and meat production. The result is that most of our food supply is tainted with chemicals and is composed of overly processed foods. The natural vitamins and fiber have been stripped out for processing ease and have been added back in for fortification.

E **Fact**

"Certified organic" is a subset of organic foods. It's a government-regulated process that requires producers to follow specific rules and methods in their growing. If you will be eating the skin or leaf of a food, like certain fruits or vegetables, organic versions are safest. Skins and leaves are more likely to have been exposed to and to have absorbed chemical and pesticide residues.

Locally Grown and Sustainable

Genetically modified foods, including grains and vegetables, are making the public uneasy. No one knows what the long-term effects of growing and eating these products will be. Over-fishing the seas has caused a shortage of many types of fish. To compensate, businesses are trying to cultivate fish in farms, where fish are no longer free to swim and eat what they want. Instead, they are kept in pools or tanks and fed processed food. Without having to swim much for their supper, their fat layers are increased, and consequently, so is their flavor and nutrient content.

Small farmers, dairy farmers, and ranchers are making a comeback. Not only are consumers demanding organic and naturally raised products in their local grocery stores, but they're learning from eating out at independent restaurants that products grown locally taste better. Many chefs around the country, especially today's younger cooks, are learning that it makes sense to support locally grown and raised products.

E ssential

The best products often come from small, local farmers, who grow products and raise animals in a natural, organic way. If you establish a relationship with local farmers, you'll have the highest quality ingredients at fair prices. The result will be wonderful dishes to serve to happy customers.

Chefs feature pasture-fed beef and heirloom tomatoes on their menus, in addition to a wide array of locally available products, for several reasons:

- **The products taste better.** Instead of buying tomatoes that are bred to survive sixty days from the vine to the consumer's sandwich, local ingredients are grown with natural fertilizer and bred for flavor. They won't last nearly as long as their commercial cousins, but they sure are juicier and have more flavor.
- **It makes good economic sense.** Supporting locally grown products supports the local economy and creates jobs.
- **It makes environmental sense.** Shipping goods over long distances requires massive amounts of fossil fuels. The less distance a product has to travel, the less fossil fuels are burned.
- **The products are healthier.** Handmade cheese isn't bright orange because small producers don't use chemical colors and additives. When was the last time you saw a cow give orange milk? Small producers can't afford expensive pesticides and chemicals. They rely on old-fashioned methods to grow and make what they produce. Like caterers, they are driven by passion to make the best product they can.

- **Natural and organic ingredients can command a price premium.** While the organic and natural market is still small, and demand is strong for these artisanal or handmade products, these ingredients can cost on average 20–50 percent more than conventionally grown or raised ingredients. Restaurants can charge more for these ingredients and make a higher profit margin on some of their dishes.

The people who buy organic eggs and milk at the supermarket and who eat grass-fed beef and wild Pacific salmon at restaurants are the same people who entertain clients, friends, and family and hire caterers. The demand for natural, local, and organic ingredients has spread to the catering industry through its clients. No longer can you get away with buying conventional ingredients from big conglomerates.

E Fact

The Organic Trade Association (OTA) in Greenfield, Massachusetts, estimates that 23 percent of U.S. consumers buy organic products weekly. The market for organic poultry, meat, and fish has doubled within the past few years.

Know Your Local Cheese Makers, Growers, and Ranchers

Caterers need to know who grows the best fruits and vegetables in their area and who raises the best chickens and beef. While more time and care has to be taken with food procurement, the good news is that you can establish a close relationship with local growers. As a small local business, you have a lot in common with your suppliers. You work hard and struggle to make the best product available, just like they do. You can help each other promote your businesses. You can tell your guests where you bought the ingredients for your delicious leek and cheddar quiche, and your local grower can recommend you to cater area celebrations.

All cooks know that fresher, tastier ingredients end up making fresher, tastier dishes. No matter who the chef is, there's no way that canned tomatoes and tinned tuna end up tasting like line-caught tuna and ripe heirloom tomatoes. Using the freshest ingredients makes the caterer's job easier. Foods can be cooked simply, allowing their natural flavors to flourish. There's no need to mask or create flavors with sharp spices or heavy sauces.

✓Expertise

Dan Barber, a young New York chef, is a master of using sustainable ingredients. At Stone Barns, about an hour's ride north of Manhattan, he slaughters his own pigs and grows his own vegetables right on the old Rockefeller estate.

Consumers are demanding healthy, organic, and local foods, and this is not a fad that will disappear next year. This trend should be reflected in your cooking philosophy, as well as in the ingredients you use and the dishes you serve. Using more locally produced ingredients means certain things will be in and out of season during various times of the year.

Catering as Edutainment

As clients ask for better and more sophisticated ingredients, caterers are responding to rising requests to teach about food and cultures through entertainment, or edutainment. Some high-end affairs around the country use their multimillion-dollar catering budgets to demand that their caterers and event designers re-create entire cultures, buildings, interiors, and atmospheres for their events. From new product launches to black-tie charity balls, today's events require caterers to be more creative than ever.

While your potential clients' catering budgets may not have nine figures—or even six—ideas and themes that start out at big events get media coverage and are copied and scaled down for other catered events. Clients who attend grand galas often challenge their local caterers to do a smaller version of what they saw. The more you as a caterer know about your food, its origins, and how it's made, the more value you can offer your clients.

Increasingly, clients expect the food to be the entertainment. People are interested in tasting things from around the world, and it's possible to offer clients varietal food tastings of exotic foods.

✓Expertise

Some entrepreneurs offer guided tastings as entertainment for private and corporate events. One such innovative firm is New York Food Tours and Events, which teaches clients all over the New York, New Jersey, and Connecticut area about different types of handmade and varietal foods. It offers tastings of varietal honeys and cheeses and guides food and wine pairings.

The more you can offer quality ingredients, delicious dishes, and knowledge about what you're serving, the more valuable and irreplaceable your services will be to your clients. In this way, you can distinguish yourself from other caterers.

The catering industry may be larger than you thought, but that means it has room for professional players who offer something different. Whether it's your ability to turn an average room into a tropical beach or your gift for instilling a passion for locally grown and handmade foods in your clients and guests, there's a niche in the industry for you. Composed of mostly small and medium-sized players, the catering business is an industry that rewards hard work, attention to detail, and creativity. Recipes aren't trademarked, and neither are décor schemes or serving methods. Draw inspiration from other events, menus, and dishes. Improve on them and make them your own.

Chapter 3

Required Skills for a Caterer

Catering might seem like the right career move as you're lying in bed envisioning how you could've done a better job with your friend's holiday buffet than she did. But there's a lot more to running a catering business than meets the eye. Not only do you have to be a skilled chef, a mover of delicate and perishable items, a master planner, and a savvy entrepreneur all at the same time, but you have to do it looking as cool and stress-free as possible with a smile on your face.

Is Catering for You?

The catering business is not for the lazy or risk averse. For those who love sitting behind a desk all day, catering is not the profession for you. If you love keeping busy, juggling many things at once, working under tight deadlines, orchestrating projects, and bringing enjoyment to others, then maybe catering could provide the right fit for you.

⚡ Alert

Caterers must be able to work well under stress. People who love catering enjoy the constant time pressures and are always faced with new challenges, from being short staffed and pleasing demanding clients to dealing with late or incomplete deliveries. The fun comes in solving problems, pulling off the event on time, and pleasing a client.

Above all, becoming a caterer means starting and running your own business. Cooking is just one aspect of being a caterer. You must do a lot of preliminary work before you even step into the kitchen. Starting a catering business entails developing a concept, planning menus, marketing your services, and convincing a client to pay you for catering their event.

The Many Hats of a Caterer

Caterers wear many hats, and only one of them resembles the familiar white chef's hat. There are many responsibilities to be fulfilled, including marketing and sales, planning, and financial management.

Professional Chef

At the beginning you'll have the lofty title of executive chef, but you may also be sous chef, line cook, prep cook, and dishwasher, too! You'll need to be knowledgeable about all aspects of food safety and handling, as well as kitchen safety and accident prevention. You'll also have to establish a control system to minimize waste, spoilage, and theft.

E Fact

Kitchen safety encompasses many practices. You already know the obvious (keep cleaning chemicals away from food), but there may be some things you haven't considered. If you are lucky enough to have some say in the design of the kitchen, make sure the floors are water resistant and made of nonslip materials.

You'll be purchasing ingredients, determining food costings, and writing the menus. You'll have to master each station of the kitchen to develop and test recipes, to minimize food costs, and to ensure your recipes work consistently well for large numbers of servings.

Project Manager

To begin a project such as organizing a party for eighty-five people, you'll have to consult with the client, plan the menus, order supplies from vendors, plan out the preparation and event timelines, hire extra help if necessary, arrange for transportation and/or delivery, handle the contract and monies, and cook and prepare the food. In addition you'll have to arrange for rentals and any décor, entertainment, or audiovisual needs that you're hiring subcontractors for.

Much of catering is figuring out how all the components are going to come together as one at precisely the right time. Everything for a catered event has to be planned down to the finest detail. Caterers who run events create timelines not by the day but by the hour, so they know what has to happen when. This may sound like overkill, but it's not. If you've ever had a wedding or thrown a party, you know how quickly time can go by. Someone has to plan when the toasts are going to be made and let the speakers know when to begin. Someone has to tell the kitchen when the main course is to be served to 400 guests and has to warn the kitchen if there's a delay. If no one orchestrates the event, the day will turn into chaos.

Customer Service Representative

Caterers have to be cheerleaders and problem solvers every day. Not only do you have to understand your client's needs to develop a menu and proposal he likes, but you have to work with him, often over a period of months, accommodating questions, changes, and special requests.

E ssential

The real customer service savvy comes the day of the event, when you're tired from hours of preparations and you have to be all smiles and full of energy. Catering demands that you be able to defuse a situation without ever appearing flustered, and you exhibit patience as you strive to please your client's every whim all the time.

Last minute problems always arise, and you have to stay flexible to deal with them. Rain delays many of the guests, so the serving timetable gets pushed back and your filets are in danger of drying out. Six people who said they weren't coming to the party suddenly appear at the front door, yelling "surprise," and they need to be fed.

Someone else remembers he's allergic to shellfish and needs an alternative to the bouillabaisse you're serving. Your client's schnauzer has somehow managed to knock your cookie platter off the counter and onto the floor. You have to quickly invent a dessert alternative.

Professional Server and Cleaner

Until you can afford, find, and train an excellent staff, you're the chief bottle washer and cook. You'll have to set up the party, making sure you've brought everything from the vegetable side dishes to the toothpicks. You must also help serve the guests.

E Fact

> Every good caterer must include basic repair tools and cleaning supplies in her equipment lists. Everyone on your team should know where duct tape, clean rags, all-purpose cleaner, fresh batteries, and other handy items are stowed.

For a large party, you'll need to hire serving help to provide drink refills, restock rolls, and clear away used plates, cutlery, and glasses. You'll have to oversee your staff, making sure they are servicing the guests and attending to their needs. After the party, you'll have to clean up the site, gather the trash, and repack your supplies so that you find everything for the next job.

Marketing Manager

Every caterer has to assertively market herself. With such a highly competitive industry, you can't expect the phone to start ringing as soon as you announce you're a caterer. You have to spread the word about your services and your new business as creatively and as inexpensively as possible. You'll have to learn to be an astute guerrilla marketer in order to grow your client list.

Salesperson

You have to venture out into the market to sell yourself and your services, so there's no room for shyness. You'll pick whom you want to sell to, determine what to charge them, and negotiate with clients. You don't get to practice your kitchen magic if you don't sell your services. Like it or not, selling becomes more important than cooking, especially at the beginning.

The Caterer's Skill Set

Wearing a multitude of different hats is all in an average day for a caterer. As long as you're an adept quick-change artist, you'll be a great caterer. This career requires a certain type of personality, versatility, and skill. Before you commit time, energy, and money and quit your day job, have a heart-to-heart with yourself and ask yourself these questions.

Are You a Detail Person?

It should really rankle you to see things done sloppily or haphazardly, but you should be able to revel in things that are done cleanly and to exact specifications. If you notice nitpicky details like lint on a friend's shirt or fingerprints on a glass when you're seated at a restaurant, you have the crucial eye for detail a successful caterer needs. Maybe you critique how dishes are plated when you eat out, or perhaps you find that nothing exasperates you more than surveying your Aunt Mary's Thanksgiving feast and knowing everything is cold because her timing was all off. These little signs show you that details are important to you.

If you'd like to strengthen your attention to detail even further, take classes in pastry decorating, accounting, and other disciplines that require exact detail. If you enjoy these classes, then there's hope that you'll excel at catering.

Do You Have a Good Memory?

You easily remember what needs to be done and when it needs to happen, and you recall your colleague Nicholas from the Nashville office commented on his love of natural peanut butter the one time you met him last year. Even if you can't remember Nicholas from Nashville, you can compensate by taking complete, timely notes about client requests and deadlines and invent mnemonics so that you can remember clients' names. You'll also need to be very organized and keep an accurate calendar and timelines for projects. Managing with sticky notes plastered everywhere won't work.

E ssential

Write everything down. Keep track of your daily schedule, and keep a file for each of your clients with meticulous notes about what they want, what you've agreed on, and when their payments are due. Keep a calendar on your wall with the dates that each payment is due. Otherwise, you'll lose track of your accounts receivable and have trouble managing your cash flow.

Even with a great memory, you'll have a lot of projects with many details, tasks, and steps to complete. You'll need to find an organizational system that works for you in whatever mode(s) you prefer—handwritten, computerized, or on a personal digital assistant (PDA).

Many organizational companies provide binders and software for computers and PDAs. Most binder systems have special pages that allow you to record detailed to-do lists. You can easily take meeting notes and cross-reference lists and ideas so that you keep organized for clients. There are forms to help you track bills, phone calls, and other details. Project management forms break up responsibilities into smaller, manageable actions to prevent you from becoming overwhelmed.

PDAs are commonplace, and many business owners and managers wouldn't last a day without them. If you're technology friendly, enjoy using a tiny keyboard, and feel the need to be continually connected to everything, maybe a PDA is for you. If you're just getting computer savvy and don't use many features of your cell phone, don't feel compelled to run your business on a PDA. If you're not absolutely comfortable with it, it will cause you more frustration than it's worth.

Some companies also offer seminars that will teach you skills for staying focused on goals to prevent you from getting bogged down in details. These seminars are particularly helpful if you feel like you're not accomplishing as many important things as you should during a given week or month. Calendar planning software can help you to stay organized by reminding you about important events you have scheduled on a particular day. You can input tasks and journal entries and plan things far in advance.

 Fact

Project management software loaded onto your computer can help you manage your various client events. There are software programs designed especially for caterers that allow you to keep track of everything from event floor plans to outstanding client accounts.

Are You Action Oriented?

You cannot wait to start new projects, and you begin work as soon as possible to make the most use of the time you have before your deadline. Catering requires a take-charge attitude and a person who likes to get things done.

Skilled procrastinators need not apply. Catering requires an awful lot of meticulous planning and execution. All-nighters may work for some jobs, but there's no way you can cater a dinner for eighty starting the night before.

Are You a Project Planner?

You are always the one who plans evenings out for your spouse or friends. You single-handedly plan your vacation itinerary and pack for the whole family. Feeling comfortable managing large, complex projects at work or for a volunteer position is an important indicator that you can handle the rigors of catering.

If you haven't professionally managed multifaceted projects before, take a course or seminar in project management. Get some practice in planning and organizing a large event by volunteering for a charity or taking on a new project at work. The more events you plan and run, the more efficient your technique becomes. And the more projects you manage, the more you'll be able to juggle.

Do You Enjoy Logistical Planning?

Do you like to think about how all that luggage is going to fit into your car, or how you're going to get the cake, punch bowl, and soup in good shape to your cousin's party? If you don't naturally think like a logistician, take a course in logistics planning for the food service industry. Logistics planning is a part of project planning, and in the off-premise catering business, it's a huge piece.

Are You Organized?

People admire how much you accomplish in a day and marvel at the fact that you can find what you're looking for 95 percent of the time. Your children and partner depend on you to be the organized one, and you always show up for appointments on time and meet your deadlines. Organization is a key part of catering. Often you'll be working on multiple jobs at the same time. You'll need to be able to keep them straight in your mind.

Do You Have High Energy and Stamina?

Caterers need to have the ability to run around and do many things at once for hours on end. If that's not you, you'll have to get into decent shape. Start an exercise regimen of walking fast enough to get your heart rate elevated, but slow enough that you can carry on a conver-sation with a person next to you. Start with a mile a day and build up to walking five to six miles a day within one to one-and-a-half hours. You'll also need to do weight-bearing exercises at least three times a week to be strong enough to lift heavy pots and platters of food.

Catering requires a lot of physical work. Your body needs to cooperate when you ask it to transport food and supplies and stand for hours on end over a hot stove.

Do You Enjoy Prep Cooking?

A prep cook is at the lowest rung of the cooking staff in the restaurant or commercial kitchen. He is in charge of preparing or prepping the ingredients that will be needed for the day's meals. In short, the prep cook does the peeling, chopping, trimming, cutting, weighing, and measuring. It's grunt work, plain and simple.

You should consider chopping vegetables, deveining shrimp, and making sandwiches for the gang part of what makes catering fun. You can develop skills to make food preparation more efficient, but caterers inevitably spend a lot of time preparing food.

E ssential

Catering requires excellent knife skills. You'll need to mince, chop, slice, and dice efficiently and safely. While food processors can help, you'll still have to cut herbs and onions by hand and trim meats and fish. High quality knives are a worthwhile investment.

Do You Enjoy Working with Your Hands?

Your hands feel empty unless you're doing something with them. Perhaps you use them to make meatloaf, sculpt, or garden. Maybe tinkering with car engines or repairing broken clocks is more your realm of expertise. Whatever you feel most comfortable with, you're not afraid to get your hands dirty. If you pride yourself on having soft, callous-free hands, ask yourself if you'd be happier and have a greater sense of fulfillment working more directly with your hands. Catering might be your chance. Take some pastry decorating classes, a craft class, or a sculpture class to discover if you relish feeling different textures and producing something with your own hands.

Are You a People Person?

Meeting new people and networking come naturally. Does this sound familiar? Caterers need to be generally outgoing people, so if you fit into this category, catering could be a good profession.

 Fact

Caterers work with many different kinds of people. Even if you choose a very specific niche, such as catering for local business meetings and picnics, you will likely encounter a wide variety of client management styles that run the gamut from strictly professional to indecisive to possibly even rude and overbearing. You need to be able to work with all of them.

The thought of going to a party or making a sales presentation should make you feel a little thrill of anticipation. Catering is a people business. There's no way to avoid it. You're providing a service in addition to food, and you're going to have to work with a lot of people. You'll be marketing yourself and your business, continually selling and meeting with your clients.

Are You Flexible?

Caterers must be able to go with the flow and manage change well. One thing is certain in the catering business, and that is that nothing is certain. Things change minute to minute, and you have to be flexible and adapt quickly to current circumstances. Surprises are the norm, from unavailable ingredients to inclement weather to unexpected guests.

Scoring

If you've been truly honest with yourself and answered yes to all of the questions, ask your spouse/partner, work colleagues, and friends the same questions and see if they agree with your assessment. If they agree that you'd make a great caterer, it's a good sign that your gut reaction is right. If you answered no to one of the questions, don't despair. You still have the potential to be a good caterer, but you'll need to modify your behavior and compensate for skills you lack. If you answered no to more than one or two categories, catering may not be the career route that would best complement your skills.

Acquiring Chef Skills

There's no faking chef skills such as knife techniques, kitchen shortcuts, kitchen safety, and efficiency. If you weren't taught by a professionally trained chef, it's worth your time and money to take an intensive class in chef training. The class will pay for itself in the time you save prepping for catering jobs and the money you save not wasting ingredients.

Alert

Unless you've worked in restaurant kitchens, you need to learn how to work safely in a commercial kitchen. There are good reasons why chefs either go to school or work their way up in a restaurant kitchen: Cooking for large numbers of people requires safe food handling, efficiency, technique, and timing.

Cooking dinner for eight at home is one thing, but being paid to cook and serve a meal for people you don't know is another. The people who hire you will be examining what you do and how you do it. They'll be looking to see how clean you and your habits are. The last thing you want to do is get someone sick from undercooked or spoiled food.

Acquiring Business Skills

It's a good idea to study up on basic business skills such as cash management, computer skills, proposal writing, and sales and marketing techniques. You don't want to learn about them after you've started your own business; a trial-by-fire method will only waste your time and money. Either take a practical class or get a part-time job where you'll be able to learn and apply these skills.

Alert

Some colleges and universities offer courses specifically geared toward aspiring caterers. Take classes in both food preparation and catering management. You'll learn time-saving kitchen skills, as well as how to run a profitable business.

Don't make the mistake of thinking that the catering business is mainly cooking skills. It's not. It's a profession that requires a multitude of skills.

Cash Management

You'll need to know how to keep bank accounts, how to invoice customers, track accounts receivable, negotiate with vendors, and prepare costings for each menu and profit and loss statements for each job. Speak with your bank to find out what programs they have to help you manage your accounts. Some banks even provide training for small business managers.

Computer Skills

In this day and age it's unrealistic for anybody starting a business not to use a computer. You'll need to know how to use a word processing program to write proposals and marketing materials.

Essential

Caterers need to be Internet-savvy to survive in today's business climate. Clients will most likely want to correspond with you electronically, and your Web site will attract clients to you.

Easy financial management and bill-paying software programs can make managing your business easier. Consider accounting software, calendar management programs, or special catering software.

Proposal Writing

Good writing skills are a must. You won't be able to sell your services if you can't write a solid, succinct, and creative proposal. Check with local colleges and universities to find out whether they have any proposal-writing workshops or classes.

Marketing

You'll need to understand the basics of marketing—whom to target, how to price your services, what kind of products and menus to offer, and how to understand your customer. With this knowledge, you will be able to compete in your area and find a defendable niche. As with proposal writing, see if any local colleges or organizations offer basic marketing classes.

Sales

If asking people to buy something from you makes you queasy, you'll need to overcome that feeling to be a caterer. Having a catering business requires you to sell yourself. You must first believe in yourself and what you have to offer. If you don't have confidence in yourself, you can't expect anyone else to have confidence in you, either.

E Fact

You'll need to know the basics of selling strategy and technique. Learn the mechanics of a sale: how to approach a prospective customer, ask questions, and listen carefully to your client's needs; submit a proposal; close the deal; and follow up after the sale is completed.

It's crucial to be honest with yourself about the skills you lack or need to improve. If you strengthen your skills, you can avoid nasty surprises after you've launched your catering business. Identify your skill gaps, and find ways to educate yourself. There are many resources to take advantage of and many opportunities to gain knowledge, from local community colleges and cooking schools to adult education programs. Another way to gain skills is to seek a part-time job or internship at a restaurant or catering company. Whatever route you choose, make sure that you get some hands-on, practical training. Distance learning via the Internet is not recommended for learning how to debone a fish or assemble a wedding cake!

Deciding Not to Be a Caterer

If you're dejected after reading this chapter, evaluate why. Is it because you're overwhelmed? Is it because you didn't realize all that's involved in starting a catering business? If that's the case, then make a list of the skills you need to acquire and start looking for classes and people that you can learn from. Instead of starting your business this year, it makes better sense to start in eighteen or twenty-four months when you're better prepared. You'll have a better chance at success.

E ssential

If you decide that catering isn't for you, starting a personal chef business might be the answer (see Chapter 7). Personal chefs generally work fewer hours and can design their own schedules.

If you realize that you're not cut out for the catering business, that's fine too. It means you took an honest inventory of your skills and abilities and realize that you won't enjoy the whole business of catering. Chances are you now have a better understanding of your strengths and weaknesses and have a better idea of what you'd like to do. Maybe it's food styling, event planning, or starting a cookie business from home. Catering is only one way to channel your passion for food and entertainment.

Chapter 4

Getting Started as a Caterer

Local regulators may think it's nice that you make the best finger sandwiches in town, but their priority is making sure you have the correct licenses, permits, and insurance to operate legally. If you don't observe the proper legalities, you could be slapped with expensive fines or even shut down. In addition, you need to know the laws concerning safe food handling, operating in a commercial kitchen, paying employees, incorporating, and registering your name. This chapter gives you an overview of all of the rules and regulations you'll need to know.

Licensing and Other Legal Issues

Since caterers deal with potentially hazardous foods—foods that can cause illness if not handled properly—the kitchens they work in must be licensed, and caterers must be trained in food safety. Only commercial kitchens can be licensed. Caterers cannot work from their home kitchens and transport food elsewhere.

Commercial Kitchens

Commercial kitchens are specifically designed for large-scale food preparation. They have special layouts, which keep raw food separate from cooked foods. They have special ventilation systems, heavy-duty equipment meant to be used to cook large amounts of food, special nonslip floor mats, and other special features. Worktables are made of stainless steel for easy cleaning. Commercial kitchens have specific sink requirements and must use only commercial refrigeration units. There are also regulations for lighting fixtures, screens, restrooms, and dumpsters.

E ssential

Commercial kitchens are regulated by county or by state health departments. Every kitchen is inspected at least once a year. An inspector will check to make sure that dry and refrigerated ingredients are stored and handled properly, refrigerators maintain the right temperature, there are no signs of vermin, insects are kept under control, and the chefs adhere to correct procedures, such as properly cooling and reheating foods and washing their hands.

Research which agencies regulate licensing, inspection, zoning, and building codes. Start by contacting your state's Department of Health and/or the Department of Agriculture and Markets. Local municipal zoning and planning boards determine the allowable size of a facility. Local building codes will dictate the volume of business allowed and drainage issues.

Safe Food Handling

Since mishandling food can be dangerous for consumers, every caterer must be trained in food safety. Perishable foods, if given the right conditions, will grow dangerous bacteria. In an effort to prevent food-borne illnesses, the food industry developed a standard seven-step system called Hazardous Analysis Critical Control Point (HACCP). This system is taught in culinary schools and food service seminars around the country, and every professional cook needs to know it and follow it. The seven steps are:

1. Assess hazards and potential risks.
2. Identify critical control points, including cross contamination, cooking, cooling, and hygiene.

3. Establish procedures to ensure safety is maintained at all critical control points.
4. Monitor critical control points, using the correct tools.
5. Take corrective actions as soon as a critical control point is in jeopardy.
6. Set up a record-keeping system to log all of your flowchart and temperature checks.
7. Maintain the system to make sure it's working.

ServSafe courses taught by the National Restaurant Association are available online at *www.nraef.org*. These courses teach the HACCP system, basic microbiology, and methods for ensuring safe cooking and serving practices.

Licensing Requirements

Exact licensing requirements vary from state to state and county to county, so you'll have to check with the local county offices. In New York, for example, commercial kitchens are inspected and licensed by the Department of Health. Specific information about how to safely handle raw eggs, cool food, and avoid problems is available at *www.health.state.ny.us/environmental*. This information is applicable to all caterers and personal chefs regardless of where they operate. Every state will have a similar license procedure; to find your state's specific procedures, visit your state's government Web site.

Liquor Licenses

In order to serve liquor of any kind, you'll need to carry a liquor license. Liquor licenses, like commercial kitchen licenses, are overseen on the state level, and requirements and availability vary from state to state. Each state has its own liquor license authority, and the licenses are granted at the local level depending on your specific location.

Liquor licenses are not easy to get and are often expensive. They also increase your liability and will add to your insurance premiums. Some states only resell existing licenses rather than issuing new ones, while others can put a moratorium on issuing new licenses in certain areas if the local authorities feel that there are too many in too small an area.

Fact

According to *Event Solutions* magazine, just over 38 percent of caterers had a liquor license in 2003. Some liquor licenses will let you serve hard alcohol, wine, and beer, but some restrict you to only beer and wine. Check with your attorney about the laws in your area.

If you plan to apply for a liquor license, consult a lawyer experienced in handling local liquor permits. State statutes often have specific requirements for locations to qualify for a permit. An experienced lawyer can help you navigate through the process more quickly and easily and can advise you on how to best meet the statute specifications.

Finding a Commercial Kitchen

In order to operate legally as a caterer, you'll have to cook in a licensed commercial kitchen. This will provide you with proper working conditions and large-scale equipment. If you don't have access to a commercial kitchen, there are several ways to find a suitable location.

Shared-Use Commercial Kitchens

This segment of the market is relatively new and small, but it's growing. New York State, for example, has about a dozen shared-use commercial kitchens. Some are run as not-for-profit businesses. These kitchens rent out time to caterers and small food manufacturers who don't have their own kitchens. The people who run the kitchen maintain the licenses and permits with the local authorities and pay for the location's insurance. In return, they charge an hourly fee for using their cooking facilities.

Check to see if your area has a shared-use commercial kitchen. If not, find out where the closest one is. Some resources with location listings are in Appendix A.

Underutilized Commercial Kitchens

Many churches and community centers have commercial kitchens and are willing to rent time to local entrepreneurs. If you're doing kosher catering, visit the synagogues in your area, the Jewish community center, and other local Jewish organizations to see if there's a kitchen that you can use.

Catering Commercial Kitchens

It's not unheard of for a caterer with their own commercial kitchen to rent time to other small caterers. If you need the kitchen when the caterer is busy, however, you might be out of luck.

Restaurant Kitchens

This isn't an ideal option, since restaurant kitchens are usually quite busy during many hours of the day, but if you can find a restaurant that is closed during the day and only serves dinner, you might be able to work in the kitchen in the morning before the cooks come in to start prepping for dinner.

School Kitchens

It never hurts to ask. Call local schools and colleges in your area and ask if they have a commercial kitchen. Talk to the person who manages the kitchen and see if you can negotiate to work during times that the kitchen is empty or when the school is closed to students.

Insurance

The type of catering company you have will determine what kinds of insurance coverage you need. All caterers need a standard general liability policy; professional liability policies are used in other industries, but not for catering. The standard general liability policy will have a "products" and "completed operations" clause, which will provide coverage for your food products and catering jobs. The policy should also have "bodily injury" and "property damage" clauses to protect you if someone becomes ill or if the venue gets damaged.

"Personal injury" and "advertising injury" clauses should be included to protect you if you get into a scuffle with a client or are sued by someone who says you made a false claim in advertising or marketing your services.

E ssential

General Liability

Unfortunately, it's not easy for a new business owner to find an insurer who will write a policy for him. Most insurers require that a business be up and profitably running for at least three years. The amount of coverage will be based on the business's annual receipts. Generally, start-ups aim to get a policy that will provide $1 million of coverage for each occurrence. The excess liability companies are the firms that are the likeliest to write these types of policies, since they're in the business of taking on greater risk. Companies like AIG, United States Liability, and the Hartford write these policies. It's easier for a catering firm to get insurance coverage if it doesn't directly serve alcohol, since there are fewer liability issues involved.

E Alert

Workers' Compensation Insurance

If you employ other workers, you'll need to have workers' compensation insurance. Every state's regulations vary. In some states you need to have a minimum of three full-time employees in order to be mandated to carry this type of insurance. Workers' compensation insurance covers you in the event that one of your employees is injured on the job.

✓Expertise

One caterer was hit with $30,000 worth of fines because she didn't realize she had to pay workers' compensation for her employees. She had been paying her employees as independent contractors, and it didn't matter to the authorities that she wasn't aware of the law.

Finding a Lawyer

If you're starting a business, it's important to consult with an attorney. You'll need help forming a formal business structure, finding a location to lease or buy if you're not going to rent time in a commercial kitchen, and making sure you understand all the local regulations for operating your type of business.

Hopefully, your attorney will be able to address all of your issues, but you may need to consult a legal specialist. For example, if you want to purchase a liquor license for your catering business, you may need to find a lawyer in your state who specializes in obtaining such licenses for food industry clients.

Hiring a lawyer should be done with care and consideration, since she'll be one of your trusted advisors. Don't just pick a name out of the yellow pages; network to find a good corporate attorney who has experience with small businesses in the foodservice industry.

If you find an attorney you like but she doesn't have much small business experience or food experience, keep looking. Unless you negotiate a flat rate, you'll be paying your attorney by the hour, and if she's unfamiliar with the proper forms and permits, it'll take her more time and cost you more money. With lawyers, most of what you're paying for is expertise and experience. Don't feel compelled to use an aunt or the friend of a friend just because she's a lawyer.

E Fact

The Internal Revenue Service defines small businesses as commercial operations with less than $5 million in revenue per year. The IRS publishes an annual resource guide to help small business owners. It includes information on starting and running a new business and filing taxes.

The best way to find an appropriate attorney is to ask friends and business acquaintances who have food businesses in your area for a referral. You can also ask your accountant, other attorneys, and your banker. Referrals are the way the legal profession works. Today, with the proliferation of e-mail, it's easy to send out a message that will reach a large number of professionals quickly. If someone has a good attorney, they will e-mail you the necessary contact information.

Don't go to a large law firm where the rates will be higher. An attorney at a small or medium-sized firm who has experience working with restaurants will do fine. Once you have three or so referrals for good attorneys, call and ask a few questions:

- Ask him what his billable rate is and how much he charges for paralegals and associates.
- Get references. Call a couple of clients to find out how efficient the attorney is and how quickly he returns calls and attends to important matters.
- Determine the type of practice. Try to find an attorney who works with a variety of small clients so that you won't be the smallest fish in the pond.
- Find out where the attorney went to school, how long he's been practicing, and in what states he's admitted to the bar.

Meet with at least a few different attorneys to get a sense of their style, experience, and how eager they are to have you as a client. There should be no charge for an introductory consultation. Interview each attorney and ask the same questions. The most important thing, aside from finding a competent and licensed attorney, is finding a person whose opinion you respect and who will listen to you. You need to find someone you're comfortable with. If your gut tells you that one of the attorneys is smart, tough when she needs to be, and diligent, that's the attorney you should hire, even if she's not the cheapest.

E ssential

Network with local business owners and local associations. If there's an active chamber of commerce group or other business networking groups, ask them for a referral. Call your local National Association of Catering Executives (NACE) chapter or ask the Small Business Development Center (SBDC) at the local university for a recommendation.

Your Business Structure

Whether you start as a personal chef or a caterer, you'll have to decide on a formal business structure. You can operate as a sole proprietorship and file an extra schedule, or form, with your personal income tax, or you may choose to form a corporation and file a separate tax return for the business. This may seem like a dull task that can wait, but without formalizing a company structure, you can't open a bank account for the business or get additional investors.

While setting up a corporation is more expensive initially than operating as a sole proprietorship, there are benefits to operating within a corporate entity. Corporations provide protection if someone should try to sue you, or if the business goes bankrupt. Corporations also offer certain tax advantages.

There are three types of corporations, each with its benefits and limitations—the limited liability company (LLC), the S corporation, and the C corporation. Discuss the types that are available in your state with your attorney and work with her to decide which type will be best for your business goals. Some types of incorporation allow more investors than others.

Sole Proprietorship

Running your new catering or personal chef business as a sole proprietorship means that you are the sole owner, and that you may file your business's tax return on your federal and state returns on a Schedule C.

While this makes paperwork and tax filing easier, there are downsides to operating under a sole proprietorship. Under this type of structure you can't have any partners. Also, since you're not incorporated, you are personally liable for any lawsuits that may be filed against you. Say, for example, that a client claims you're responsible for the food poisoning that sickened all of his guests. He could sue you directly and go after your personal assets.

Also, if the business goes bankrupt, you will be held personally liable for any payments due to creditors. This means that if there are outstanding loan payments or unpaid vendor bills, you, as the sole business owner, are personally responsible for any monies owed, and your personal assets may be used to pay off debt. Any gains or losses from the business get funneled into your adjusted gross income.

Limited Liability Company

A limited liability company (LLC) takes advantage of the liability protection of a corporation and the tax benefits of sole ownership. The LLC structure offers more flexibility in the management of your business than the C corporation or S corporation options. Many restaurants and catering businesses choose this structure. Check with your financial and legal advisors to confirm that this is the way to go.

E Alert

Even if you are able to get some insurance coverage added onto your household policy or are eligible for additional liability coverage on a business insurance policy as a caterer, you still are more vulnerable than if you incorporate and run your business as a corporation.

S Corporation

With this type of structure, you incorporate under state law; becoming an S corporation on a federal level is optional. If the company does incorporate at the federal level, there are additional tax benefits. S corporations operate under a limited number of investors. Setting up this kind of corporate shell is somewhat complex, so you will need some expert advice.

C Corporation

A C corporation is a legal entity that exists separately from the business owners. While corporations, of course, can be sued, the corporate shell provides the owners legal protection. In most cases, personal assets cannot be confiscated. In C corporations, all gains and losses are absorbed by the corporation. While the C corporation will cost anywhere from $500 to several thousand dollars to set up, depending on the lawyer you use, it is worth the investment if you plan to be in business for at least a few years.

Accounting

You will have to set up a basic accounting and record keeping system for your business. There are many software choices for tracking expenditures and balancing your bank account. By buying a basic off-the-shelf software package, you'll save money. These packages have all the necessary features you need to set up sales, purchase, and create general ledgers to manage your accounts and petty cash. Software systems will be programmed to adhere to the Generally Accepted Accounting Principles (GAAP) rules, which you and your accountant should follow.

E ssential

You'll need to set up a chart of accounts for coding the elements used to classify, record, budget, and report information. The National Restaurant Association publishes *A Uniform System of Accounts for Restaurants*. You can purchase the book at *www.restaurant.org* and adapt it to your catering business.

When using general-purpose accounting software, you'll have to put in your own descriptions, such as expense items for food, beverages, and linen rental. Which headings you choose will depend on how you wish to analyze them later, so discuss this with your accountant.

Bank Accounts

As soon as you have a business structure, open a business checking account. Don't try to operate a business with your personal checking account. Commingling assets and operating in a nonprofessional manner will only get you into trouble later on when you have to pay taxes and figure out your profit.

Open a business account at a bank that caters to small businesses so that the fees you pay will be minimal. Hopefully, you'll be able to establish a relationship with this bank. As they get to know you and your business needs, you'll be able to approach them for lines of credit, loans, credit cards, and other important services.

☀ E Alert

Most likely, the money in your business account won't earn interest. This won't make much difference at the beginning, but as you grow you may want to open an interest-bearing savings account. You can keep most of your money in the savings account and move money into the checking account as needed.

If you don't have the final name for your catering business, you can open the bank account under the corporation's name and file a DBA certificate with your state later. It's simpler if you can open the account with the final business name. That way, the information on the checks will match your business's name and avoid confusion.

Payment Methods

Accepting credit cards is a convenience that customers will appreciate. Credit card sales must be processed or settled in order to transfer the money to your bank account. There's a fee for this, and fees vary from processing company to processing company. With recent innovations like PayPal, sole proprietors can easily accept credit card payments. You'll need to open an account with PayPal and provide your banking information. Fees for credit card processing will range from just over 1 percent to more than 3 percent depending on the type of credit card and the volume of sales that you process.

State Sales Tax Issues

While state laws may vary slightly, you'll need to pay sales tax on the catering sales you make. Since there's no tax on most food items, the state expects to be paid once you turn raw ingredients into edible dishes. Since you'll pay sales tax on food wrap, food trays, and other equipment when you purchase it, you don't have to charge your customers sales tax on those items. Just include the prices of those items in your selling price for the event.

When you cater for a nonprofit organization, a certified 501(c)(3), or another legitimate tax-exempt organization, you must get a current copy of their tax status and keep it in your files with the paid invoice for that job. If you are ever audited, you will be asked for proof of why you didn't collect or pay sales tax.

Finding an Accountant

Finding an accountant is much like finding an attorney. Try to find a small business accountant who is familiar with food businesses or at least has retail and service businesses as clients. Use a certified public accountant (CPA), an accountant who has passed a regulated exam and meets the requirements of this industry-recognized accreditation. Ask for recommendations from other small business owners. The American Institute of Certified Public Accountants is also a good resource for finding CPAs in your area. Visit their Web site at *www.aicpa.org*.

Financing

The good news is that starting a catering business doesn't have to cost a tremendous amount of money. If you find a licensed commercial kitchen to work in, you'll only need to purchase a limited amount of equipment. Budget several hundred dollars to build a Web site and to print up business cards. Set aside some funds for filing permits and buying accounting software, but huge amounts of cash aren't necessarily required. Client deposits will pay for up-front ingredient costs.

Try to use savings for your start-up costs. Borrowing money from your credit card is not a good choice. You'll end up paying exorbitant interest rates varying from 18 percent to more than 25 percent. If you have trouble making payments, you'll negatively impact your credit score. If you don't have enough in savings, borrow from friends and family. If the person expects to be paid back, type up a simple loan agreement that you'll pay back the loan X amount per month after the first year with X amount of simple interest added. A 6–8 percent simple interest rate should be satisfactory.

Bartering

Bartering your services with others is a great way to save on start-up costs. If you can find a Web page designer or attorney who'll accept your catering services in return for professional help, then you'll save cash. Bartered agreements need to be spelled out in writing and need to be equivalent in dollar amounts for both parties.

Small Business Administration

The Small Business Administration (SBA) guarantees loans made by banks. Find a bank in your area that is certified by the SBA or a preferred SBA lender. The SBA has a Micro Lenders program that lends small businesses relatively small amounts of money. The maximum amount is $35,000, and the average loan size is about $13,000. Apply through your local bank. Loans must be paid back within six years, if not sooner, and interest rates vary from 8 to 13 percent.

The SBA also has many helpful resources for entrepreneurs on its Web site, *www.sba.gov.* You'll find forms for starting a business, determining your total start-up costs, and other forms. These forms, once filled out, will feed right into your business plan.

Small Business Development Centers

These entities are usually affiliated with universities. They employ professionals, experienced volunteers, and talented students. SBDCs offer help to small and start-up businesses and can assist business owners with writing business plans, marketing ideas, developing new products, and exploring finance options. SBDCs help students get entrepreneurial and consulting experience, and in return, local small businesses can get some valuable free or low-cost help.

Catering Software

You may want a computer software program to help you organize all of your business requirements. Using a catering-specific software package like CaterEdge, CaterEase, or Synergy, will make routine duties easier than if you build your own spreadsheets. They alleviate one major headache: costing. These software packages can import ingredient costs right into recipes to make menu costings easier. They will also be able to track the profit of each item and calculate your average profit of sold items.

While buying industry-specific software will cost you more than using standard office software, it will make your job easier. The three main software packages are similar in functionality, but their prices differ. CaterEase and CaterEdge seem best suited for small catering businesses and are the most affordable.

All of the software packages offer either online demonstrations, trials, or product tours. In general, they allow you to do the following:

- Create proposals and contracts
- Track sales prospects
- Manage contact information
- Cost recipes
- Measure inventory
- Create invoices and handle accounts receivable
- Run custom reports
- Schedule and manage event labor

They are often compatible with major office software programs. Some of the software can analyze your profit and loss by job and help you manage your bottom line.

CaterEdge (*www.cateredgesoftware.com*) is designed for small off-premise caterers. CaterEase (*www.caterease.com*), another industry leader, offers several versions to choose from. Visual Synergy by Synergy International (*www.synergy-intl.com*) is manufactured by a company that specializes in hospitality software. Look at each system and see which interface you like best. Compare the functions and abilities of the three systems, and buy the one that's easiest for you to use.

Chapter 5

Researching Your Business Opportunity

In order to launch a successful business, you'll have to do your homework. You'll need to gather essential information—who your potential customers are (your targets), how much they're willing to pay for various types of catering services (a competitive survey), and where gaps exist in the marketplace for you to enter (positioning).

Types of Research

There are two main types of research in business: primary and secondary. Primary research is research that you conduct yourself. It's original research where you design the research study, collect the data, analyze it, and draw conclusions.

Secondary research is collecting information that already exists. These types of data include demographic information like how many people live in a certain zip code, the average household income in your area, and how many new businesses have been launched in the last year. Some secondary data is free, while you may have to pay a fee to access other data. With the Internet, a tremendous amount of data is instantly available to you. You can research your local chamber of commerce, local publications, and many official records online.

There are advantages and disadvantages to both primary and secondary research. Doing the research yourself allows you to tailor the process to your specific needs. However, you may be able to draw the same conclusions and save yourself time and money by analyzing data that's been compiled by someone else. Using secondary data may be more convenient but may not answer all of your questions. In the end, you may get the best results with a combination of primary and secondary research.

If you're unfamiliar with conducting primary research or using secondary research data properly, you can take a class to make yourself more comfortable. Local community colleges offer classes in market research and basic marketing. At the very least, you can buy a book on market research techniques. Appendix A has some helpful suggestions.

Take Advantage of the Public Library

Your local library is the best place to start your research. Reference librarians can help you find the resources you need, and they can often give you valuable Internet searching tips. If your local library doesn't have a good business reference section or doesn't subscribe to online databases, call a nearby university or local community college and ask if you can get a day pass or an online password to do some research. They should accommodate you, particularly if you're an alumna and/or a local resident.

The good news is that with the Internet and broadband connections, you can do much of your research from the comfort of your home computer. With a current library card, you can access online business databases from your local library. Libraries all over the country allow local residents to use subscription-only databases from home.

Free Library Databases

Reference USA is an indispensable free database, and most libraries in North America subscribe to it. This database contains information on more than 13 million businesses and 120 million U.S. households. You can access thousands of listings from yellow pages and business white pages, corporate annual reports, and chamber of commerce data, plus a wide variety of business and trade magazines. The database is continually updated, so the data you collect will be current.

Once you log into the database, you can easily do a custom search to find caterers in your area. In a matter of seconds, you'll get a printable list of competitors. You can sort them by zip code, sales volume, or number of employees. You'll get the company name, phone number, and location.

Knowing the North American Industry Classification System code for the type of businesses you're looking for will help. Your librarian will have a book that lists these codes. The code for catering is 722320.

Ⓔ Fact

Canada, the United States, and Mexico started using the North American Industry Classification System in 1997. It is a way for the three countries to track and share statistics relating to different industries. In the United States, NAICS replaced the four-digit Standard Industrial Classification system, and many search databases still use the SIC codes.

Other popular databases include Predicast's PROMPT, which allows you to do a keyword search and produces relevant articles. The EBSCO Regional Business News database also allows you to search by keyword and will allow you to print articles from hundreds of publications in PDF format, right from the original publication.

By using these databases, you'll be able to research your competition, keep track of what they're doing, and learn about their owners. If you do your homework, you'll be better able to position your business and defend it from other caterers.

Useful Directories

Ward's Business Directory of U.S. Private and Public Companies lists companies by name, geographic location, and industry. The *D&B Million Dollar Directory* is also a very helpful volume. You can search by industry or zero in on particular companies to find quarterly sales figures and employment information. Both of these directories will give you a better picture of the catering market in your area.

Census Data

Visiting the government's census Web site, *www.census.gov*, can be very helpful, if somewhat confusing. You can find the population count for your area as well as information on small businesses across the country at *http://factfinder.census.gov*.

Qualitative Versus Quantitative Data

There are two main types of data: qualitative and quantitative. Chances are you'll find value in both types as you research your catering business.

Qualitative data can't be precisely measured or stated in terms of numbers. If you interview someone and ask him what he liked about a certain caterer, his response would be considered qualitative data. If you design a survey and ask people to rank four different caterers, their answers would also be qualitative data because you'd only be able to tell which caterer is ranked the highest. (Since the rankings mean something different to each survey respondent, the actual rating values would have little meaning.)

E ssential

Demographics are the measurable physical or personal characteristics of a population, such as age, sex, marital status, family size, education, income, and religion.

Quantitative data is measurable data. It can be represented in terms of actual quantities or figures, such as prices and sales figures. If you send an e-mail to a target list and ask people to mention a code when they place an order with you, you'll be able to quantitatively measure exactly how many people replied compared to how many e-mails you sent out.

Quantitative data is easy to work with because the numbers give you immediate feedback. Qualitative data may not feel as concrete, but it offers a valuable insight into your local market that you can't get from a page full of numbers.

Doing a Competitive Survey

Surveying and analyzing the catering competitors in your area is one of the most important pieces of research you can do. Without knowing what the offerings are, what the prices are, how much to pay servers, and whether to levy a service charge, you won't be able to price your services competitively.

Pick Your Targets

After you have done your preliminary research, you will be familiar with the major caterers in your area. Focus on the most popular and largest caterers first. Then look for specialty caterers.

If you're located in a relatively small area, you'll be able to include almost every caterer in your competitive review. However, if you want to start a catering business in a metropolitan area with a population of more than 100,000, narrow your search and pick representative companies to survey. Choose ten to twelve caterers at the most for your competitive review. Choose caterers who represent the catering market in your area. Choose a couple of very high-end businesses, a couple in the middle of the market, a couple at the lower end, and a couple of specialty caterers.

Collect Data

Begin by studying the Web sites of your fellow caterers. How detailed are they? How many pages do they usually have? What kinds of photos do they have? What do you like about them? What's missing? Can you e-mail the caterer directly from the Web site? Are prices listed, or do you have to call for information? What kind of concept and positioning do they have? Is there something that makes this caterer unique? Looking at the Web sites will give you a better idea of what each caterer is trying to accomplish and how they fit into the local market.

Set up a spreadsheet for yourself so you can compare the data on your potential competition. Make a separate column for each of the following categories:

- Company name
- Type of business (e.g., specialty, on-site, off-site)
- Owner or manager's name
- Company phone number
- Company Web site
- Average price per person for a seated/buffet lunch
- Average price per person for a seated/buffet dinner
- Service charge information
- Number of years the company has been in business
- Notes on the company's reputation (e.g., friendly service, decadent desserts, creative food stations)

Create a separate "information sheet" for each business in your competitive survey. Call each one and have them prepare a proposal for you. Tell each one you're planning a dinner party for 100 guests. Have a total budget in mind for the entire party and give the same budget to each caterer. Talk with each company, noting who talks with you and how the conversation unfolds. Is it the owner or a sales associate? Is the person professional, friendly, and articulate? What kind of rapport does she establish with you? Pay attention to the questions she asks you. They are your key to determining whether she understands your vision for your dinner party.

Don't feel guilty about asking other caterers for proposals, but be courteous and make sure not to call them during a peak time such as immediately before Thanksgiving or at the height of wedding season. Here are some sample questions to ask:

- How long have you been in business?
- What kind of facility do you work out of? Do you have your own commercial kitchen or do you share a commercial kitchen with others?
- What kind of catering jobs do you specialize in? Do you tend to do more formal dinner parties or catered outdoor picnics—or are you equally comfortable with both?
- How long before the event starts do you arrive?
- Who are your clients? (Get names and at least two to three references.)
- What are your ideas for the dinner party? What can you do with the quoted budget?

Ask caterers for a detailed proposal. You should receive the proposal within a week. If you don't, there's something wrong. Either they're too busy for new business or they don't have their act together. Either way, it's a good sign for you that the local climate could support another caterer.

Evaluate the Proposals

Read each proposal carefully, quickly noting what you like and don't like about each one. What is written well? What is missing? What is confusing or misleading? How was the proposal delivered? How did it look? Is the proposal comprehensive and clear? Are there any surprises? Is dish rental included in the price? Are table linens included? Does the proposal include everything you asked for? If you're unclear about anything, call the caterer back and ask for clarification.

Compare the proposals and examine the following. Record information on your spreadsheet:

- What is the per-person charge?
- How many entrée choices are there? How many side dishes?
- Is the price of staff included? How much does each staff person cost?
- How much deposit is needed?

- Is a service charge added on to the bill? If so, how much?
- What forms of payment are accepted?
- What other charges are there, if any?
- What type of menu did they provide? Continental? Italian? Ethnic?
- How receptive was the caterer to your ideas?
- How much creativity is there in the proposal? What suggestions did the caterer provide?
- Did the caterer want to see the event space before she sent you a proposal?
- What was left out or unclear?
- Did you get the sense that the caterer really wants the job?

Essential

Ask to see photos of the caterer's jobs online, or meet with him in person. See how each caterer sets up his buffet stations. Does he use chafing dishes, or does each dish come out plated from the kitchen? How much food does he put out? Just enough or plenty for the hungriest of groups?

Once you have all the information from the competition compiled, you'll start to see some patterns. You will notice price ranges. You'll also start to see patterns in the kinds of food that the caterers in your area provide and the types of customers and functions they cater.

Hopefully you'll start to see a niche where your business can fit. Maybe all the caterers offered similar types of food, and there's a need for the type of healthy, fresh cooking you specialize in. Or maybe most of the caterers focused on formal dinner parties, and there's room for you to enter the market specializing in more casual catering for brunches and buffet dinners.

Identify Opportunities

From the competitive information you've gathered and evaluated, and from your assessment of what kinds of food you like to cook and serve, you'll now want to conduct some of your own primary research to further define your catering concept.

By now, you should have at least a couple of ideas of the type of catering services you'd like to offer. Conduct your own research to help you determine which concept will be the best received in your area. If your concept involves relatively expensive prices, ask questions about how much people would be willing to pay for top-quality food and service. If your concept involves ethnic cooking, ask people if they enjoy eating new foods, what kind of food they most enjoy eating, and whether they like spicy foods.

While you want a concept that is different from the other caterers in the market, you don't want a concept that is so unique and original that it's ahead of its time. If customers don't immediately understand what you're offering, you'll have a hard time selling proposals and making your business work.

Conduct Your Own Research

One of the easiest and best ways to get feedback on your business idea is to write a short one- to two-page survey, and give it to a group of friends, acquaintances, and work colleagues to fill out and give back to you anonymously. Ask people to hand the survey back to you. If you let people take the survey home and mail it back to you, you'll get far fewer back. Even if you give them a self-addressed stamped envelope, most people won't return the survey. So don't try to conduct a mail survey. E-mail surveys work well and are easy to set up. Check *www.grapevinesurveys.com* and *http://freeonline surveys.com* for do-it-yourself online surveys. If you're not sure you'll get your written surveys back, call your friends at home and ask if you can interview them for five minutes over the phone.

The results you get from your survey will tell you whether your ideas will find a receptive audience or whether you need to go back to the drawing board.

Writing a Survey

Try writing your own customer survey and hand it out to people who you think might be your target audience. Give it to people as they go into or out of a local gourmet store. Give them a pen and clipboard, and ask them to fill it out for you on the spot. Thank people for their time; give out a wrapped cookie, chocolate bar, or dollar bill along with your business card to everyone who returns a completed survey.

☰ ᛓ ☰ Alert

If most caterers in your area don't include a service charge as part of their bill, make sure to ask your survey respondents whether they would appreciate a service charge instead of tipping or whether they'd object to such a charge.

Make sure that the survey is no longer than a page or two, as people won't take the time to answer more than that. Have a combination of open-ended questions and specific-answer questions. Ask people to check a box if you can use their e-mail address to contact them with special offers and news about your business.

Here are some examples of questions you may want to include in your survey:

- Have you ever hired a caterer?
- If yes, for what type of event and when was it?
- Were you happy with the job they did?
- What could they have done better?
- If you could find a caterer who could cater a party in your home for a reasonable price, would you hire them?
- How much would you be willing to spend per person for a catered meal?

$15–$25	*$26–$40*	*$41–60*	*$61–80*
$81–99	*$100–$115*	*$116–$130*	*More than $131 per person*

- Rank the most important things you look for in a caterer.
  __ *Good food*
  __ *Reputation*
  __ *Reliability*
  __ *Friendly Service*
  __ *Ability to provide rentals, entertainment, flowers, etc.*
  __ *Price*
  __ *Other* _____
- Do you entertain at home? If not, why not? If yes, when? For what occasions?
- What kind of food do you like to serve your guests?
- How many people do you usually entertain?

Test out your concept ideas. If you want to specialize in corporate catering, ask the respondents if their company or workplace uses caterers for lunches, parties, or other office events. If you want to cater weddings, ask respondents what they'd look for in a wedding caterer.

Ask each respondent for his or her income, education level, age, whether they've traveled outside the United States, and anything else that may help you learn about your potential customers. This is potentially sensitive information, so you may want to make the section optional.

Digesting the Data

Once you have collected at least twenty-five to thirty-five surveys from a variety of people (not just your family and close friends), start another spreadsheet. Summarize the most important qualities your respondents sought in a caterer. What were the top two most important attributes? What were the majority of respondents willing to pay for a caterer?

How did the respondents feel about your concept? Did they seem to understand it? Were they open to it? Analyze the data. You might learn something you didn't anticipate that will help you modify your concept. If you think you have to change your concept, develop a follow-up survey and ask another group of people to fill it out.

Focus Groups

Once you have developed your concept and position, you should conduct a focus group to see how potential customers react to it. Focus groups are unscientific, but they are good for providing feedback. Focus groups are a form of qualitative, or directional, research, where an objective moderator leads a discussion of a small group of potential customers or buyers.

If you have examples of your menus and photographs of some of your signature dishes, have the moderator show these items to the group to get their feedback on the concept.

Listening to feedback on your ideas won't always be easy, but it should be interesting. You can glean valuable insights from listening to others discuss your concept. The group may have worthwhile suggestions. Analyze the feedback from the focus group as you did the written surveys. Determine whether your concept needs to be revised, and schedule another focus group if your plan needs a major overhaul. If you received positive feedback from your focus group with suggestions for minor changes, you are ready to move into the development phase.

Chapter 6

Developing a Concept

Every caterer has a business concept that's reflected in his menus, his pricing, and the way he does business. Some caterers have more interesting concepts than others. Many caterers stick to the basics and serve customers with typical offerings like salmon, chicken, and beef entrées. Other caterers offer their clients a unique take on ethnic food, outdoor picnics, or kosher eating. Put your market research to work to imagine and test a concept that will work for you.

Identifying a Concept

Your catering concept is limited only by your imagination and by your talent. The possibilities are nearly limitless. How do you know what kind of catering business to launch? Here are a number of factors to consider when developing your concept.

Make Your Concept Different Enough . . .

If there are a lot of traditional full-service off-premise caterers in your area, don't merely copy them and jump into the fray. Instead, try to develop a catering concept that will stand out from those other businesses. Check their menus and offerings. If they focus on formal occasions and offer standard fare like roast chicken, grilled steak, and poached fish, check your research and see if prospective clients would be likely to use you if you started a barbecue catering business or a home-style catering business. What if you emphasized high-quality ingredients, offered vegetarian menus, and focused on less formal events like office picnics or graduation parties?

The key is to develop a concept that you can own and one that is different from what the others are doing. Develop your concept so that it will be hard for the competition to copy exactly what you're doing. One way to do this is to focus on your particular skills and personality. Remember, there's only one of you, and you can't be duplicated. This is a plus when you start your business.

Take stock of your skills and figure out how you can differentiate yourself. Maybe it's doing cooking demonstrations as part of your events. Maybe it's your unusual menus and your ability to cook an array of ethnic specialties.

E ssential

Your concept can be a hybrid that includes a combination of style and food. You don't need to pick one aspect for your concept. Just make sure you don't muddle your message by trying to offer too many things at once. You can't be all things to all people, especially when you're starting a small company.

The average consumer should be able to distinguish your concept from the competition. If she can't figure out what you do or what's different about you, she won't call you. You can distinguish yourself by the look of your Web site and the layout and offerings on your menu.

... But Not Too Different

While you need to differentiate yourself from your competition, don't be so different with your concept that customers won't understand what you do. If you're too weird or too avant-garde, you'll have to spend too much time educating your clientele. Opening a raw food catering business in Pocatello, Idaho, for instance, may not fly. Do your research and make sure friends easily understand your concept. In the end, the best concepts are usually variations on a theme, not a totally new theme.

Good Concepts Are On-Trend

Strong concepts take a current trend and run with it. For example, you could take advantage of the growing demand for Latin and

Asian foods and the increased popularity of locally raised ingredients. Good concepts leverage the popularity of a growing trend, not a fad that will disappear along with your business.

Consider Pricing and Profitability

Be careful that your concept will allow you to offer menu items at prices that the market will bear. You may have a great idea for a high-end catering business, but if you're planning to open in an area inhabited by poor students and struggling artists, you better make sure that customers who can afford your prices will be banging down your door. Better to design a catering menu that the locals can afford.

$\equiv \overset{\backslash | /}{\underset{\equiv}{E}} \equiv$ **Alert**

Don't cut your prices or try to be the low-cost caterer in town. A larger catering company can always drop its prices to run you out of business. Focus on your unique talents and offerings.

If there are similar caterers in other parts of the country, check what prices they charge and compare them to the cost of living in your area. Talk to some caterers in other areas of the country and find out what kind of customers they have, and if they've been able to raise their prices in the last year. Ask if their business is growing at a healthy pace.

Some concepts look good on the drawing board, but in reality they can't make money. Either they require too much time in the kitchen, they are too labor intensive, or they're so specialized that the number of clients will be small unless you live in a huge metropolitan area.

Run some preliminary financial forecasts. Assume you will charge prices that are comparable to the other caterers in your area. Investigate some local vendors and see what prices they'll charge you. Figure in fixed costs and estimate how many jobs you expect to work each month. Your concept needs to be flexible enough that you can make adjustments to it. Don't invest in a lot of specialty equipment before you can test your concept and gauge demand.

Make Sure You Love the Concept

Any successful caterer will tell you that he created his concept because it's the type of food he loves to cook, eat, and see others enjoy. If you create a concept because you think it'll be popular or an investor convinced you it will be, but you don't enjoy cooking that type of food, go back to the drawing board. With all the time, energy, and money you'll put into your business, you need to love the idea and be passionate about the menus.

Positioning and Marketing a Concept

Once you have a business concept, it's up to you to describe and market your catering business. You'll need to position your business and your newly created brand in the marketplace among all of the other catering companies, restaurants, and gourmet food businesses in your area. The way you position your company in the hearts and minds of potential customers will determine who your closest competitors are.

Fact

Positioning is the way you create an image or identity for your services, products, brand, and company. It is the "place" a product occupies in a given market as perceived by the target market. You will need to study your target market and your competition carefully before you decide how to position your business.

Differentiate Your Position

Make sure your position is differentiated from other catering operations in your area. You don't want to start a new business and have to fight head-to-head with an established catering business.

To determine the right positioning for your business, you have to map out the positions of the competition and determine where there's a void or an opportunity that you, your skills, and your concept can fit into. Whatever category you fall into, you will need to utilize strategic market positioning to convince customers to buy into your vision.

Catering Positionings

Your business could fall into one of several categories. Each category markets itself to a specific segment of the catering market. Regardless of where you see your business, you will have to be innovative to differentiate it from the rest of the competition.

Middle of the Road

Your concept is to provide catering for the average banquet. You'll feature roast chicken and farm-raised salmon dinners. Your prices will be competitive with other caterers. This is both a blessing and a curse. The competition in your area will likely be fierce, and you will compete with on-site banquet caterers as well as off-site caterers. On the other hand, demand for the type of catering you provide is steady, and your services will be highly recognizable to your potential clients.

✓Expertise

Simply Homemade, a company in Massachusetts run by E. Tracie Ritchie, offers buffet-style catering for 20–200 people. The menu includes baked ham, sausage and peppers, and apple crisp. Nothing is elaborate or constructed. All the dishes are things your mom made when you were growing up if you had an Italian-American mom in New England who loved to cook.

Premium

You want to target the top 20 percent of catering clients. Your menus will be upscale but not outrageously decadent. You'll feature items like filet of beef, bay scallops, and heirloom tomatoes, but maybe not Wagyu beef and farmstead cheeses. You will have to work hard to avoid being lumped into either the middle-of-the-road or ultra-premium group. You will have to be especially careful with pricing if there are few or no other premium caterers in your immediate area.

Ultrapremium

You'll focus on the top 5 percent of all catering clients in your area. You'll emphasize exclusivity and feature special ingredients like Maine lobster tails, Kobe beef, and line-caught salmon. Your prices will be high and so will your level of service. Clients will expect the very best from you.

✓Expertise

Feast & Fêtes is the catering business operated by celebrity French chef Daniel Boulud, who runs the acclaimed New York restaurant Daniel. From intimate dinners to lavish galas, the company provides the haute cuisine available at the restaurant combined with person-alized service.

Specialty/Niche

A specialty or niche positioning includes everything from being your town's only ethnic food caterer to specializing in diet or sugar-free catering. You need to work hard to promote your image. Be particularly careful that your idea is innovative rather than obscure.

As a specialty or niche caterer, your challenge is not to differentiate yourself from your competition; it's to make your services known and understood. Your marketing materials must address what you offer, why clients will value you, and how you will make their event special. You could rely on a successful gimmick, such as Douglas Coffin's pizza truck. The tricky thing about gimmicks is that they have to work. They need to become an integral part of your company's identity, so that they automatically associate your company and your gimmick.

✓ **E**xpertise

Another alternative is to specialize in a unique service. Gail's Vegetarian Catering (*www.gailsvegetarian.com*) in Wheaton, Maryland, focuses exclusively on creating elegant vegetarian meals for clients and specializes in catering vegetarian weddings in the Washington, D.C., area.

Differentiation

Most caterers offer a combination of good food and good service and try to differentiate themselves in one way or another, but some caterers are able to make a name for themselves simply through great food or great service.

Cuisine and Service

New York caterer Liz Neumark, the founder of Great Performances Catering, has grown her business to become one of the largest off-premise caterers in the city. The company focuses on ingredient quality and has purchased its own farm. It is starting to grow its own vegetables so that it can offer the freshest produce to its clients.

Danny Meyer, a New York restaurateur who recently started a large catering business called Hudson Yards Catering, is known for training his servers and staff well and for gracious service in his eateries. People will want to use his catering not only for the great food and interesting location but for his reputation for friendly and professional staff.

Specific Locations

Off-premise caterers develop relationships with the venues they use. These relationships vary from informal to formal. Some caterers will negotiate to have the exclusive right to cater at a club or museum and others will be a preferred vendor for a certain venue.

✓Expertise

Abigail Kirsch Catering differentiates itself by the variety of locations it can offer clients. Each venue attracts a different type of client, so the company can offer the right venue for almost any event, explains Kimberly Sundt, the corporate director of marketing and sales.

As a new caterer, you may not be able to develop an exclusive relationship with a specific venue, but you can work with smaller venues to build a reputation.

Mapping Your Competitors' Positionings

A positioning map will give you an idea of where your competitors "sit" in the marketplace and where there are gaps. Mapping isn't exact, so don't worry about being precise. Draw a horizontal X-axis on a blank piece of paper, halfway down. Cross the X-axis with a vertical Y-axis midway through, so that you have four quadrants. Label the X axis "Price." The left side of the axis is low price and the right side is high price. Label the Y-axis "Quality." The area above the X-axis represents high quality, and the bottom is lower quality.

Based on their prices and the types of events they primarily do, pick a point on the chart that represents where each competitor would lie. Chart at least ten companies. Then chart yourself, based on your proposed prices and the types of events and the quality you plan to offer.

If you are near your competitors, it means that your positioning is very similar to the other companies. If you lie very close to another point on the map, it means that you'll be directly competing with that point. The best position would be somewhere off of the straight line that forms when you connect the dots of most of the other companies. Being on a different line shows that you have a unique positioning.

E ssential

Alternatively, you can label the Y-axis "Type of Events," with the top half denoting formal events and the bottom reserved for informal. Since these positioning maps are two-dimensional, you may want to draw a few different maps, charting your competitors on a few different attributes.

Checking the Concept Against Your Skill Set

Now that you've charted your desired position in the marketplace and found a unique place, you'll also need to make sure that your new concept meshes with your skill set. Using the list of skills discussed in Chapter 3, make a list on the left side of a piece of paper. Record the skills required for your concept in order of importance until you've reviewed all the skills mentioned in the chapter.

Label the right side of the paper "Strength of My Skills," and list your skills according to how good you are at each one. If your top skill is menu design, list it first. If your pastry decorating skills are your second best skill, put it second. If your cooking skills are next, list them third, and continue down the list until you go through all the required skills. If you feel that you're equally good at two skills, then list them next to one another on the same line.

Compare the lists on the left and on the right side of the page. If the lists are vastly different, that tells you the skills required for your concept are different from your current skill level and ability. You may want to re-evaluate your concept. If your skills match relatively neatly with your concept's required skills, you are probably on the right track.

Testing Your Positioning

The last test you should do before you start to develop your marketing and sales materials and launch your business is to conduct an informal focus group. Focus groups are a type of qualitative market research. They're used by many companies to get feedback from customers. They're unscientific, but they're good for providing feedback on your concept.

To run an informal focus group, invite eight to ten of the people who filled out surveys over to your home or another private location. Make sure to invite an equal number of men and women, and avoid intimidating or extremely outspoken people. Put out some simple snacks and drinks and have a friend who does not have strong opinions about your business moderate the discussion. The discussion should be taped; videotape is best. You should excuse yourself and leave the house and come back in an hour.

The moderator should show a printed copy of your business concept to each member of the focus group and then ask the group what they think of the concept. The moderator should ask non-leading questions and be careful not to influence the group's answer. The moderator should ask, "How do you feel about Jane's concept?" and let the group speak, one by one. She shouldn't say, "You don't like the concept, do you?" Also, if there's someone in the group who has a strong opinion, the moderator should make sure that that person doesn't dominate the discussion or bully the others in the group into agreeing with him. Include the following questions:

- Do you like this presented concept? Why or why not? Please be specific.
- Would you be likely to hire this type of caterer? Why or why not?
- What would you change, if anything, about this concept?
- When would you be likely to hire Jane if she launched this business concept?
- Who in this area operates a business similar to Jane's?

The moderator should collect the hard copies of the concept and then ask each person to write down the name of the business and the type of catering it offers.

The moderator should summarize the feelings of the group for you in a three-page summary with a conclusion. You should sit with the moderator and watch the focus group tape and read the summary report. Try not to take any criticism of the concept personally.

If the group loves your concept, that's great. If they have suggestions, evaluate them fairly and adjust your concept. If the group didn't think your concept would work, listen to the criticism and reassess. If the group couldn't remember the name of the business or accurately describe the key components of the concept, think about another name and tweak your concept.

☀ Alert

Focus groups are directional only, and they can be wrong. More often than not, however, you can glean important information from the group's comments if you listen to their suggestions carefully.

If the group thought you needed major changes to your concept, do some more research and bounce the concept off of some industry professionals. Have another focus group with different people and see if the feedback is better.

Chapter 7

Being a Personal or Private Chef

Rather than offering your services to a different client each week and catering large events, you might choose to be a personal or private chef. A personal chef usually cooks for one client a day, making a week's worth of meals at a time that can be easily reheated or eaten as is. Personal chefs usually work on their own, set their own schedules, and, in general, have a lighter workday and less stress than most caterers. Private chefs work part-time or full-time for a particular client, cooking for them, their friends, and family.

Personal Chefs

Most personal chefs start their business on a small scale, renting time in a local commercial kitchen. As their business grows, they find they need to purchase or build their own commercial kitchen. Once you have your own commercial kitchen and catering insurance, you'll be able to cook all your clients' meals at your location and deliver them on a weekly basis, allowing you to accommodate a greater number of clients and grow your business even larger. With your own commercial kitchen, you'll also be able to cater your client's parties and have the option to cater larger off-premise events too.

Since being a personal chef doesn't involve all of the business and logistical aspects of the catering business, some people who have the goal of starting their own catering business begin as personal chefs. By doing this, they gain experience cooking for a client for a fee. They can also experiment with marketing techniques and build their cooking resume.

Getting Started

If you want to start as a personal chef, get a professional cooking job or two under your belt and onto your resume so that you're a credible candidate. Cooking for friends and family isn't the same thing as cooking on demand for paying clients. You'll also want to develop a portfolio of meal menus for prospective clients. Develop a roster of breakfasts, lunches, and dinners, so that you have plenty of variety for clients to eat a different meal every day for at least three weeks. If you plan to target athletes or people on special diets, make sure to develop appropriate menus.

Lifestyle Benefits

Some people become personal chefs because they like the lifestyle. Often, chefs who begin their careers working in restaurant and hotel kitchens start their own personal chef businesses when they're in their forties and fifties after years of line cooking take their toll. Typically, middle-aged chefs suffer from arthritis and joint problems in their wrists, knees, and hips. Women in particular choose to start their own chefing business, so that they can enjoy their family and be around for their children.

E ssential

A personal chef will usually have five clients at a time, cooking one day during the week for each client. An experienced personal chef can shop, cook, store, and clean up for a client in a six-hour day, making the job quite manageable.

Personal chefing is a great option if you want to have direct input on helping people eat healthier. For clients, knowing that they'll have a delicious home-cooked meal to sit down to whenever they get home is a big relief. Personal chefing also provides a more relaxed atmosphere for chefs who are passionate about cooking but don't necessarily thrive with the pressures of catering. With personal chefing, unlike in the restaurant business, no one is sitting at a table, waiting for you to finish cooking their entrée so they can eat.

✓Expertise

Jim and Brian Davis run a thriving personal chef and catering business called Brian's Kitchen and a cooking school in Rockville, Maryland. In the beginning, the father-son team needed some help. Although Brian was a professionally trained chef, he didn't know anything about personal chefing. Jim turned to the Internet and got advice from a professional personal chef association.

Private chefs have to work out their schedules with their client. They may be needed all day, or parts of the day, and may sometimes have to work weekends. Private chefs will often cook meals and serve them immediately to clients seated in a nearby dining room.

Make sure your commercial kitchen is licensed and you have the necessary permits and licenses for your vehicle, such as commercial plates. Laws vary from state to state, so check with your municipality to see if it requires a business license for a meal-serving business.

Types of Personal Chefs

Most personal chefs prepare a variety of dinner entrées and side dishes for clients who want wholesome meals ready to eat whenever they choose. That's a pretty broad spectrum, and you may want to specialize in making meals for people with special requirements. It can be challenging to make delicious and filling meals without common ingredients like dairy or gluten, but if you can earn a reputation for cooking spectacular meals under such restrictions, you can gain a foothold in the market.

Consider some of the factors in specialized chefing, and keep in mind that you can concentrate on multiple areas:

- **Dietary requirements.** There are many people who are on restricted diets, and they can depend on you to make sure they can still eat delicious meals with the right nutrition. Clients may have specific food concerns such as lactose intolerance or celiac disease, but personal chefs can also carve a niche for themselves by cooking for clients with other conditions, such as high blood pressure, heart disease, diabetes, and cancer.
- **Family situations.** Young families with infants and small children present special challenges, especially if the children are picky eaters.
- **Diets.** Clients may want you to prepare meals that are wholly organic or vegetarian. Others may adhere to the Zone Diet or the Atkins Diet. You may not be asked to stick to a particular diet at all, but some clients will ask for meals that are low-fat, low-carbohydrate, or low-calorie.
- **Kosher diets.** Clients on kosher diets will want you to use only kosher products and follow kosher practices.
- **Athletes.** Athletes often require specialized diets to maintain their physique.

E Fact

Some vacationers splurge on personal chefs when they go on vacation. Often, when clients hire a yacht with a professional crew, a private chef is included as part of the crew. His job is to tailor every meal to the vacationers' specific requests. The same is true of exclusive villas.

With baby boomers aging and older adults living longer, the opportunities for personal chefs will dramatically increase over the next twenty years. Adults who can no longer cook for themselves and who must stick to specific diets will increasingly be hiring personal chef services to work with their doctors and nutritionists to keep them healthy.

The Personal Chef Industry

In a survey commissioned by the American Personal and Private Chef Association (APPCA), as of June 2006, there were approximately 9,000 personal chefs in the United States, and the APPCA represented nearly 4,000 active member chefs. The industry started in the 1980s and is still in its infancy.

Personal chefs in the United States are estimated to serve 72,000 clients a year, generating an annual revenue of $300 million. Industry predictions project that if the present rate of growth continues there will be nearly 25,000 personal chefs serving nearly 300,000 clients and contributing nearly $1.2 billion to the American economy annually within the next five years.

E ssential

Knowledgeable parents are refraining from feeding their families unhealthy fast food meals. Those who don't have time to cook for themselves are increasingly turning to personal chef services to prepare family meals. This represents a growing segment of the personal chefing market.

The personal chefing industry is growing quickly to keep up with demand. Many busy professionals find that they'd rather spend time eating dinner with their families than shopping and cooking. Additionally, with nutritional and health concerns for their families, they'd rather have a personal chef create healthy, balanced meals than have to rely on ordering out. Many singles, too, particularly men, use personal chefs to cook nutritious meals, which allows them to use the time they gain to go to the gym or socialize. Many have such hectic work schedules that they have little time or energy to devote to meal planning.

Planning Menus

Personal chefs cooking in clients' homes have to plan their menus ahead of time so that they can shop efficiently and plan their cooking dates and be sure to complete the week's meals during the time the client is away. Menus are customized for each client and accommodate each client's unique likes and dislikes. As a personal chef, you'll meet with a prospective client and have her fill out a detailed form, called an LDA form (Likes, Dislikes, and Allergies). You'll gather information about the client from her eating goals, her daily routine. This will allow you to plan meals to distribute the calories throughout the day. It will also tell you what details you should pay attention to, such as whether she likes her poultry with or without skin and bones and how finely she likes her vegetables chopped.

E Alert

Personal and private chefs must know if any of their clients have any major food allergies. Make sure to ask your client and fill out any allergy information on the LDA form. Major food allergens include milk, eggs, fish, shellfish, tree nuts, wheat, peanuts, and soybeans.

Personal and private chefs are expected to make everything from scratch. As a personal or private chef, you cannot use tomato sauce from a jar or chicken stock from a can or box. Sauces, stocks, soups, and everything else is made from scratch. Unseasoned stocks and sauces, however, can be made ahead and brought to the client if you have access to a licensed commercial kitchen.

Planning Ahead

Personal and professional chefs, like caterers, must be efficient. You'll only have three to four hours to cook five entrées and a variety of side dishes for your client. In order to accomplish this task, you'll have to plan menus carefully. Since you'll be working on home equipment, you really won't be able to sauté more than two things at once, so plan at least one baked dish, such as a casserole or lasagna; one roasted dish, such as roast chicken, meatloaf, or roast beef; and possibly a fifth entrée that is marinated and then grilled or broiled.

Fact

Personal chefs can cater parties for their clients as long as the party is in the client's home and the cooking is done in the home's kitchen. A personal chef can't buy or serve alcohol, nor can she transport food to another location.

Your menu planning should incorporate how long the dishes will take to cook, so that you can use your time in the client's kitchen wisely. Make sure to start soups and long-cooking dishes like rice and beans on the back of the stove first. Then prepare your casseroles and baked dishes, attending to the sautéed and grilled dishes last.

Individualized Menus

Making entrées and side dishes to customers' specifications is an essential part of a personalized chef service, so make sure to use and fill out detailed information forms for each client.

Private chefs will usually have to present clients with a suggested menu for special events and will offer a few options of a client's favorite foods during an average day. Sometimes clients will request something special for a meal. Private chefs, like personal chefs, will have to get to know their employers' likes and dislikes intimately.

Typical Clients

The following is a list of the customer segments that hire personal chefs. Target these groups when marketing your service:

- **Dual-income families with kids.** Today's busy, active families are discovering that they can spend more quality time together eating dinner rather than having to wait for mom or dad to shop and then make dinner.
- **Dual-income, no kids (DINKs).** Active, professional couples with a lot of disposable income hire personal chefs so they can spend what little free time they have enjoying leisure activities with each other.

- **Single professionals.** Both busy men and women are finding that personal chefs can provide them with wholesome, ready-to-eat meals at any time of the day or night.
- **People with health issues.** People who can't shop or cook for themselves and who require meals to meet a certain number of calories or a particular type of diet can depend on personal chefs to help them reach their goals.
- **Older adults.** With adults living well into their eighties, nineties, and beyond, many people who live on their own can no longer shop or cook for themselves, and hiring a personal chef means that they can continue living independently.

Before you begin your career as a private or personal chef, think about which of these segments you would feel most comfortable cooking for and which you have the most experience working with already.

Private Chefs

A private chef works exclusively for one client, either full-time or part-time.

Many celebrities and other public figures prefer having a private chef cook for them at home since they are always recognized when eating out and have trouble enjoying a quiet meal in a restaurant with their families.

E Fact

It's a good idea to keep a list of ingredients that your employer or client dislikes or is allergic to posted where you plan menus and where you cook. You can have these lists laminated in plastic at a FedEx Kinko's store so they won't be damaged by wet hands or kitchen spatters.

Some private chefs who work full-time for a client may also function as an executive estate manager, coordinating general household maintenance and attending to other noncooking duties. Personal chefs working for executives and diplomats have to be familiar with the rules of etiquette and how to treat guests of various nationalities and customs. The private chefing experience will vary greatly depending on the client. Some clients, of course, will be more demanding than others.

Pricing Your Services

Personal chefs usually charge by the day, and the rate varies according to where the chef works. In smaller cities and larger towns, rates are generally $175–$200 per day plus the cost of the food. The chef is responsible for doing the shopping; bringing the groceries to the client's house; prepping, cooking, and storing the meals; and cleaning up. In larger urban areas, a personal chef will charge $250–$300 per day plus the cost of the food.

The traditional personal chef package for clients includes five entrées with four servings of each entrée and two side dishes per entrée. Snacks, breakfasts, and desserts cost extra. The price for this standard package varies across the country, though the going rate in a large urban area is currently $395 per week (or per cook date at the client's house).

That equates to $20 per meal, a fair price for the client considering the time, effort, and skill put into the meal and its high quality. That price includes the shopping, delivery, storage, and cleanup, so point that out to your clients if they balk at your price. Twenty dollars is less than what it would cost the client to eat out at most decent restaurants in their area.

E ssential

Most clients choose to eat out or cook for themselves on weekends, so most personal chefs don't include weekend meals in their basic plans. If a client wants meals for seven days, negotiate with him. You might have to cook for him two days during the week, depending on how much variety he wants and how large his family is.

Contracts and Price Sheets

Unlike catered events, detailed proposals aren't necessary for personal chefing. Since you won't be planning an elaborate event, you'll just need to prepare a general pricing and terms sheet outlining your cancellation and additional charge policies.

Computer software can help personal chefs keep track of each client's likes and dislikes. Whether you use catering-specific software or general office software, keep a list in Microsoft Word or in a spreadsheet that spells out each client's preferences for everything from her desired type of storage containers to her favorite types of fruits. By keeping a detailed list and referring to it before you cook for each client, you'll be able to deliver a very high level of customer service.

Communication with Clients

Just as in the catering business, personal chefs are only as good as the last meal they cook. If the client isn't happy, he won't continue to use you. To prevent clients from leaving, ask each one for feedback a couple of days after you've made the week's meals. Ask what he liked and didn't like and have him note anything he wants you to change. Not everyone will give you honest feedback, but it will keep many clients who would have left. Make sure you note his concerns on his personal profiles and address them next time.

 Fact

You must meet with a prospective client in her home kitchen to see what condition the appliances are in, what kind of cookware she has, and how the pantry and refrigerator are stocked. This will give you additional insight into what the client generally likes to eat.

Collect feedback from customers either by phone or e-mail. Add specific notes to the profile you have stored on your computer. If one client didn't like a certain recipe of yours, make a note. Ask the client if she has a recipe she'd like you to follow.

Establishing some basic policies up front will save you a lot of time, money, and heartache. For example, take a valid credit card number from every client when he books a cook date or a delivery date with you. Charge customers a flat cancellation fee if they cancel a cook date less than forty-eight hours in advance, and print this on your price sheet. Most people won't cancel on short notice if they know they'll have to pay a fee. Charge a small surcharge if clients want every meal stored in individual portions rather than family portions.

To increase revenue, offer to bake a dozen cookies or a celebration cake for your clients for a flat fee. Print up a simple flier telling them that your cookies and cakes are great for school and office parties and are perfect for snacks and a well-deserved dessert. Charge $10–$13 per dozen for large, freshly baked cookies with real chocolate, nuts, and fruit bits. Charge $20–$45 for a homemade personalized layer cake.

☀ Alert

You may want to charge your clients a travel supplement if you have to travel more than twenty-five miles from where you live. Keep in mind that that's a fifty-mile round trip, so plan stops carefully, allowing for travel time. Try to schedule cook times that aren't during rush hour.

Another idea for adding revenue to your business is to ask clients to provide a shopping list of additional items to give to you at least forty-eight hours prior to a scheduled cook date. You can charge a nominal fee for picking up extra groceries, and it's easy for you to pick up the items when you're doing your other shopping. You can add the cost of the groceries to your client's bill for the week. Just limit the number of items you'll pick up. You're a personal chef, after all, not a grocery delivery service.

Professional Personal Chef Associations

Joining a professional association for the industry will provide you with insurance coverage, a professional network, and an efficient service to match you with clients in your area.

American Personal and Private Chef Association

The American Personal and Private Chef Association (*www .personalchef.com*) is a twelve-year-old organization headed by executive director and personal chef Candy Wallace. APPCA provides education and training to people who want to have their own chefing businesses. The organization also provides its members with general liability coverage and matches chefs with clients as part of its service to its members.

E ssential

Professional organizations charge annual dues for membership. Chefs' organizations are no different, but the benefits of membership outweigh the cost. Gaining accreditation from one of the organizations will allow you to expand your career beyond chefing. You can stray from the kitchen into the classroom and teach aspiring chefs how to cook if you desire.

APPCA has local chapters around the country. The organization offers two-day skills seminars throughout the year in cities across the country. For those who want to study at home, it offers DVD-based programs as well.

United States Personal Chef Association

The United States Personal Chef Association (*www.uspca.com*) is the other professional organization in the industry. Although the USPCA is older, it's not run by a personal chef. Like APPCA, this organization provides its members with general liability insurance coverage for property damage and bodily injury while cooking in a client's home. It also provides seminars, networking opportunities, and a way to market yourself through *www.hireachef.com*. The USPCA offers certification, and once you have met the requirements, you have a recognized industry qualification, which will set you apart from those without it.

Opportunity Areas for Personal and Private Chefs

There's no sign that Americans will have more time to shop and to cook anytime soon. With the average work week getting longer and scheduled activities for kids on the rise, personal chefs will continue to be in demand. Additionally, as the population continues to age, there will be an increased need for personal chefs to cook for those who can't but still wish to live independently. As the personal chef industry continues to develop and expand, more and more people will want to benefit from its services. You can adapt to the market by adding high-demand items and services.

Sugar-Free and Low-Fat Desserts

Most clients don't ask for desserts in their meal plan. If you can offer reasonably priced delicious desserts that are sugar free, you can target your services to the growing diabetic market. Modify some of your regular dessert recipes and use Splenda and other sweeteners that are okay for diabetics. This will differentiate your company from others.

Kosher Clients

If you're in an area with many professional Jewish singles, families, and older adults, you might want to target personal chefing services for clients who keep kosher. There are more than 2 million people in the United States who keep kosher homes, and these people tend to live in just a few cities. The biggest area of Jewish population in the country is the Metropolitan New York region, which includes Northern New Jersey, Long Island, and Southern Connecticut. Los Angeles, including Riverside and Orange Counties, is the second largest, and Miami–Fort Lauderdale is the third-largest market. The greater Philadelphia metropolitan area and the Chicago area round out the top five markets.

You need to understand how a kosher kitchen is organized and know which ingredients can be mixed together and which must be avoided altogether. Once you understand how to cook in a kosher kitchen, you can cook in clients' homes. The key differences between a kosher and nonkosher kitchen are:

- **There are separate sets** of cookware, silverware, utensils, and plates for meat dishes and dairy dishes.
- **Only kosher cuts of meat and fish may be used.** Unkosher cuts of beef like sirloin and filet mignon cannot be used. No pork may be used. Shellfish may not be used.
- **Dairy may not be mixed with meat.** Milk, for example, may not be used to coat chicken, veal, or any other kind of meat. Cheese may not be used with meat, so a traditional lasagna recipe must be modified. Fish are considered pareve—not meat or dairy—but it may not be eaten or cooked with poultry.

Often, kosher kitchens have a split sink. One side is used for dairy dishes and one side for meat. The two must be kept separate at all times. Kosher kitchens may also have separate ovens, dishwashers, and refrigerators. Talk to your clients to find out the details of their kitchens.

You can charge a premium for cooking kosher meals in a client's home because the restrictions will make extra work. You'll have to cook some pareve meals like fish and vegetarian casseroles and some separate meat meals and dairy meals. Most likely, cooking for kosher clients will take a bit more time, so charge accordingly.

Vegetarian and Vegan Clients

The number of people in the United States who define themselves as vegetarian or vegan is growing. Approximately 7 percent of Americans are vegetarians, and this market is expanding as people become more and more concerned about their health, their food's health, and the environment's health. The market for vegetarians is estimated to be between 21 and 25 million people in the United States. If there is a growing vegetarian population in your area, you may want to specialize in vegetarian cooking.

There are several different types of vegetarianism, so check with each client to make sure you know what you can and cannot cook. Some vegetarians do not eat dairy and eggs, while others eat one of the two, and still others consume both. Strict vegans abstain from eating anything with animal products. This includes honey, which is made by bees.

Chapter 8

Developing a Catering Menu

Devising your menus should be fun. Be creative and make sure to put your own special touch on your offerings. Include variations of what you cook or bake best. If you're known for your wonderful Asian fusion hors d'oeuvres, be sure to feature them whenever possible. There are tens of thousands of catering menus out there; practically every restaurant, deli, grocery store, and gourmet store has their own, not to mention every caterer. Study the ones in your area and make sure yours stands out.

Menus That Sell

Creative and innovative menus are an integral part of the total experience you create for your clients. Aside from your reputation and your talent, your menu is one of the most important marketing and sales tools that you have. Your menus play a major role in whether or not you get hired, and they reflect the image and tone of your business. Menus are the perfect place to tickle your clients' senses with mouthwatering descriptions of your dishes. They should look professional, but they should also stand out in the pile of competing menus your potential customers will collect.

Always keep in mind the two most important aspects of your catering business: your target audience and the food you will serve them.

Target Audience

You should have a collection of menus from other catering companies left over from your competitive research. Borrow from their best ideas and adapt their offerings to what you think your customers would like. Look through cookbooks and magazine articles. Scour local gourmet food shops, and study their prepared food cases. New ideas will start coming to you.

The way your menu is organized and laid out will help attract clients' attention. Make sure the menu is easy to read and understand, but try to be innovative in how you present the information. If your concept stresses offering many of your delicious side dishes with every meal, feature them in the center of the menu and list the main dishes off to the side.

☀ Alert

Make sure your menus are geared to your target customers. If you're targeting corporate picnics and barbecues, don't include quiches, seared *foie gras*, or hot soups on your menus. Include appropriate dishes and put your own signature on each recipe you serve.

Use fonts and outlines to highlight various features of the menu. Remember, your menu is your most important marketing piece after your Web site and business card. It has to reflect the personality of your business.

Tasty Inspirations

Before you begin to write your menu, you must decide what dishes you will offer. You may already have ideas for some dishes, but you will need a full menu of choices for your customers.

Keep a journal of menu ideas. Paste in photos of appetizers, soups, entrées, desserts, and beverages that appeal to you. Add recipes that you'd like to experiment with. Make notes about what you think would work for a large group, for a buffet, for a catered brunch. Keep adding to the book and referring to it as you develop your menu. You can buy a blank journal at most stationery and office supply stores; using a three-ring binder gives you the flexibility of moving pages around to help you visualize your menu. Make sure to copy the pages of your journal every few weeks and store them in a safe place in case the journal gets destroyed, damaged, or lost.

E ssential

Menu Creation

Writing and rewriting your menus is not something you can do in a morning, an afternoon, or an evening. Set aside time every day over a period of weeks—or even months. If done correctly, innovative menus will help you grow your top line, while your chef skills will ensure that you can deliver your menus in an efficient and profitable manner.

Menu Mainstays

Now that you have a good idea about your concept and what types of foods you'll be offering, start with a clean sheet of paper or a clear spreadsheet and label it "Classics Menu." Begin by listing the dishes you think you'll make the most. For example, if you plan to specialize in catering bridal showers and other brunch/luncheon parties mainly for women, then list the salads, quiches, sandwiches, desserts, and beverages that will be the mainstay of your menu. If you plan to specialize in barbecues, list pulled pork and ribs along with the specialty coleslaws, potato salads, homemade baked beans, and other specialties you'll be offering. Your classics menu should reflect the pillars of your catering business. These are—maybe literally—your bread and butter. They will always appear on your menu, and repeat customers will recognize and request these staples.

Grandiose menus with many exotic ingredients don't pay off unless you're a top caterer charging $150 or more a head. Smart menu design uses the same ingredients over and over again in clever ways so that food buying can be done efficiently. A well-thought-out menu will have chicken breast in one dish, for example, chicken stock in another, and gizzard stuffing as a side, so that the entire chicken can be used.

Ⓔ Fact

If you use catering software like CaterEdge, CaterEase, or Synergy, you can develop your menus right in the software, and it will be easier for you to do cost analyses.

Seasonal Items

Make a list of seasonal items that highlight the produce of spring, summer, winter, and fall. Every season, you'll want to add a few of these items to your classics menu so that your menu stays fresh and not dated. For example, in winter you may want to offer some heartier fare, liked a spiced pumpkin soup, while for summer luncheons you'll want to offer a couple of cold soups like watermelon gazpacho.

For Thanksgiving, Christmas, and New Year's (or for Rosh Hashanah and Yom Kippur if you're a kosher caterer), you'll want to create streamlined menus to help you get through the busy holiday season. Offer plenty of roasted meats and vegetables that aren't labor-intensive and dishes that can be prepped and made ahead of time like pies, tarts, soups, and cranberry sauce. Some items can be made ahead and frozen, so you may need additional freezer space starting in your busiest seasons.

If you don't start out with catering-specific software, put your menus in a word-processing program on your computer, since you'll need different versions. Once on your computer, you can easily customize and tailor your menus as needed for clients. The menus will need to be modified depending on the size of the group, the location, and the type of event and venue.

Premium Menu Items

After you develop the key items and holiday specialties, start a list of "premium items." Premium items are upgrades to your standard fare or contain special ingredients, and they will cost more. For example, a filet mignon, goat cheese, and arugula sandwich would be an add-on item, replacing your standard roast beef, field greens, and horse-radish mayonnaise sandwich.

Developing a premium item or add-on approach for your menu will help you up-sell customers and increase your revenue per head. Know what customers in your market are likely to request, and have a versatile menu that will help you meet their needs.

E ssential

Use specific adjectives to energize menu items. Try hot, crisp, tender, velvety, sizzling, delicate, silky, creamy, crunchy, chilled, tender, and savory.

Sources of Food

Customers are more concerned than ever about where their food is coming from. Organic and locally grown ingredients are one of the fastest growing segments of the food industry, so your menus, pricing, and selling strategy should take this trend into account.

Locally raised, free-roaming, grass-fed meats are also in vogue, as are exotic imported meats like Kobe beef and kangaroo steaks. A wide variety of fresh game is also available from suppliers. Offer these ingredients to clients who are looking for something truly different, and develop a couple of different versions of menus featuring these premium-priced products if they fit into your catering concept.

Ethnic Goes Mainstream

The usual roast chicken dinner won't cut it anymore. Customers are drawing inspiration from the recent influx of exotic ingredients into local restaurants and grocery stores. They hear about items like pickled shallots and chanterelle mushrooms, and they want savvy caterers who know how to cook with them. Increasingly, clients want specialized themes—not just a Caribbean theme, but the foods of

Jamaica, for example. As a caterer, it's challenging to stay up-to-date on the trends, but it gives you the flexibility to experiment with new dishes.

✓Expertise

The City Bakery Catering Company in New York and Los Angeles specializes in fusion cuisine. One hors d'oeuvre, pork tenderloin with hummus and radish on paratha, mixes foods that are not traditionally served together. Middle Eastern hummus is not usually served with pork, and it's generally eaten with pita bread, not Indian paratha.

Caterers are using ethnic ingredients in new and unusual ways, creating fusion menus for their customers. Fusion cuisine blends ingredients and techniques from different cooking traditions to create truly unique flavors. There are few boundaries with fusion cuisine, but it does require an understanding of the tastes and traditions of multiple cuisines.

Artisanal and Farmstead Cheeses

Cheese has been reborn in the United States in the last decade. Rising numbers of restaurants offer cheese trays on their menus, and more small domestic dairies produce artisanal or farmstead cheeses. Customers are coming to expect high-quality, flavorful cheeses. It's no longer acceptable for a caterer to offer a cheese tray composed of Brie, Jarslberg, and Port Salut.

Handmade or artisanal foods command premium prices. Source some local cheeses and artisanal chocolates and offer these on your menus as premium items. Educate your clients about these items and offer a cheese course at appropriate events. When it's appropriate, offer to do a guided cheese tasting for your clients. If you can't do it yourself, invite a local cheese expert in from a dairy or from a cheese shop.

Offering artisanal and farmstead cheeses is a way to up-sell your customer and increase your profits. As a caterer, you'll need to know something about cheese and how to serve it with honeys, preserves, Marcona almonds, and other accoutrements.

Dark Chocolate

The fine chocolate market—especially dark chocolate—is growing as consumers realize that all chocolates are not created equal. Customers are demanding better-quality chocolate and more exotic chocolate desserts, and caterers are rising to the challenge with Meyer lemon and sea salt truffles and chocolate-dipped cocoa nibs.

Tea

No longer just a hot beverage for ladies, fine tea is now part of all types of beverages, from cocktails to frozen smoothies. Caterers can no longer serve iced tea made with commercial Lipton tea bags. This gives you the freedom to explore other options, such as young white teas and Japanese green teas.

Even bakeries have taken advantage of the trend, making dozens of sweet and savory items flavored with green tea, jasmine tea, and chai. As you're developing your menus, experiment and see how green tea can fit into your dishes. Whether it's tea-infused poached chicken breast or Matcha-dusted chocolate truffles, green tea is a trendy ingredient that will spice up your menu.

Preliminary Costing

Every item on your menu needs a price. Keep track of how much every ingredient costs and how much labor each dish will require. Menu prices should also reflect associated business costs, such as overhead. Once you have established these costs, you will add a markup, which is where your profit will come from. The next chapter discusses the specifics of pricing your menu, but prices can be fixed according to a rough formula:

- **Food costs:** 20–30 percent
- **Labor costs:** 5–10 percent
- **Overhead:** 15 percent
- **Markup:** 45–60 percent

Remember, gratuity is always added on top of your price. You give your client a price and explain that a service charge is added on top to cover the gratuity. Generally, service charges range from 17 to 25 percent.

Determining costings will be a long and tedious process when you start your business, but it has to be done correctly. You can't guesstimate costings and run a profitable business. Catering software can make the tedious job of costing menu items easier. Let the software do the calculations for you.

Costing Food

Costings must be done based on your final recipes. If you change a recipe, the costings will no longer be accurate. You'll have to estimate costs for salt, spices, and other ingredients—even water. It doesn't matter if it's only a few cents; enter a cost for each ingredient. If it's not free for you, it shouldn't be free for the client.

Determine how many servings your recipes will yield. Try to have the same yield for all of the recipes on your menu. This will make pricing easier for you. For example, if you base your standard recipes on thirty-six servings, you can calculate the cost of buying ingredients for thirty-six portions and price each dish accordingly. Using a recipe that works for a large number of servings means you won't have to alter the recipe to cater larger jobs, but don't base your recipes on too large a number. You'll end up underestimating your per-serving cost, since you'll overestimate the discount you get by buying in bulk.

If you use nine pounds of salmon in your baked salmon dish to get thirty-six servings, you'll have to price the exact type of salmon you use for your classics and premium menus. If you use farmed salmon on your classics menu, find an average price per pound from the two or three most likely sources you'll purchase the fish from. Don't use the lowest price you find, and don't use sale prices. If you want to offer wild Pacific salmon on your premium menu as an upgrade, price that type of fish. Calculate the average premium over the farm-raised fish, and record that information on your spreadsheet.

It's better to overestimate the cost of a dish than to underestimate it. If you're too conservative with costings, you may end up losing money.

Labor, Overhead, and Up-Selling

To determine labor, you need to know how many man-hours it takes to prepare and serve each item on your menu. Calculate a weighted-average for determining a labor cost for a specific event. To know your overhead cost, list each of the fixed and variable charges you pay annually or every month. This list should include your rent, energy costs, insurance premiums, and other costs that you pay day in and day out, whether or not you have a catering gig.

Determine a price for up-selling a customer, and record it in a separate column on your spreadsheet or as a separate item in your catering software, so you'll be prepared when you meet with clients. Be prepared to offer potential clients other options to make their event even more special. If it turns out that the client has a big sweet tooth, for example, have a price ready for a complete chocolate decadence buffet, rather than just a price for a standard cake.

Since food and overhead costs tend to go up on an annual basis, you'll need to adjust your costings every year and raise menu prices as needed.

Truth-in-Menu Laws

Federal "Truth-in-Menu" laws require that caterers and other menu planners accurately describe dishes and fairly represent prices and other charges on their menus. Accuracy in menu development involves more than honestly describing an entrée and precisely stating a price. It also means being careful when describing many food attributes, including the preparation style, ingredients, origin, portion sizes, and health benefits. Make sure you can deliver on everything you put on a menu. If you promise an eight-ounce aged sirloin steak, make sure it weighs a half pound before cooking and that it's an aged sirloin, not a fresh rib eye.

Ⓔ Fact

The National Restaurant Association has published "A Practical Guide to the Nutrition Labeling Laws," to assist foodservice operators as they develop menus. This guide outlines everything you need to know about nutrition claims you can make for your menu items.

Here are some specific guidelines for describing menu items.

Brand Names

You cannot use a copyrighted or registered trademark to identify an item in your menu unless you use the specific product in your dish. If you use round, candy-coated chocolate bits in your cookies, you can't describe them as "M&M Cookies" unless you use genuine M&M's. If you use a generic product, this is your chance to get creative with names and descriptions; chances are your customers won't miss the brand names.

Means of Preservation

You can't call something "fresh" if it has been previously frozen—ever! This includes everything from shrimp to frozen juices to pies.

Merchandising Terms

Don't say anything you serve for your catering business is "homemade." It wasn't actually made in your home kitchen. That would be an unlicensed facility! Use words like "home-style" or "traditional" instead.

Points of Origin

The point of origin refers to the original spot where the product was grown or harvested, such as Maine lobsters or Florida stone crabs. Make sure the product labels you use are accurate.

Price

Cover charges, service charges, and mandatory gratuities must all be contained in contract or by letter. They should never be hidden or go unmentioned in negotiations.

Product Identification

Sometimes a product must be substituted at the last minute when the item in the initial agreement is not available, not delivered, or too expensive. Be certain to state the correct products being used, but reserve the right in your contracts and on your menus to substitute similar items in extraordinary circumstances, such as E. coli outbreaks, commodity price increases, or delivery problems. If the item you end up using is less expensive than what a client ordered off of your premium menu, refund the difference.

Alert

Often you'll be selling menus and event pricing months in advance. Prices on certain items may increase before you actually order the ingredients and cook and serve the food. Make sure that your prices have enough padding, or margin, to cover an increase in gas usage over the holidays, for example, or a rise in orange juice and milk prices.

Quality

Grades of meat and poultry products should refer strictly to USDA-recognized terminology (Prime, Choice, Select, Standard, and Commercial) or accepted variants (Grade A, Good, Number One, Fancy, Grade AA, and Extra Standard).

Quantity

Steaks are often sold and listed on menus by weight. It is acceptable to use the weight of the raw meat before cooking on your menu.

Type of Preparation

Use the proper terms for the cooking methods you are using to prepare a particular food item—for example, baked, broiled, fried, sautéed, smoked, and roasted.

Fact

Make sure your terminology accurately reflects the ingredients you're using. Pay particular attention to the following words: winter, spring, summer, fall, harvest, rainbow, prime, choice, USDA grade, extra large, jumbo, fresh, natural, whole, original, and signature.

Verbal and Visual Presentation

Be certain that the descriptions given by the waitstaff or written on the menu, or photographs reproduced on menus or table tents, represent what the customer receives.

Caution Statements

It's helpful to include a warning regarding any potentially harmful items on your menu. Customers should be warned about raw foods and common allergens like nuts and gluten.

Basic Menu-Writing Guidelines

Be as descriptive as possible. Your menu should tease your customers into feeling like they can almost taste and smell your dishes simply by reading the descriptions. This is also your opportunity to showcase the quality of your ingredients. If you're using Kobe beef, take credit for it. If the honey you serve is from a private farm in New Hampshire, include it in the description. However, be careful not to stretch the truth. If you're using fresh frozen veal, don't call it fresh, since it's not.

Include your firm's name, phone, e-mail, and Web site on each page of each menu. Just like mail-order catalogs, pages get ripped apart and separated, and you don't want a client hunting for your contact information. If you haven't been trained in professional menu design, it might be helpful to take a class to learn how to design a menu that will be both intriguing and efficient.

E ssential

Don't be afraid to get creative. Include digital pictures that realistically portray what you're selling and serving. Use terms like *starter* or *prelude* for *appetizer, main* instead of *entrée,* and *finale* or *just desserts* rather than *desserts* or *dessert stations.*

It's All in the Details

Pay attention to the paper you use. Match the paper to the client. For an elegant black-tie wedding, emphasize your professionalism with beautiful handmade off-white paper. For a celebratory barbecue, show off your playfulness and creativity. Choose a more informal yellow paper the color of corn on the cob, roll the menus up, and attach decorative corn holders to the ends. For business luncheons, use a heavy-duty paper, and include your client's logo on the menu. Always send a hard copy of all menus and proposals and multiple copies if you're dealing with committees. A good source for paper is *www.paperdirect.com.*

If you e-mail your menus, don't assume they will look the way they appear on your Web site when they are printed from someone else's computer. You may want to e-mail them to clients in a PDF format. This will ensure that they stay formatted and look good.

Triple check all spelling. Prospective clients may not say anything, but if there are misspelled words on your menus, it reflects poorly on you and your attention to detail. Make sure that you have a couple of food dictionaries on your shelf within easy reach, and consult them while you write your menus. *The Food Lover's Companion* by Sharon Herbst is a great resource with thousands of food, wine, and culinary terms.

In all correspondence with your customers, always be sure you spell the client's name right. Is it "Terry" or "Terri"? You may not be sure, but your customer will certainly notice if you get it wrong.

Prices on Menus

Very high-end caterers should not print prices on their menus. Each and every event is customized, and the price is determined by any number of factors such as the date, the number of guests, the location, the client's ability to pay, and the urgency for the catering. Prices should be reflected in your proposal with the specific menus attached and premium ingredients stipulated.

E Alert

Be sure to quadruple-check all of your prices, menu additions, special requests, up charges (for special or unusual ingredients), service fees, and other details before you send a proposal to a client for signing. If you send out a proposal and forget to charge for something or undercharge for something, it's too late.

For drop-off and moderately priced caterers who deal with lots of clients on a daily basis, prices should be printed on your menus and should be updated when necessary. Costing and pricing each order would be inefficient.

Customizing Menus

When writing custom menus for proposals, start with a menu you've done for a similar type of event if possible. This way, you can customize menus in a matter of minutes, not hours or days. As you work more and more jobs, you'll have at least a few dozen separate menus in your computer—from ethnic menus to barbecues to picnic and cocktail party menus.

Writing menus should be challenging. Consider that your menus reflect your business, so if you hardly change them from season to season and year to year, your business will be dated rather than cutting edge. Menu writing requires concentrated effort; don't try to write your new fall menus while prepping a job. Block out time on your schedule for tasting new menu recipes, menu writing, menu analysis, and costing.

Creative Design and Presentation

Be creative in the way that you deliver your menus to the client for approval and at the event. One sure-fire way to get a prospective client's attention is by delivering some of your food as samples with the menu. Make sure to deliver something that will hold up during transport and taste good at room temperature. Deliver the food with china, flatware, and linen napkins, and serve the customer. If you have to leave the china and flatware, follow up and try to close the deal when you return for pick-up.

At the event itself, make the menu an extension of the theme. For example, if it's a 1950s party, put the menu in a record album cover. For Kentucky Derby–themed parties print the menu like a racing program. If you're doing a proposal for a picnic, pin the menus to a red-and-white checked cloth napkin and deliver them rolled up in a fun napkin ring.

Menus for Place Settings

Printed menus that are set at each place setting should be printed on card stock. They can be scored and folded in half or printed only on one side. The ideal size is 4" × 6". The day, date, and occasion should be written at the top of the menu. Wines and beverages may be listed to the left of each course or directly underneath. Kosher menus should have the name of the specific kosher supervision at the bottom. Careful proofreading is essential to avoid reprinting costs.

Chapter 9

Pricing Your Services and Menus

To sell your catering services, you must set prices for them or customers *can't* buy them, and they must be the right prices or customers *won't* buy them. Your pricing will help to position you in the marketplace, informing potential customers about the expected quality of your food and service. Correct pricing will help you attract customers and maximize potential profit. Pricing can be complex, so this chapter focuses on setting prices with confidence.

Pricing Strategy

Your prices must be consistent with your concept. If you're planning to be a high-end wedding caterer but your prices are competitive with the catering department of the local grocery store, then you haven't priced yourself correctly. Your prices must accurately reflect the level of quality and service you're going to offer.

In business, there are two main pricing strategies:

- Being the low-cost producer
- Providing differentiated goods and services

Low-cost producers are able to provide consumers with the lowest prices for goods. They make their money by being extremely efficient, selling high quantities of products at a relatively low margin. For example, Wal-Mart is a low-cost producer. It is not feasible for caterers to be low-cost producers, simply because one caterer cannot provide the volume of service necessary to discount prices as deeply as a low-cost producer does. Caterers follow the second pricing strategy, providing unique goods and services.

Differentiated Pricing Strategy

You need to charge prices that reflect the ingredient quality and level of sophistication of your offerings. Being the lowest-cost caterer in your area will only spell disaster. Larger, more efficient caterers will drive you out of business by matching or beating your prices, and setting low prices will cut into your profit. These two factors will make your business venture very short-lived.

Your best option is to follow a differentiated pricing strategy. This method of pricing is as much of an art as it is a science. While you must be sure to cover all your costs and include a profit, how much you charge for your products depends on many factors. Prices for differentiated products are signals to potential customers. If your prices are high, some customers will aspire to use you, others will be unable to afford you, and another customer segment will be your main target, since you'll be right in their price range.

Catering, like most food businesses, is a business of pennies; if you don't price your products and services correctly, you won't be profitable.

Differentiated service providers like caterers must choose where in the competitive price range they'll be. It's safest to be in the middle of the range. A good rule of thumb for pricing your menu and service is to be about 10 percent above the average competition in your area.

Location is a prime factor in pricing. You must consider the local cost of living, competitive prices, what you're offering, and who you're targeting. In general, caterers located in large urban areas, where the cost of living is higher, will charge more than caterers located in places with a lower cost of living.

Variations in Prices

Depending on the caterer, a similar meal can have a wide price range across the country. Three differently positioned caterers in three different cities, for instance, can serve a similar three-course dinner of salad, grilled salmon, and dessert. The prices they charge can vary tremendously depending on the type of the event, the event venue, the city or town, and the type of caterer.

Caterer A, a middle-of-the-road caterer in Rapid City, South Dakota, serving a seated dinner at a museum might charge $25 a person without wine for salad, grilled salmon, and dessert.

Caterer B, a premium caterer in Cleveland, Ohio, might charge $80 a person for a similar meal. The table settings might be fancier, the side dishes might be more elegant and might include more expensive ingredients like shiitake mushrooms and fingerling potatoes, and the desserts might be more elaborate, but the meal would be essentially the same. Some wine might be included in this price, but not enough to account for the price difference.

E Fact

According to *Event Solutions* magazine's latest *Fact Book*, the average food cost per person for a fully catered event is $16.20, while the average price per person for a fully catered dinner is $38.62.

Caterer C, a high-end Manhattan caterer serving a similar meal at a seated black-tie charity event at a small New York City museum, could charge $140 per person. While this price would include the cost of alcoholic beverages, wild Pacific salmon, heirloom vegetables, and a Valrhona chocolate tart for dessert, the higher food costs don't by themselves account for vast price difference from the South Dakota and Ohio caterers.

Caterer C can command such a high price because of the level of service it offers, because of its stellar client list and reputation, and because of the high cost of living in New York City. The cost of living in Cleveland is much higher than in South Dakota, and the cost of living in New York City is nearly double the cost of living in Rapid City. This means that the cost of transportation, rent, supplies, and labor are highest in New York City, and that translates to higher catering prices.

The Rise of the $40 Entrée

As restaurant prices increase and menu pricing breaks new barriers, catering prices will follow the trend. In 2006, restaurants around the country broke the $39 entrée barrier and started to charge $40 and over for main courses. Steak and lobster have long been among the most expensive dishes, but pasta and fish dishes in urban markets around the country are starting to command $40 price tags at upscale restaurants and even national chains.

E ssential

Offering more expensive price points with your menus will raise your total revenue. If you offer a client a choice between menus priced at $150, $130, and $115 per person, for example, the $130 menu looks cheap next to the $150 menu and makes it much more attractive.

The fact that casual upscale restaurants are charging these prices signals that catering prices will continue to go higher. As long as chefs continue to experiment with their menus to serve items no one else has and use organic and heirloom produce, farm-raised meats, and wild fish from high-quality purveyors, meal prices will climb. As long as your service is commensurate with the higher prices you're charging for food, your customers will pay them.

Both Ends of the Spectrum

If you're going to be a price leader and charge higher prices than your competition, you must offer food and service that is truly extraordinary. Being at the lower end of the price range forces you to compete on price.

Catering is a service business, and you need to price yourself accordingly. You're creating an ambiance; you're providing entertainment and using your creativity to design an event. What you offer is a unique product, not a commodity, so your prices must reflect that.

☀ E ☀ Alert

If you're premium priced, everything about your company must signal premium quality. From your name, logo, menu layout, and staff attire, all must consistently signal that you're a premium provider.

You don't want to price yourself too high, or you'll scare away potential customers. Similarly, you don't want to price yourself too low, so that you're way below what the market will bear. There are two methods you can use to price your services: top-down and bottom-up.

Top-Down Pricing Method

The first step to determining your pricing is to compare the pricing data you compiled in your competitive survey. Make sure that you're comparing similar services. Try to pick caterers that are close to your concept and your type of catering. You'll be able to tell which caterers are similar to you by comparing their menu prices to yours and by comparing their service fees to yours.

It's important to study how caterers in your area price themselves. Make a spreadsheet and track the answers to these questions for each competitor:

- How much do they charge for serving staff?
- How much is an additional server?
- How much is a bartender?
- How much do they mark up outsourced products like liquor, specialty cakes, and ice sculptures?
- Do they charge a fuel surcharge for jobs more than twenty miles away?
- What extra fees do they charge?

Once you know how other caterers charge, you can make an educated decision about how and what you want to charge. Depending on your marketing strategy, you'll want to either be priced competitively with your colleagues or priced above them if you're planning to offer a more premium catering service.

E Fact

If you are trying to premium price your services, charge at least 20 percent more than the average price of your direct competitors. This alerts customers that you intend to provide superior service, and you will still be in your target audience's price range.

There's no simple mathematical formula to follow for calculating the exact price of your catered meals. The cost of each ingredient you use is quantifiable; you pay an exact amount for thirty-six chicken breasts, for example. The other costs associated with catering are not as tangible. You must also figure preparation labor and transportation into your calculations, but the fixed dollar amount you choose to charge for these components is subjective—and so is the final price you charge your clients. The right price exists between the cost of your materials, labor, and overhead, and what the market will bear. An efficient way to calculate this is to find comparable sales and determine what services in your area can command.

E Alert

The only labor cost that should be included in your menu costings is the labor that is required to make, or prep, a certain menu item or dish. The labor to serve the menu item or to run a buffet is billed to the client on a separate line item of your bill.

Often, like a consultant, you need to convince your client that you are worth the fee you command. Once you show your client what you can do, he'll gladly pay the fee you request.

Bottom-Up Pricing Method

The bottom-up pricing method is a more tedious process than the top-down method, but it is important nevertheless. Only by carefully measuring your costs will you be able to check that your prices are correct and measure your profit. Every caterer will have a different cost structure based on individual factors such as overhead, labor force, marketing expenses, and location. If you lease your own kitchen and employ a dozen people, you'll have a different cost structure than if you rent space in a commercial kitchen and work on your own.

It's very important for you to cost everything from the price you pay to secure supplies, ingredients, and labor. First determine the total cost of every dish that you offer on your menu. Once you know what your total costs are, add the necessary amount of profit to arrive at your final price. Only by doing careful cost analyses will you be able to know how much ingredient and labor cost increases will affect your profit margin.

The amount of profit you'll make on each item will vary. Try to sell as many higher-profit items as possible, and only offer the lower-profit items to satisfy client demands. As long as you hit the average annual profit number, you're doing fine.

Ingredient Costs

Start by making a list of ingredient items, preferably on a spreadsheet on your computer. Create headings like "Dairy Items," "Meat, Poultry, Fish," "Vegetables and Fruits," and "Pantry Items." Continue until you have all the headings that you need to cover all of your ingredients. Under the appropriate heading, list every item that you'll use regularly in your menus.

Vendor Costs

Fill in the cost for each item, and in a separate column list the portion size in ounces. Your list will be long. Make sure to list the size and grade of the item. For example, list a dozen organic large grade-A eggs and sixteen ounces of full-fat sour cream. If the fish you use is farmed, make a note. If the beef is grass-fed, record it. Prices rise over time, so date your spreadsheet.

E ssential

The Web site ✑*www.foodservice.com* is a great resource to help you with ingredient prices and other useful information. To access all of the industry information and resources, register for free online.

Make sure that you fill in total prices you will pay, and don't use a price for a higher quantity than you'll typically buy or a price paid by a higher-volume caterer.

Cost Every Dish

You'll have to cost every dish. Start with your recipe and fill in the costs from your ingredient cost sheet. Calculate the cost per serving. Include your best estimate for prep time and multiply that by your labor cost. If you have an assistant prep that dish, calculate the labor cost based on her wage. If it's a dish you do yourself, you must factor in your labor. To determine your hourly labor cost, compare yourself to the salary of a local chef with a similar amount of experience.

Use these components to cost each dish:

- Food cost
- Food production labor
- Overhead
- Soft costs

Soft costs are variable costs and generally include supervision, profit, freight, software, and other intangible items.

Compare the Two Pricing Methods

Compare the prices, item by item, that you arrived at by each method. In some instances, the two prices for a dish will be close. In other instances, the prices may be rather far apart. If the bottom-up method produced a price that is higher than the top-down method, then you'll probably have to lower the offering or menu price of that item and make a lower amount of profit on that item. If the bottom-up method produced a price that is lower than the top-down method, you can raise your price to what the market will bear for that item. This is where you'll make greater profit and how you'll be able to raise your average profit number.

Fact

Only by tracking the number of items sold and the actual profit per item will you be able to calculate and measure the profitability of your business venture. Use a spreadsheet program or catering-specific software to track your financial performance.

You'll need to have a sense of how price sensitive your customers are and for which products they're the most price sensitive. When researching your concept and positioning, make sure to include pricing questions in your surveys and in your focus group discussions.

Price sensitivity is the extent to which price is an important criterion in your customer's decision-making process; a price-sensitive customer is likely to notice a significant price rise and switch to a cheaper supplier. Price sensitivity varies among market segments and across different products. Some clients might object to the price you charge them for a can of domestic beer, for instance, while they won't question the charge for free-range organic chicken.

Cost Controls

Knowing how to control food, labor, and other costs is a crucial part of running a thriving catering business. Costs for ingredients, labor, equipment, fuel, and other business components will continue to rise. While you will be able to raise some of your prices from time to time, controlling rising costs will be a significant challenge. The more costs you can control and the more you can save by running your business intelligently, the more profitable you'll be.

Maximize Kitchen Efficiency

The more quickly you can prepare food for a job, the better. The lower your total labor costs, the more competitive you'll be. Over time, you'll learn how to efficiently prep for a job and how to best use your staff's talents.

Be Your Own Butcher

Butchering, cutting, trimming, and deboning your own whole birds, whole fish, and larger cuts of meat will save you money. Rather than paying for filets or Frenched lamb chops, it's important that you know how to prepare these cuts yourself.

Minimize Waste

The more you know about how to maximize food use and minimize waste, the more profitable you'll be. Don't over-peel fruits and vegetables, know how to work with cheaper cuts of meat for stews and soups, and utilize all parts of fish, meat, or vegetables in stocks, purees, and dips.

Control Portion Sizes

One common pitfall is serving sizes: Caterers often serve too much or don't keep portion sizes the same. If you're serving filet of beef to 125 people, it's important to weigh each piece and make sure that everyone gets the same portion. For buffets, it's important to have items sliced and cut into one serving size. All pies and casseroles should be precut. Have staff serve guests expensive items like lobster tails, filet slices, and large shrimp from the buffet.

Other Fees

The catering business has relatively low margins. The trend in the catering business over the last several years is to charge clients a service charge on top of the negotiated price per person for the meal. Assessing a service charge as a percentage of the total bill is the method many caterers choose to make their real money. Service charges range from about 15 to 22 percent. Charge your client based on the pre-tax amount of his bill.

✓**E**xpertise

Caterer Bill Hansen explains that if he didn't charge a surcharge, he wouldn't make a profit. The costs in the catering business are so high that if he had to depend on menu prices and the generosity of client tipping to pay his staff and his bills, he wouldn't be able to make a living. Most upscale caterers agree with him, and the trend has spread all over the country. The service charge covers staff tips, overages, and other soft costs.

Explain to your clients when you first meet with them that instead of tipping, a service charge will be added to the bill. Most people like the fact that they don't have to worry about tipping when they're caught up in their event.

Staff Pricing

You will need to provide staff to serve and clean up for parties. Most caterers bill clients separately for this and don't include the cost of staffers in their menu prices. If you decide to bill customers separately, you can bill them a flat rate, an hourly rate, or a percentage-based fee for servers. According to Catersource, the average national hourly rate is around $20 per hour per server, and the average percentage fee is 17 percent of the bill.

Labor costs will vary across the country depending on the local labor market. In a very competitive labor market like Manhattan, a waiter/bartender/butler will make $19–$25 an hour, with a four- to five-hour minimum. This means that if the event is shorter than four to five hours, the caterer is required to pay the staff for the entire shift. Highly experienced staffers working as shift captains will make $30–$50 per hour.

Surcharges

Charging your client a surcharge for a special service or a large unexpected cost out of your control is perfectly reasonable. If a client wants a dinner party in twenty-four hours for 100 people, for example, you should charge an "expedite fee," since you have to drop everything else to do her event.

Credit Card Fees

If a customer wants to pay by credit card, make sure you charge him a credit card processing fee. Check with your credit card processing company to find out what the fee will be, and charge that fee to your customer. If you don't, you'll be losing 1–4 percent of the invoice right off the bat.

Credit card fees vary depending on the type of card used, the amount of the charge, and the processing company used to transfer the monies.

Pricing Outsourced Items

There are times that you may want to offer an outsourced item at cost to a solid repeat client. In general, though, since you're hiring the outsourcing vendor and arranging for the special cake, flower arrangements, or chocolate fountain, you should be compensated for your time. Charging 10–15 percent over the price the vendor charges you is reasonable. Charging 30 percent or more is greedy. Remember, you want to provide this service as a convenience to your guests.

You can charge a corkage fee per bottle for wines the client buys. Corkage fees vary from $5 to $15 per bottle, depending on the cost of the bottle. Corkage fees cover the cost of training your staff to serve alcohol in a professional and responsible manner.

In catering, every little fee adds up—both the fees you pay to run your business and the fees you charge your clients for your services. It is up to you to scrupulously record your exact costs and adjust your prices if you need to.

Chapter 10

Developing a Catering Business Plan

It's important to take the time to write a solid business plan. It will be your road map during the first couple of years of running your business. While business plans vary in length and complexity, almost all business plans include the following: an executive summary, a mission statement, a business overview, a market analysis, a competitive analysis, a marketing plan, an operations plan, and a financial plan.

Why You Need to Write a Business Plan

By writing a detailed and thorough plan, you'll be able to flesh out the financial and marketing plans for your business. A well-thought-out plan will serve as a blueprint for your business, helping you organize and run your business more effectively and enabling you to achieve your goals and objectives.

A business plan will help you run your business. Your well-written business plan will be the primary document you give potential investors if you need to raise money through outside investors or loans. They'll look at your concept, your marketing plan, your resume, and your financial statements to make a decision. In the future, you will also be able to use your business plan to see whether your goals have become reality. Assess your strengths and weaknesses, and revise your business plan as necessary.

Show your plan to some successful businesspeople whose opinions you trust to get their feedback and ideas. Befriend an established caterer or two and let them look at the plan to see if they think it's realistic.

Fact

Financial Models

Even if you don't need investors to assist with your initial costs, you still need to develop the financial statements to have an idea about how many catering jobs you'll need to do to make a profit. Assemble a budget showing your planned monthly expenses, as well as any large capital expenditures you'll need to make for any equipment or for a vehicle. You'll also need to do a cash flow analysis to understand how much money you'll need to run the business.

Essential

Running the financial models will let you know how much business you need to generate to make a profit. It will also help you gauge whether the prices you've set are appropriate and reasonable. By constructing a budget, you'll be able to tell if your business plan is in line with industry standards.

More than half of new businesses fail within the first year. You should do everything you can to avoid being part of that statistic by carefully planning. Make sure you start with eight to twelve months of operating expenses in the bank. An established bank account and an affordable line of credit can help keep you afloat until you establish yourself.

Launching Your Brand

By developing a detailed marketing plan, you'll have a step-by-step guide for how to introduce potential customers to your services and your new brand. By breaking down the plan into actionable tasks and creating a marketing calendar, the job of marketing your business and launching your brand won't seem as daunting.

Marketing Your Business

You need a detailed plan of action for promoting yourself and your services. The marketing plan should have a strategy for delivering and disseminating your marketing message. The concept you have developed for your business is the key to preparing this section of your business plan.

Market Analysis

Here you'll want to discuss the catering business in your area. Use all of the data you collected when you researched your business opportunity. Consider these questions:

- How large is the existing catering market?
- Is it growing, and if so, how much?
- Have any catering businesses recently closed?
- What market trends will affect your business?

Assess the local market you're about to enter and analyze its ability to support another catering business.

Within the marketing plan, you should have a marketing and promotions budget. In general, marketing and promotions should be estimated as a percentage of sales, broken down by month. As a rule of thumb, plan to spend approximately 5–10 percent of Year 1 sales on the marketing budget for your first twelve months. This will be a relatively high marketing budget, but if you don't spend the money to introduce your services and get the message out, clients won't know about you and sales orders won't come.

 Fact

The cost of any samples that you hand out should come out of your marketing and promotion budget, not your food cost budget.

One of the most important goals of your marketing plan is to create awareness of your services and your brand. If last month your business didn't exist, then no one knows you're in business now. Your awareness level is zero. Your job is to let as many people as possible know about your wonderful catering services. Whether it's standing outside a busy local rail station a few mornings handing out mini muffins with your catering menus, or paying for printed postcards announcing your business and Web site, it all comes out of your marketing and promotion budget.

Competitive Analysis

Delve a little further into the catering market in your area. Identify the competition one by one and answer the following questions for each one:

- What kind of catering do they specialize in? Do you see any open niches in the market?
- How large are they?
- What are their sales strategies and techniques? How successful are they?

Conclude this section with a few paragraphs on how you will make your business stand out from the competition.

Market Plan

You've analyzed the overall catering market and your direct competitors. Now it's time to explain exactly how your business will fit into the market and deal with other caterers.

Start the marketing plan by defining your strategy. Do you want to conquer your local catering market and become the number one caterer within five years or would you rather find a profitable niche within the local market?

Next, specify your objective. The marketing objective is to generate Year 1's sales goals in your sales plan and to create awareness and generate sales. Specify how many people you're going to contact to let them know about your business and how much of the overall market you expect to capture. For example, if the local catering market is valued at $50 million a year and you want to grab a 1 percent share of the market within five years, that means you'll have to generate $500,000 in sales by Year 5.

Aiming to grab 1 percent of the market may seem easy, but in reality it's not. Catering is a very competitive business, and your competitors aren't going to lose sales to a newcomer easily. From your five-year sales forecast, you'll be able to judge whether a 1 percent market share is attainable or whether it will require explosive growth.

E ssential

Outsiders will want to know your strengths, weaknesses, opportunities, and threats (SWOT). A SWOT analysis will identify your business's advantages and disadvantages and your ability to seize openings in the market and deal with threats. In Chapter 12, you'll do a SWOT analysis. Refine your analysis and include it in your business plan.

You'll be introducing the world, or at least your area, to a new brand. Describe your brand's personality in a paragraph or two, so that readers can get an idea about what your brand will stand for and what familiar brands it will resemble. Include a few photos of your signature dishes and buffet setups, as well as some sample menus, brochures, and business cards to complete the section.

Sales and Promotions Strategies

Map out your plan to catch customers' attention and explain the costs and time commitment involved in your chosen tactics. You can cold call accounts, use past clients or personal contacts, and conduct mailings. You will need materials to send or give prospective clients, and you need to construct a one-minute sales pitch. Advertising is costly, so be creative with your marketing tactics in order to conserve funds.

E Fact

Building a new business and a brand takes time and effort. At the beginning, unless you have a prearranged agreement with former clients or contracts with new clients, you probably won't have a catering job every week. As you gain momentum, you should have a couple of jobs on the weekends and a job or two during the week.

Once potential clients know who you are, you need to convince them to pick you to cater their event. Invite them to a tasting party and offer discounts or a gift certificate to anyone who refers a new client to you.

Describe how you will come up with new menus and dishes and how you will introduce new services to your clients. Take into account the unique aspects of your particular market.

Strategic Relationships

Investors and lenders will want to know if you have a competitive advantage in the industry. You can gain a competitive advantage by being the first in your area to offer a certain type of catering, one that addresses a demand that none of the other local caterers focus on. You can also gain a competitive advantage from your experience and your relationships with other business leaders.

If you ran the catering operations for the best caterer in town and are now striking out on your own, you may have an edge over someone who doesn't have that experience. If you have strategic relationships or partnerships with event planners, corporate meeting planners, or are closely allied with a company that markets to engaged couples, that would give you an edge when getting new clients. Acknowledge your strengths and play to them.

Your Marketing Tactics Calendar

The marketing plan should be written by month, and you should have several complementary efforts or tactics happening at once. Spend most of your marketing money in the months leading up to your busy season.

✓Expertise

If you plan to specialize in graduation party catering, make sure you promote your services to parents by March, since they'll be planning their child's graduation party for May or June. Make sure you're not too early, either. Marketing your Thanksgiving menus to private homes in August, for example, is too early. Better wait until the beginning of October to start marketing your catering items for Thanksgiving dinner.

In order to reach your target, plan on using at least a couple of different avenues. For example, to reach parents of graduating seniors, reach out to local schools and see if you can participate in school fairs or could distribute your chocolate chip cookies along with a printed menu to the senior class. Also try to reach the parents by direct mail, e-mail, or by using your professional contacts. Local florists, photographers, party disc jockeys, and chair rental companies are frequently asked to provide services for graduation parties, and they all make good leads.

Your sales, promotion, public relations, and guerrilla marketing tactics should be planned out and marked on your calendar. Make sure your efforts complement each other and you have time to execute them.

Operations and Staffing Plans

You'll need a brief "Operations" section in your plan to explain where you'll get your supplies and ingredients and how you'll transport your prepped ingredients to your event locations. This section will cover the logistics of your business. It tells outsiders how the business will actually function and accomplish what it sets out to do. It's the nuts and bolts of the operation. Topics you'll address here are:

- Who will be in charge of business operations? Accounting? Staffing? Will it be you or will you hire someone else to help you?
- Will you hire employees to help you cook and serve food? If so, how many? Will you pay them or will they receive internship credit from a local school?
- Will you buy or lease a vehicle?
- Will you do most of your own ingredient shopping or will you rely on setting up accounts with foodservice vendors?

Outline whether you will run the company on your own or whether you will have someone to help you. This plan will show how you can fill the orders and jobs you expect from your financial statement. Lenders will want to know what happens if you're ill. Explain who will fill in for you. This is also the appropriate place to lay out how many people you plan to hire, how you will pay them, and whether you will need to hire additional support to cope with busy seasons.

The Financial Plan

Your financial plan is a model, which means it will certainly change, but it's important to put your estimated sales forecast down on paper to see if your menu, pricing, and sales estimates make sense. Consider whether it will be possible to generate as much business as you've projected given your resources, especially if you're going to be the primary salesperson and caterer. To give yourself an idea, research the amount of business other local caterers with similar resources generated in their first few years.

The first step in writing a solid business and financial plan is knowing what kind of catering services you'll offer. The concept, the menus, the pricing, and the competitive survey you've developed all contribute to a strong financial plan. In Chapter 6, you created a concept for your business and studied your key competitors. In Chapter 9, you took the time to carefully cost your menus and develop a cost estimate for preparation labor and overhead.

Your financial plan should include the following:

- Summary of financial needs
- Sales forecast
- Profit margins
- Income statement
- Balance sheet
- Cash flow forecast
- Capital spending plan

Summary of Financial Needs

Start the financial portion of your business plan with a summary of how much money you'll need to operate the business for the first year. If you need to raise some of this money, specify how much you're looking for and how it will be spent. Show a breakdown for how much will be used for leases and equipment and how much will be used for operating expenses. If you have applied for loans, include information on loan repayment in this section.

If you need to borrow funds or lease equipment, it is likely that you will have to personally guarantee the payments. At the beginning of your business venture, you will not have much leverage with credit terms because you are an unknown entity.

Prior to your first month of operation, you'll need to have kitchen time lined up, a preliminary proposal with costs saved in your computer, sample menus that have been costed and priced, your business name registered, and a Web site ready to be published or launched. Explain how you will pay for all of these expenditures.

Sales Forecast

It will take more than a year for you to gain momentum and have a flow of steady jobs. By knowing what kind of catering services you're going to offer, you'll have a rough idea of how much revenue you can expect. Start with a blank spreadsheet with the months written across the top.

For Year 1, start with the month you expect to launch your business. If you plan to start catering jobs in April, then list April as the first month in your Year 1 Sales Forecast. To determine the number of events you'll cater each month, look at a calendar and focus on the number of weekends and holidays in the month. Enter the number of possible jobs you think you'll be hired to do each month. Be conservative with your estimate, showing moderate growth.

E ssential

Remember that the business plan is only a plan, and your actual business will be constantly changing. As your business changes, update the sales forecast for Year 1 in your business plan to keep track of how you're doing and how close you are to generating a profit.

Your concept and location will dictate your busy seasons. If you're located in a resort area where the population swells in the summer but declines drastically in the winter, you'll have to factor that into your sales forecast. If you plan to be a wedding caterer, expect to be slow the first quarter of the year, peak in the second and third quarters, and slow down again in the fourth quarter.

Once you guesstimate the likely number of jobs a month, you'll need to forecast the average dollar amount of a job. If you assume that all jobs will average out to be medium sized, you can approximate the number of guests each job will have, determine an average price per person based on your menu pricing, and figure out an expected total revenue figure by multiplying the numbers together.

 Fact

There are many off-the-shelf software programs available to help you write the business plan. They provide templates for the financial models and other sections of the plan, and you can input your own data and carefully customize each model and template.

Spreadsheet programs like Microsoft Excel and business plan software are great for this because it's easy to change your variables and assumptions and get a new revenue figure with just a few clicks of the mouse. Your financial plan is a starting point, and it's better to be on the low side than on the high side. Once you have a revenue estimate for Year 1, figure out estimates for Years 2 and 3. Grow Year 2 by 30–40 percent to be conservative.

You're starting with a base of zero, so you'll be expected to grow quickly. In Year 3, project growth to be around 20 percent, since you'll be starting with a higher base sales figure.

Catering Industry Profit Margins

After you've gotten a sense for how much revenue you can expect, it's time to put together a cost estimate, forecasting how much your expenses will be. Expenses tend to be high; catering involves a lot of labor, and food is expensive. Margins are low compared to other service industries like consulting and accounting.

When you start out, your food costs are likely to be high as you figure out exactly how much food you need to order. Your gross margin is likely to be on the low side during your first few years, as you learn the business and increase your efficiency. Reflect this in your financial plan.

Ⓔ Fact

Remember that you won't get every catering job you propose. You'll need to pitch, on average, at least two to three jobs for every contract you land.

Start a spreadsheet to track your monthly expenditures. It should mirror your sales spreadsheet, but it will track the cash going out of your pocket instead of coming in. Fixed costs, or overhead, include things like rent, insurance, utilities, and computer costs. They don't generally change with the amount of catering jobs you get, and they don't disappear even if you're having a slow month. Variable costs fluctuate according to how much business you have. The more sales you generate, the more variable costs you'll incur. Variable costs include food costs, labor costs, and anything else that will increase as the number of events you cater increases.

✓ Expertise

There are certain industry standards and rules of thumb for catering costs. According to Jo Herde, director of food and beverage operations for Great Performances catering in New York, the catering business tends to be more profitable than the restaurant business, especially if you can sell liquor to your catering clients.

An experienced, efficient, smoothly operating caterer can expect to spend 27–29 percent of sales on food costs, 9 percent on overhead, and 16–17 percent on production labor, resulting in a gross profit margin of 8–12 percent.

Income Statement

Once you have your estimated revenue and costs broken down by month, you'll be able to estimate by month how much you'll make or lose. This is known as a profit and loss forecast (P&L) or an income statement. After you've developed your Year 1 P&L, you'll need to model projections for years 2 and 3.

E ssential

It's normal, even expected, that your total costs will be more than your total revenue in Year 1. New businesses that break even in Year 1 are doing very well. It's more common to lose money in Year 1, break even during Year 2, and show a profit in Year 3.

Your income statement tallies your total expenditures versus your total income. You should be conservative in your estimates. This may result in final figures that look less robust than you may like, but this keeps you from overestimating your profits. Following is an example of a general income statement.

Sample Income Statement for the Year Ending December 31, 200X

Income	
Gross Sales	346,400
Less Chargebacks/Discounts	1,000
Net Sales	**345,400**

Cost of Goods	
Merchandise Inventory, January 1	160,000
Purchases	90,000
Freight Charges	2,000
Total Merchandise Handled	**252,000**

Less Inventory, December 31	100,000
Cost of Goods Sold	152,000
Gross Profit	**193,400**

Interest Income	500
Total Income	**193,900**

Expenses	
Salaries	68,250
Utilities	5,800
Rent	23,000
Office Supplies	2,250
Insurance	3,900
Advertising/P.R.	8,650
Telephone	2,700
Travel and Entertainment	2,550
Dues and Subscriptions	1,100
Interest Paid	2,140
Repairs and Maintenance	1,250
Taxes and Licenses	11,700
Total Expenses	**133,290**

Net Income	**$60,110**

Adapted from www.smallbusinessnotes.com

Run a few different financial forecasts. Make sure your business will make money with up to 40 percent less business than you project in Years 1 and 2 and with 50 percent more costs. With spreadsheet programs, it's easy to change your numbers and calculate different scenarios. Don't rely on the best-case scenario. Things happen: supplier prices rise, you may get fewer bookings during a crucial holiday season, a competitor may launch a large advertising and promotional campaign. You need to be able to buy the necessary ingredients and rent the right type of equipment and still be able to make money.

Balance Sheet

You'll need to prepare a balance sheet showing your assets and liabilities and the difference between them. The balance sheet is a snapshot of what your business is worth. Under liabilities, show any outstanding loan payments and any leases for a facility or equipment, in addition to other monies owed to vendors for supplies.

Under assets, record accounts receivable (amounts your customers owe you) and any inventory you may have. If you own any large equipment or a vehicle, you can list it here. List available cash in the business bank accounts.

Cash Flow Forecast

This is a financial forecast that will show how you manage the cash coming in versus the cash going out. At the beginning, you'll most likely have a negative cash flow—spending more money than you're bringing in—until you have enough clients contacting you for jobs to cover your expenses. That's why it's important to start with a positive amount in your business bank account to cover at least eight months of expenses, so that you have enough money to last while you spread the word about your businesses and start getting clients.

Capital Spending Plan

This lists any large equipment you may have to purchase or lease to start your business. This may include convection ovens, a vehicle, or a walk-in fridge. Clearly, the less you have to spend on major purchases, the sooner you'll generate enough revenue to pay for your costs and break even.

✓ Expertise

General Business Information

The business plan must include a description of your business as well as information on you and your assets. The executive summary, mission statement, and business overview will help you organize the rest of the business plan. Potential investors will flip to these items first; if what they read doesn't pique their interest, they won't read further.

Executive Summary

Now that you have considered your financial, marketing, and operational plans, you know what it will take to make your business succeed. Highlight the most compelling portions of your business plan and summarize them in this section. Outline your vision for your business, and take a few paragraphs to explain how you expect to accomplish your goals. Make bulleted lists of objectives and keys to success. Include charts and graphs showing projected revenues. Clearly state why your business will succeed and what gives it a competitive edge in the catering market.

Mission Statement

Your mission statement encapsulates your long-term plans. It provides a focus for your business plan. A mission statement should spell out your optimistic vision and state your commitment to your business and the community you serve.

Business Overview

Write a one-page description of your business so that a potential investor or lender can quickly understand what it is you're trying to do and what it is that's going to set you apart and enable you to succeed. Start with the concept you have developed.

As part of the business description, include a paragraph on your business mission. Address these questions:

- How will your company compete in the marketplace?
- What services will you provide? Outline the focus of your catering business, whether it's formal or informal, centered around large weddings or moderate home parties.
- How aggressive will you be in capturing market share?
- How will you contribute to the local community? Will you support community organizations and local school teams? Will you strive to use as many local ingredients and services as possible and recycle as much of your materials as possible?

Resume

Include your personal resume targeted toward cooking and food-service businesses. Highlight past experience that will help you in your new endeavor. Highlight past project management, sales, public relations, finance, and, of course, cooking and event-management skills.

Potential investors and lenders will look at your resume to assess your track record and skill set. Based on your resume, the rest of the business plan, and the personal impression you make, they'll decided whether you have what it takes to create and run a successful business. Whether they're right or wrong, one thing is for sure—it's their decision to make, and they'll make up their mind quickly, so make sure to present yourself in the best possible light.

Personal Financial Statement

Create a statement that includes all your personal assets and debts. Debts include any outstanding bank loans, credit card balances, student loan balances, personal mortgages, car lease payments, and any other monies that you may owe. List all of your real assets in a separate section. Include any real estate that you own and the current market price of any stocks, mutual funds, or bonds in any investment accounts, including retirement accounts. You don't have to list any spousal or child support that you receive or the value of any trust accounts, but listing those amounts will help you get loans.

Chapter 11

Proposal Writing

The only way you'll be able to sell catering jobs is by writing a clear, concise proposal that reflects your client's vision and adds your own creative touch to their idea. The proposal is a business document that contains all the details about the event, including the amount of money you will charge and a payment schedule. The proposal, in almost all cases, will serve as your contract with the client.

The Customer's Needs

It is essential that you correctly and fully reflect the client's needs in your proposal. In order to completely understand the client's requirements, you'll have to meet with him in person, preferably at the location where the event will be held. Meeting the client face-to-face is important. Seeing how he describes what he wants, studying his body language, and viewing the site will enable you to meet and exceed his expectations and deliver a high level of customer service. Meeting the client and seeing his location will also allow you to more accurately price a proposal and get a feel for the client's style.

E ssential

You can learn a lot from visual cues when talking to someone in person. It's hard to talk to someone you don't know over the telephone and be sure you're on the same wavelength. When people speak to each other directly, they tend to emphasize or clarify words through physical cues, such as facial expression, gestures, motions, and posture.

Address potential challenges with the site in your proposal, say if a space is unusually large or the kitchen is far from where you'll have to serve the food. In your proposal, suggest how to make the large space intimate, and plan the menu and logistics so that you can serve food efficiently and at the appropriate temperature with an inconveniently placed kitchen.

Analyze the equipment at the site, and make notes during your visit. If the stove is old and unreliable and the refrigerator tiny, plan your menu and storage needs accordingly. Bring insulated containers for storing refrigerated items, and you may need to do extra prep. You may also need to bring propane-fueled burners to finish sautéing your main dish.

When you meet with the client, bring photos of some of your plated entrées and various buffet displays—anything that can help describe catering options. Offer to meet with the client when it's convenient for him. If he can only meet you at 7 A.M. before he leaves for work, then meet him at 7 A.M. and bring some fresh muffins or scones to get the meeting off to a good start. The easier it is for the client to work with you, the more likely he is to hire you and continue to use you and recommend you.

Ⓔ Fact

Show your boilerplate proposal to your lawyer to get her comments. Add wording to your proposal stating that the signed proposal will only be considered valid when a deposit is received. In certain cases, you might want to require that the client provide you with a valid credit card number, which you'll keep on file.

Only when it's impossible to meet with a client in person should you discuss all the details with him over the phone. If he prefers to deal with you exclusively via phone, make sure to listen to him very carefully. Hear what he's saying and how he's saying it. Summarize what he's asked you to do before you hang up so that you both know you understand each other. Don't cook or do anything else while you're speaking with a client or potential client. Make sure to ask him all the specifics so that you can write a thorough proposal. Explain to the client that the only way you can guarantee a smoothly run event is if you see the venue and examine the on-site equipment prior to finalizing the menu and other event details. E-mail is only recommended for specifics once you have landed the job.

Creativity and Flair

It's important that you do more in the proposal than merely repeat what the client asked for. Remember, you're being hired for your creative flair in addition to your efficiency and logistical abilities. Creativity and an effort to make the client's event truly special translates into a proposal that is easily distinguished from the competition and makes the client happy and loyal to you. You'll be hard to replace with another local caterer if you deliver comprehensive and creative proposals to your clients. Make sure to write proposals when you have the time to focus on them to ensure that they're your best work.

In your proposal, recap the client's key requests or parameters in a paragraph or in bullet points. Follow that with a section entitled "Suggestions." Build on the client's desires and show how you can make the event unique. After seeing the event space, let the client know how you envision the setup and how the event will flow around it. If the client wants a chic, casual atmosphere, for example, suggest where to seat the guests, where to set up the bar, and where to place the buffet. Suggest specific décor elements to help reinforce the mood of the party. If you think it appropriate, suggest floral decorations, rearranging furniture, or using another room to serve cocktails and hors d'oeuvres if you need more space.

E ssential

To leverage your proposal suggestions, recommend the floral designers, wine merchants, and other vendors with whom you have partnerships. You will save the client time-consuming legwork, and you will get to work with vendors you know you can depend on to execute your vision.

All of your proposals should have a standard design and have the same subheadings. Design a proposal and use the blank template for all proposals. You can refer to previous proposals, but using a blank template ensures that you won't inadvertently include components from an old proposal in a new one. If you're e-mailing a proposal, make sure it prints out properly formatted and looks professional.

Creative Menu Suggestions

Clients will look to you to create and execute an exciting menu for their event. Many clients want to offer their guests something new and unique. Be creative in the food choices and pairings and in serving them. If the event is buffet style, describe how your buffet will have distinctiveness and drama and will be more than a boring line of stainless steel chafing dishes. Include a photo or two of similar buffets you've designed. Maybe you can suggest a theme for the buffet that will tie the event together.

If your client wants a poultry entrée for her dinner, think beyond the typical roast chicken. Suggest a Thai chicken breast with coconut milk and star anise if you like cooking Thai, or a red wine poached duck breast served with a piece of crisp honey-and-herb-roasted chicken on the same plate.

Clever Table Seating and Décor

If a client is having a seated dinner, think of a distinct way to decorate the table and seat the guests. If it's a Thanksgiving dinner, turn small, colorful squash into place-card holders by making a slit at the top of each one. They'll be easier to see than if they are laying flat on the table. Serve your soup in hollowed-out squash gourds, and decorate the table with whole chestnuts and other nuts with their shells on. Roast the nuts and make them part of the dessert by offering guests bowls and nutcrackers. Serve chocolate dipping sauce and spiced sugars so that guests can coat their nuts and can enjoy them with their tea and coffee.

Make sure that each of your suggestions has a price or price range associated with it. This way the client can pick and choose from your list of suggestions and can easily understand how each one will affect his budget. For example, if the client only wanted a simple crudités platter and assorted nuts for arriving guests, and you think that passed hors d'oeuvres would be a worthwhile addition, let the client know your reasoning and give him a couple of pricing options. Let him choose between four different room-temperature hors d'oeuvres, or eight different hot and cold hors d'oeuvres for a slightly higher price.

Components of the Proposal

The entire proposal should be two to three pages, written clearly and concisely. Enclose two copies of the proposal, both with your signature. Have the client sign one and mail it back to you with a deposit or let her fax it to you and mail the deposit separately.

Alert

Remember to proofread all proposals very carefully before sending them to a client. Nothing will turn off a client more than misspelling a name, making typographical errors, or including something from an old proposal.

Once you've written a few detailed proposals and have them saved on your computer, writing additional proposals will be easier. You can base a new proposal on an old one rather than starting from scratch.

Proposal Basics

Send each proposal with a cover letter. Thank the client for her interest, and make a personal connection by recalling something from your meeting or conversation with her. Spend a few sentences summarizing her vision for the event and what you will do to make it a reality. Tell her when you need the signed contract and deposit back from her, and conclude by providing your contact information and letting her know she can call you with any questions.

Each proposal should have the following components:

- **Event Overview.** Map out in detail exactly what you envision for the event and how it will flow.
- **Menu.** Provide a menu with options that the client can choose from.
- **Caterer's Responsibilities and Client's Responsibilities.** All food, beverages, materials, and labor should fall into one of these two categories. Make sure everything is accounted for, so that there are no surprises at the end of the event. Spell out how much cleanup you'll do, how late you'll stay, how many servers you're supplying, and who pays for the liquor. Avoid using a lot of legalese. Clients tend to get nervous and wary if the document looks like a lawyer drafted it. Use plain English, but make sure you cover all the bases.
- **Pricing.** List the price per person for the event. Stipulate what it includes and does not include. State that tax and a service charge will be added to the bill, and list your service charge percent and the applicable state and city tax rate(s). State exactly when payments are due and what forms of payment you accept. Remember to state that if an event is cancelled, the client loses his deposit.

Division of Responsibilities

One of the best ways to ensure the job goes smoothly is to make sure you spell out precisely what you'll be responsible for. State everything that will be included in your price. If the client is providing the tables, for example, spell that out under a section entitled "Client's Responsibility."

Under "Client's Responsibility," stipulate the exact date you'll need the final guest count. You'll want to include wording in the proposal stating that guest numbers cannot be changed less than forty-eight hours prior to an event, and the client must contact you directly via telephone with any last-minute changes. This protects you in the event that a client gets a lot of party cancellations just before the party starts, and you've already bought the ingredients and are preparing the food. With this policy, you'll be justified in charging the client for the agreed-upon number of guests.

List everything you'll provide, from rolls and butter to iced tea, coffee, milk, and sugar. Make sure everything is accounted for. Everything needed to feed and serve guests should be listed under "Caterer's Responsibilities" or "Client's Responsibilities." It is helpful to divide these lists into categories—food, beverages, serving dishes, and displays and decorations.

Specify what kind of cleanup you'll do. State what you will do with any waste and who will supply cleaning supplies and trash bags.

Details to Cover

Below is a list of details that should be covered in every proposal. Caterers get into trouble when they leave too much to the imagination. Don't rely on assumptions. Spell everything out.

Date and Time of the Event

Make sure you double-check that the day of the week matches the date. Events are often planned months ahead and the date may be the next calendar year, so check to make sure that July 7, for example, is indeed Saturday and not Friday.

☀ Alert

Be clear about the start and end time of the event. For example, writing a start time as 12 is ambiguous as it could be construed as either 12 P.M. or 12 A.M. Write out the exact start and end times to avoid any confusion.

Note what time you and your staff will arrive for setup, when the guests are to arrive, when you'll finish serving, and when you need to be cleaned up and ready to leave. Some clients expect the serving staff and catering crew to stay until the last guest has left. That is an unrealistic expectation. Make sure the client understands that after you have served the dessert and cleaned up the kitchen, you and your crew will be leaving.

Include language at the bottom of your proposal stating that you will do everything in your power to get to an event, but if there is an act of God like a hurricane, tornado, or other major catastrophe that prevents you from getting to the party location, you will not be held liable. Double-check the exact wording with your insurance agent and your attorney.

Specify that the event will take place rain or shine, snowstorm or blackout. If there is to be a rain date, you'll have to negotiate that with your client and charge a higher price, since you'll be reserving two days on your calendar for the event.

Length of the Event

Cocktail and afternoon tea events run two to three hours. Lunches generally run two hours. Dinners, weddings, and other parties last four to five hours from the time the first guest arrives until the last guest leaves. If your client wants the party to run longer, charge them a higher fee. If you're catering an event on a boat, for example, which won't dock for six hours once it leaves port, charge your client an extra hour of labor.

Price Per Person

Specify how much it will cost to serve each person. Be very clear what other charges will be added and are not included in this figure. If you'll be adding a service charge over and above the serving staff fee, specify that in the proposal and say what percentage you'll charge. Let the client know the service fee includes all gratuities.

If the client asks you to provide tableware and linens, specify those prices separately. If you're going to outsource other parts of the event, such as a specialty cake or liquor, list each of those components separately.

If all the details and prices are spelled out, clients are less likely to raise objections than if you combine a number of items and provide the client with a large lump sum.

You must charge state sales tax on your catering services, so list the current state sales tax and indicate which items are subject to that tax.

E ssential

Submit a proposal that comes in close to the client's budget. If you can't afford to include certain things using that budget, then include options under your "Suggestions" category. Nothing annoys a client more than disregarding their budget and submitting a proposal that's priced much higher.

The Deposit

Collect 50 percent of the expected cost of the event when the client signs the proposal and returns it to you.

State in the proposal that the pricing and terms will only be good for a period of two weeks from the date of the proposal, and the deposit must be received in full by the end of the two-week period. Explain to customers that market prices change, and you can't guarantee them indefinitely if you haven't received a deposit.

Deposits owed should be per person based on the middle of the range of expected guests. For example, if the client tells you that he expects 80–100 guests, collect a deposit based on 90 guests. Service staff is priced separately from the food. Bill for each outsourced item separately and add your surcharge.

Fact

If you are outsourcing items, you'll need separate deposits for these items.

You may accept personal checks for the deposit because you won't buy anything with the funds until they clear your bank. If the event is to be run on short notice, insist that the client pay the entire estimated cost either by certified check or by wire to your bank. Cash, of course, is acceptable as well. Just make sure to record the cash on your books as revenue.

Keep a list of the deposits you're expecting and the date you expect them to arrive. If your client fails to give you a deposit, e-mail her or call her to give her a friendly reminder. If she still doesn't send you a deposit in another week, send her a registered letter stating that her date is no longer reserved and her proposal is considered null and void.

The Balance

Collect the balance of the payment from your client at least twenty-four hours prior to the start of the event. Make sure the client wires the funds into your business bank account or delivers a certified check to you. Do not accept personal checks for a balance from a client unless she's your mother. Some clients will make excuses and tell you that they can't get you the funds before the party. Explain that you're a small business, and you must have the funds before the event to manage your cash flow. Be clear and let them know that without payment, you won't be able to cater their party.

E Alert

State in your proposal that the balance of payment must be received at least one business day prior to the event, otherwise you will not be able to provide your services. Don't accept credit card payments unless you won't get paid any other way. Make sure to charge customers the credit card fee that PayPal or another processing company will charge you.

Number of Guests

Clearly state the number of guests you'll be providing food for. Make sure the client guarantees you a minimum number of guests. If the host expects 100 people to come to his party but tells you the week before that only 20 are coming, you'll be stuck catering a tiny affair that may not be worth the effort. Also get a maximum number of guests from the client. You don't want to be stuck forty-eight hours before the event procuring more ingredients and making food for an extra 50 people if the entire party was supposed to be for 80–100 guests. Try to keep the range to within 20 percent of the total number of guests.

Some hosts will try to get their money back if they have a lot of guests who didn't show up. Explain that you've cooked the food for that number of guests and provided service staff for that number. Remind your client that the number of guests was agreed to in the proposal and that she had up to forty-eight hours before the event to make any necessary changes.

Type of Event

The proposal should clearly state the type of event. Specify whether it is brunch or lunch, seated or buffet. Spell out the formality—is it a casual outdoor picnic or is it a black-tie five-course dinner with French service?

If a client changes his mind and decides to have a buffet instead of a seated dinner, charge him a nominal fee for redoing the proposal. Credit the client the proposal fee if they end up using you to cater their event. This will discourage indecisive clients from wasting your time.

Event Location

The proposal must state the exact location of the event. List the street address and state whether it's indoors or outdoors. If it's in a park, specify if it's your responsibility or the client's to get the permit or license and who is to pay for it.

Other Considerations

Find out from the client what the occasion is and mention it in the proposal. Also mention the kind of atmosphere she wants. Your menu and style will depend on whether the event is a subdued business occasion or a boisterous birthday celebration. Will people already know each other, or does the host want people to be able to mingle? The answer affects how you want the event to flow.

Find out who the guests will be. You may need to make special arrangements to accommodate everyone. Ask your client the following questions:

- Is she expecting any VIPs?
- Are there any cultural sensitivities you need to be aware of? Are there any foods you need to avoid? Is there a specific dress code you and your employees—particularly females—should follow?
- Will the guests be evenly split, or will there be many more men than women?
- How old are the guests? Will the group be mostly adults in their thirties or in their seventies?
- Will there be any children in attendance?

Special Food Requests

You must ask the host how many vegetarians there will be and how strictly vegetarian they are. If the host doesn't know, he must find out from his guests if anyone is vegan, or if the vegetarian guests will eat fish or poultry. Special vegetarian meals should be prepared for these guests. Vegetarian guests should not have to "make do" by eating only meat-free side dishes such as rice, pasta, and vegetables.

You'll also need to know if any of the guests keep kosher or avoid other foods like pork, nuts, shellfish, berries, or egg whites because of religious practice or food allergies. Make it clear on your proposal that special requests must be made, if any, no later than one week prior to the event, so that you have time to modify any recipes and test them. Let clients know that special requests can't be changed, since they require more advanced preparation.

E ssential

With obesity rates in the United States at an all-time high, keep fat and calorie content per serving in mind when choosing recipes. Offer a lower-calorie alternative at each meal, so that guests can make healthier choices while still enjoying themselves. Avoid trans fats whenever possible and use shortenings that do not contain hydrogenated oils.

Make it a practice to ask the host if there will be any diabetic guests. This will alert you to prepare some modified recipes, allowing all guests to enjoy every dish, including dessert. The number of people in the United States living with diabetes, including children, is quickly growing. Clients will appreciate your ability to easily accommodate diabetic guests with delicious dishes. Offering a specialized menu for children will also help differentiate you from other caterers.

Take the time to familiarize yourself with foods that are diabetic friendly. Diabetics can tolerate foods that are higher in fiber and whole grains. Also, foods that don't raise the body's glycemic index too much are better for diabetics. Splenda sweetener and other non-sugar sweeteners are good choices for desserts.

Ask your client about food allergies. Food allergies are fairly common, and your host may not know every guest's medical history, but you can work to accommodate guests with specific allergies if you know about them before you begin planning the menu.

Protect yourself as much as possible from litigation by being properly insured, incorporated, and by stating on your proposal that your catering company is licensed and takes the greatest care with food safety. Individuals with allergies should be aware that foods are prepared in a facility with nuts, dairy, wheat, and berries.

Selling Additional Services

In the cover letter to the proposal, offer additional services like event planning, invitation design and envelope addressing, decorations, customized guest goodie bags, and other services if you'd like to outsource them.

When discussing ideas off-the-cuff with the client, give a ballpark price or a price range. Never commit yourself to an exact price until you've had a chance to price the whole job and make sure of your costs. A rule of thumb is to multiply your cost by four to give a price estimate to a client. (Since food cost should run around 25–30 percent of your costs, multiplying this by four is a reasonable way to get to the total cost to around 100 percent, or a bit more to give you some padding.)

Make contacts and develop relationships with other vendors before you offer to sell additional services to clients. Identify dependable vendors you know you can work with. You will take care of coordinating all of the services they will provide at the event so that the client doesn't have to. You can charge a premium (10–20 percent) for outsourcing because you are providing an additional service for your client. Outsourcing also allows you the flexibility to work directly with other vendors to make sure you share the same vision for the event. For example, you can make the dishes complement the floral arrangements by using a coordinating flower to garnish each course.

A successful catering proposal will address all of the client's specific needs and think of creative ways to solve problems the client may not even be aware of. Selling additional services is one way to let the client know you are looking out for them and are committed to making their event run smoothly.

Chapter 12

Marketing Yourself

The minute you develop your catering concept and menus and name your business, you've created a new brand. Your brand will be competing in the marketplace with thousands of other brands in the food industry from the Red Lobster brand to Dean & DeLuca Catering to Exquisite Catering by Marie in your hometown. Therefore, it's important to think of yourself as a brand, a complete package. From your appearance to your voice to your professional skills, to your inimitable style as a caterer, this is your brand to develop and grow.

Naming Your Business

There are several factors to consider when choosing a good name for your catering business. Renaming your business will waste time and money, so pick a name that can grow with you.

You're creating a new brand, so make sure the name is memorable and has positive connotations. If it's a foreign word, make sure it doesn't mean something bad in another language. (The Chevy Nova failed to sell in Spanish-speaking countries largely because in Spanish *no va* means, "No go.") Make sure the name you choose sounds like it's a food business. You may pick a great name like "Apex," but it sounds more like a technical business than a food business.

Don't choose a name that sounds like or is spelled like another brand name. If and when the owner of the original brand name becomes aware of your business name, you'll have a lot of aggravation to deal with. At a minimum, you might be served with a cease-and-desist letter warning you to stop using the name, or else pay a fee to license the name from the owner. At worst, you would be forced to go to court and spend money to defend the name.

Don't use your name for your business's name. Unless you're well known in your area and have a stellar reputation, you'd be better off creating a name that evokes the image and temperament of the concept you've chosen. Names are powerful. We often imagine what a person looks like and must be like just based on her name. Choose a name that you can imagine being one of your favorite brands and your friends' favorite brands.

If the name you choose is hard to pronounce or spell or part of an in-joke, it probably won't work well. If the name has an unusual spelling, it will make it harder for people to look up in the phone book and on line. Don't use an overly sophisticated name or one that's über trendy. Try to come up with a unique name that is easy to spell.

Choosing the right name involves finding the right balance between a name that's too broad and generic, such as "World's Best Catering Services," and a name that's too small and specific, for example, "Bob Smith's Catering."

Make sure the name is easy for others to remember. If your friends and associates can't remember the name of your business, they won't be able to tell others about it.

Domain Name Availability

You'll also want to check the Web site names or domains available for your name. If the exact name you choose isn't available as a domain, you might need to alter it slightly. You'll want to have an easy-to-remember Web site, so you may want to pick another name if your first choice isn't available.

It's easy to check if a domain name is available. Visit *www .networksolutions.com* or a similar site, type in the domain name you want, and the site will check the official registry. It's best to get a dot-com domain. Dot-net is the only other alternative, but it's not as common as dot-com. Don't bother with dot-tv or other alternatives. If you're going to be running a for-profit business, you will be ineligible to use dot-org, which is reserved for nonprofit entities.

E ssential

The longer you reserve your domain name, the cheaper it is. If you decide to reserve your name for ten years, it will only cost you a few dollars a year.

If you find the name you want available, then purchase it for at least a year. For approximately $20 you'll be able to reserve the name as a Web domain, even if you haven't registered it yet with your state. The first one who thinks up the name and registers it gets to use it, so don't take the chance of losing it.

If you find the name that you wanted to use is taken, you can find out through the Web registry who the rightful owner is. You can always offer to buy the name, but it'll be cheaper and easier if you can create another good name.

The Beginning of the Alphabet

In listings of caterers in local entertaining guides to telephone books, you'll want your business to appear near the top of the list as much as possible. If you name your business Stellar Catering Services, chances are many people will find a caterer well before they get down to *S*.

An easy way to ensure this is to make sure that the first letter of the first significant word in the title starts with one of the first six to ten letters of the alphabet. Otherwise, when browsing, many people won't even get to see your name.

Checking and Testing Your Name

It's a good idea to put the name you've chosen into a search engine or two and see what comes up. If another business appears, don't despair. Businesses are registered on the state level, so if the name you want is owned by another business that's registered in a different state and in a different industry, then you'll probably be able to use it. Avoid using the name of an existing business in a similar industry to prevent confusion, especially if the state is near yours.

When creating a name for your business, don't create only one. Create at least three names so that when you go to register your name and incorporate your business, you'll be prepared if your first or second choice is already taken.

Study the name you've chosen. Look at it backward as well as forward. Does it spell out something? Say it over and over. Does it sound like something else? What does the name rhyme with? Look up the name in several different languages, including Spanish, French, Italian, and German, and make sure it doesn't mean anything negative, X-rated, or silly.

You'll want to informally test the name with your friends, family, and colleagues. Send out a brief e-mail questionnaire. Ask people what they think of when they hear the name. Ask them if they'd use the catering services of a company with that name if they didn't know anything else about the company. Get at least twenty-five opinions back and read what they say. If the majority of respondents dislike the name, then figure out why and redevelop your name.

E-mail or call the same group back a few days after you get the responses and ask them to tell you the name of your businesses without looking at prior e-mails. If most of them remembered the name correctly and can spell it right, that's a good sign.

Putting Your Name in Print

It's a good idea to write down the names you have in mind. Play with them in different text styles and sizes on your computer's word processing program. Print out the names and let them live with you for a few days. Is the name growing on you? Does it feel right to you?

Does it seem like this has always been your business, or is something bothering you about the name?

When finalizing a logo for your business and choosing the colors, keep in mind that certain colors are more food-friendly than others. Colors that are not found in nature and are too jarring aren't ideal for food business use. Avoid neon colors, dark colors, and colors that are hard to replicate.

Plan for the Future

Make sure your name can be changed slightly and adapted. For example, let's say you're planning to use the name Akron Party Catering. You might want to consider the name Akron Party Catering & Events or Akron Party & Event Catering or Akron Full-Service Catering, so that as you expand and grow your business, your name will grow with you.

It's hard to predict the future, but the more thought you give to your business name now, the more likely it'll grow with you.

Appearance

Once you're outside your office or kitchen, clients and potential clients will be judging you by your appearance. They'll be asking themselves, "Does he look like a chef?" and "Can I trust him to run a party for 200 of my closest business associates?"

Make sure you wear a clean uniform, look professional, and are well kempt any time you meet a client, work an event, or network.

- **If you're cooking or serving food, make sure your hair is neat.** If you have long hair, it should be tied back. Another option is to wear a chef's hat.
- **Make sure you've showered.** It's easy for the smell of the commercial kitchen and food preparation to stick with you, and it's a real turnoff.
- **Make sure your nails are clean and well manicured.** You'll be the one touching your client's food, and there's nothing worse than a chef with dirty or bitten fingernails.

- **Make sure** your clothes are cleaned and freshly pressed, that you're not wearing your kitchen clogs, and that you look professional.

Remember that when you meet with prospective clients, they will be judging you and your style to see if you can be trusted with creating and executing their wonderful event. You must look the part. When you meet with bridal clients, corporate clients, and clients hosting a party in their home, look your best. Women should put on some makeup and men should make sure they are well groomed.

E ssential

Great-looking clothes don't have to cost a fortune. Buy a couple of pairs of smart-fitting slacks, a couple of shirts or blouses, and a flattering sports jacket. Mix and match pieces to create different outfits. Men can wear different ties, while women can wear different scarves to create a variety of outfits.

If you've never paid much attention to your appearance, consult a professional at a local department store or beauty shop. Some retail stores and makeup counters encourage you to make an appointment with one of their associates. This way, you can be assured of a one-on-one consultation. You have to keep in mind that you're marketing yourself, so if your "packaging" isn't right, you won't be able to sell your services. Make sure your clothes complement your figure, you're wearing colors that accent your skin tone, and your eyeglasses, makeup, hair color, and haircut bring out your features and make you look your best. It's worth investing in a new outfit or two that you can wear to meet clients and for making presentations. Clients are going to expect you to be artistic, creative, and capable of executing a stylish event. If you look dated and out of touch, clients will be hard-pressed to hire you.

Phone Skills

When you speak to people on the phone for the first time, they will be judging you as soon as you start speaking. It's important, therefore, to project a confident, upbeat, educated, professional demeanor within the first few seconds on the phone. Prospective clients will listen to what you have to say if you're commanding, but appreciative of their time. If you know what you're talking about, people will pay attention to what you're telling them.

Practice what you're going to say over the phone and get experience introducing yourself. Practice on friends, relatives, and other caterers. It's important that you don't sound nervous, as prospects will be able to hear that in your voice.

Always concentrate and listen to what the other person is saying. Don't try to multitask when you're on the phone with a prospective client. If someone asks you for a specific price or to supply something you're not sure about, don't make up an answer. Tell them you're not sure and you will get back to them shortly. Make sure you follow up that day or the next day.

☀ Alert

Speak slowly and clearly when leaving a voicemail message. Remember to repeat your phone number at the end of the message so the person won't have to relisten to the message in order to call you back.

If you reach someone's voicemail or answering machine, leave a concise but detailed message. Tell him why you're calling and when they can reach you. Give him up to a week to call you back. Then try him again, and leave a followup message saying you're following up and you'd really appreciate a call back. If the person still doesn't call you back within a couple of days, you can try to call his secretary or colleague and ask for his e-mail address. Try sending an e-mail message summarizing your services and ask if he has any upcoming events. Ask him if he'd like additional information from you. Some people will respond to e-mail and not to phone messages; it depends on how they like to work.

Don't leave more than two voicemail messages for someone you don't know if she hasn't tried returning the call. More messages will only annoy the person. There might be a good reason why she's not returning your call. Call the company or organization back and get another contact name. The original person may have changed job responsibilities or may be out of the office for an extended period of time.

Write a list of bullet points you want to convey to prospects over the phone. Make sure you convey how you and your services are different from other caterers. These points will come from the concept you've developed and from your SWOT analysis.

SWOT Analysis

Before you can start marketing yourself over the phone and selling your services, you need to evaluate your strengths, weaknesses, opportunities, and threats (SWOT). Get a letter-sized blank sheet of paper and fold it into quarters. Label the upper left corner "Strengths," the upper right corner "Weaknesses," the bottom left corner "Opportunities," and the bottom right "Threats."

Fill up the "strengths" box with bullet points of what distinguishes you from your competition and what skills of yours make you a great caterer. What you list will depend on your experience and your particular skills. If you have a background in theater design, that would make you stand out in event design. If you have experience in restaurant service, you should excel at understanding how to service customers. If you've managed large projects for a *Fortune* 500 company and brought them in on time and under budget, that will tell your clients you can manage putting together big events for them.

Essential

SWOT analysis is taught at every business school, and it's a useful evaluative skill for all types of business situations. SWOT analysis is used to evaluate competitors and new products.

For "weaknesses," be brutally honest with yourself. "Lack of experience" might be something you list if you haven't worked doing catering yet. If you are weak in one of the required skills listed in Chapter 3, make sure to list it here. If you can't decorate a wedding cake, list it. Don't worry; weaknesses can be turned into strengths through training or through outsourcing.

The opportunities box will be overflowing with all the targets and prospects you can think of. From calling local companies to see if you can meet with their event planners to introducing your catering services to local women's clubs and seeing if they have any upcoming events that you might be able to bid for, this box should be filled with prospects. List additional prospects or targets on a separate piece of paper and remember to follow up on them.

For the "threats" box, you already know most of your competitors from the research you did to develop your concept. List other threats such as a possible economic downturn in your area, a natural disaster, and other things that would cause your business to suffer. Some threats will be out of your control. Nevertheless, identifying them will help you face your biggest challenges.

If there is an economic downturn, you can always retool your menu to offer less expensive offerings or target different clients. Even during the recession of the early 1990s, people still used caterers. If corporations cut back on elaborate seated-dinner affairs, they'll still need sandwich platters. Employees and clients still need to eat, no matter how bad the economy gets. Also remember that in a recession, not everyone is affected the same way, and people still celebrate weddings, bar mitzvahs, and other events during an economic downturn.

Your strengths will form the basis of your phone and written sales pitches. It is important to know your strengths well and mention them to potential clients. Don't write down a sales pitch word-for-word to memorize; it will sound phony. As long as you know the main points you want to get across, your passion will come through and the customer will be captivated by what you're saying.

Over time, turn all weaknesses into strengths. So, if you're missing an important piece of equipment that prevents you from competing with local caterers or can't decorate a cake to save your life, find ways to borrow or rent the equipment, learn pastry decorating, or find people who can do it for you in a pinch.

Similarly, turn threats into opportunities as much as possible. If there's a caterer who's your main competition, figure out what kind of parties aren't profitable for them to do and what clients don't like about them. Maybe because you have lower overhead and are small, you can cater smaller affairs for customers. Since the big area caterer is getting impersonal, you can turn that into an opportunity for business, since some customers need hand holding, and you're great at that.

Writing Skills

Concise and professional business writing skills are required for generating new business and avoiding problems later on with clients. You must know how to write effective business proposals and contracts. Spelling, punctuation, and grammar must be correct. Nothing turns off a potential client like a poorly written letter or proposal. If things aren't written clearly, you'll have problems later. Clients may misunderstand what you are providing, when the final guest count is required, and what your cancellation policy is.

If you lack business-writing skills, take a course at the local community college. Once you get the hang of writing your cover letter and proposal, it will be easy to adapt them for other clients. Some of the newer catering software systems integrate word-processing functions into their costing and menu-planning functions, making letter and proposal writing that much easier. CaterEdge, for example, works with Microsoft Word so that you can easily e-mail proposals to prospective clients.

Software, however advanced, cannot do the writing for you. Even with automatic spelling and grammar checking, you still must know how to write clear sentences and include all the salient information in a proposal. The proposal is a tool to help get you the business, so you must offer creative proposals, meet the client's needs, and make a profit for yourself while doing so within the customer's budget.

Writing Your Catering Biography Statement

For your Web site and catering company sales and marketing information folder, you'll need a one-page biography of yourself. The first paragraph should name your business and describe what you do. The next few paragraphs should list your experience and how it pertains to catering. List some clients you've cooked for. Include any cooking training and certificates or degrees that you've earned. Mention any high-profile jobs you've catered for or well-known restaurants you've worked in. Make sure you include your contact information on the bottom of the sheet.

E ssential

Getting a professional headshot taken doesn't have to be expensive. Sears, JC Penney, and other inexpensive commercial studios are available around the country. You shouldn't have to pay much of a sitting fee. You should only be charged for the images you use.

On the bio, include a professional headshot of yourself. If you don't have one or if it no longer looks like you, you should have a new one taken. Make sure you get a haircut and have your hair color done. You want to look as youthful and attractive as possible. Have your makeup done so that your complexion isn't shiny. Make sure the photographer gets pictures in both color and black and white and that he shoots in a digital format, so you can easily use the picture on your Web site and on other printed materials.

Developing Your Catering Services Packet

Rather than printing up an expensive brochure, start out by creating a few separate pages of information and putting them in a double-sided folder that you can purchase at an office supply store like Office Max or Staples. Have some labels printed with your name and Web address and affix the label to the front of the folder. You can easily design inexpensive custom labels online and have them mailed to you. Voilà! You now have a customized presentation folder. On the inside is a slit for inserting your business card.

In the folder, you'll have your biography statement; a page titled "Services Offered," which lists the types of catering you offer (wedding, off-premise, picnics, cooking parties); suggested menus with some pricing details; copies of any recommendation letters from clients; a few photos of events you've done; and a blank contract. You can buy photo album sheets at an office supply store and print 4" × 6" photos of your food and buffet setups. This folder will be what you leave behind with prospective clients, and it is all you need to start selling your services.

Everything comes together in your catering services packet. You have a name that reflects the business image you want to project, professional photos of yourself and your services, and well-written menus and descriptions of your business.

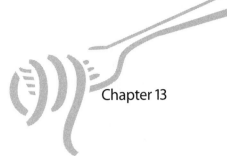

Chapter 13

Marketing Your Business

Managing a business, cooking well, and presenting food with flair are essential skills for every caterer, but it is masterful marketing that will propel your business to growth and prosperity. Understanding core marketing concepts, particularly guerrilla marketing tools, is crucial to competing in catering. This chapter discusses the techniques you'll need to familiarize yourself with your local market and position yourself so that your target audience is sure to learn about you.

The Caterer as Marketer

The term *marketing* refers to any product or service that's to be sold in a market situation, that is with buyers and sellers operating with the forces of supply and demand. Whether you're bidding on an event, cold-calling prospective customers, or speaking to a group of corporate event planners, you're marketing.

Everything in this world is marketed in some way. We market ourselves every day when we try to influence someone to do something for us. When we apply for a job or try to get a date, we're marketing ourselves. When we're trying to convince the boss to send us to London for the global sales meeting or asking our staff to please stay late, we're marketing ourselves.

When you start selling yourself and your cooking, you're marketing yourself. Your job is to:

1. Determine potential customers
2. Develop a targeted marketing message
3. Make a sales pitch

4. Close the sale
5. Deliver the products and service
6. Follow up with the customer

In Chapter 12, you learned how to evaluate your strengths and opportunities and use them in your sales pitch. In this chapter you'll learn why you need to develop a targeted marketing message and study innovative tools you can use to deliver your message and close a catering sale. In Chapter 14, you'll learn about the importance of client followup and how to monitor customer relationships.

Ⓔ Fact

During a single day, a person in a U.S. city can see 5,000 marketing messages. With so much advertising clutter, caterers must be clever in delivering their marketing messages.

From the time you get up in the morning to the time you go to bed, you see thousands and thousands of branded products. The radio ad for coffee that wakes you up in the morning, the colorfully packaged food products you eat for breakfast, the print ads you see wrapped around buildings as you walk to the ad-filled bus stop and board the ad-saturated bus itself—even in the first few hours of the day, you are surrounded by advertising. Coffee cups, pizza boxes, and even eggshells have printed messages on them trying to get you to buy a product. With all these marketing messages, how is a small business supposed to stand out and get noticed? The answer is with targeted guerrilla marketing.

The Importance of Targeting

Back when television was in its infancy and there were three networks and things like personal computers, the Internet, cell phones, and PDAs didn't exist, advertisers ran commercials that appealed to the general audience, or mass market. In the 1960s and 1970s there was no need to aim a message to a particular group, since most everyone watched the same programs, and there were few other types of media to reach people.

With the rise of cable television and specialty networks, the adoption of satellite radio and MP3 players, and the proliferation of e-mail usage and the global marketplace that is the Internet, the mass market has disintegrated. Everyone has his or her own favorite Web sites, cable networks, and specialty magazines. Marketing has evolved to new levels of sophistication to deal with the increased choices and types of media. Today, marketing messages and products can be tailored to individuals.

Essential

The major television networks are promoting their shows via the Internet. Episodes can be downloaded onto iPods and other MP3 players for consumers to watch at their leisure. The networks realize that their target audience, adults ages eighteen to thirty-four, isn't necessarily watching content during network broadcasts.

This specialization of the market is good news for small business marketers. It means that it's easier to reach customers once you know your target audience. Rather than having to spend millions of dollars on a glitzy television campaign, small businesses can target potential clients by taping and running an inexpensive commercial on a local channel that airs programming about entertaining or food. Small businesses can also devise specific marketing programs for reaching specific targets through guerrilla marketing.

Guerrilla Marketing

Guerrilla marketing takes its name from guerrilla warfare. Unlike wars fought in earlier times where whole battalions of soldiers would face each other and fight, today's wars are fought by small groups of soldiers making surprise attacks on all sorts of targets. Wars today are won one small victory at a time, rather than with one huge battle.

The reason small factions are so successful fighting battles around the globe is because of their size and use of unconventional tactics. Small businesses, by definition, are nimble. Unlike a *Fortune* 500 company with many layers of management, multiple divisions, and thousands of employees, small firms have the capacity to react quickly.

Fact

With computers, easy-to-use software, and scanners, every caterer can quickly produce customized T-shirts, brochures, fliers, business cards, and presentations for customers. If you don't want to do it yourself, use Kinko's or online services like CustomInk.com.

Out of necessity, small firms tend to rely on unconventional tactics because they can't afford traditional tools. Unconventional tools are cheaper, and by definition, newer and untested. Such guerrilla tools can have a very effective impact and can indeed compete with larger, more traditional marketing weapons.

So, like guerrilla warriors, today's savvy small-business marketers deliver a series of highly targeted messages to specific, small groups of potential customers, rather than spending their whole marketing budgets on one big advertising campaign. Guerrilla marketing uses free or low-cost tools to disseminate the marketing message.

Guerrilla Tools

There are many guerrilla tools to choose from. Here are the top ten effective guerrilla tools. Use them as much as possible.

Web Sites

Your Web site will be your virtual storefront. It will be, in many instances, the way that potential clients are first introduced to you and your business. It's the first thing they'll see, so make sure the site reflects your services and puts them in a positive light. Creating a Web site is one of the most important marketing steps you will take. In this day and age, almost everybody and every business has a Web page promoting their services. With a well-designed site, your business can appear larger and more professional than it actually is.

Through today's search engines, potential customers can easily find you. Just make sure you use the right words for Search Engine Optimization. While SEO is an inexact science, there are some general guidelines that will make you appear high in the results of search engines like Google and Yahoo.

- Include images on your site; many people search for images first.
- Be specific about the types of catering you offer. If you cater picnics and kids parties, be sure to mention that on your site.

If you don't know how to build a Web site or don't have a friend who will build one for you, it's easy to do on your own. Find a company that has the capability to sell you a domain name and host your Web site. Many companies like Network Solutions have powerful software that allows their clients to build their sites themselves very easily with little or no technical knowledge.

E ssential

There are thousands of freelance Web site designers out there. Your Web designer need not be located where you are. Everything can be done by phone and by Web. Network with everyone you know and ask for a Web designer referral.

All you have to do is sketch out how you want your site to look. Pick what you want people to see on your home page, perhaps a photo of a beautiful buffet that you catered or a photo of people eating your famous muffins and pastries?

You'll need to figure out how many pages you'd like to have on your site. Most small business sites, for example, can start with five pages:

1. Home page
2. About Us page, where you list your skills, background, current customers, mission statement, and other general information about your business
3. Menu page, which gives prospective clients an idea about the type of food that you provide
4. Recent Events and Partial Client List page, which will display photos from a variety of your events and a list of clients. If you can, get feedback from clients and ask if you can post what they write on your Web site.
5. Pricing and Details page, which spells out costs and down-payment policies; this can also include information on the geographic area you cover

Rather than paying to print full-color brochures that can easily become outdated, it's cheaper, easier, and more efficient to have information detailed on a page on your site. You can update prices, menu options, types of services, and policies as often as you'd like.

Free Publicity and Public Relations

Guerrilla marketers don't pay for public relations consultants. They generate positive PR themselves. Whether it's volunteering to cater food for the ravenous participants of a local park's cleanup day or baking a massive gingerbread cookie and decorating it to look like the Queen of England, clever caterers can get themselves on the local television news, in the newspaper, and on blogs by using some creativity and ingenuity.

If you're a wedding caterer, partner with local media outlets to run a contest. Approach a local television station or newspaper. Television stations and newspapers are always running contests to boost viewership. It will be good for them and good for you. Offer to cater a wedding for a local couple if the station will promote you for a period of at least a month. The station may give you free on-air mentions, list you on their Web site, or even run your ad or spot for free or at a very discounted rate.

Think about who you want to see your publicity efforts. If you want local society women to learn about you, then volunteer to bake the biggest cupcake that the town has ever seen for the biggest children's charity event of the year. They can serve the cupcake to the kids or auction it off for a charitable donation.

If you want event planners to notice you, then maybe you should camp outside a big event planner convention and offer each planner an edible menu. Today there are machines that can easily transfer photographs onto cookies and cakes. Put your name, phone number, Web site, and catering specialty on an edible cookie shaped like a menu to pass out to event planners. It will certainly get their attention.

E-mail and Direct Mail

You can introduce yourself for free to potential clients through e-mail. Collect a list of decision makers and their e-mail addresses. Send a group e-mail or a formal printed invitation inviting them to taste your food. Spend money and mail invitations first class. Handwrite the address so it won't look like junk mail. Your invitation will get opened and your intriguing event will get positive replies. Just make sure to let busy event planners pick from a couple of different dates and times for their special tasting. Confirm that each person is a decision maker for at least $10,000 worth of catering a year and invite a group for a special tasting.

Positive Word-of-Mouth

Generating positive word-of-mouth about your catering will be the best thing that you can possibly do to build your business. The best way to do this is to ensure that you have satisfied customers. You must follow up with clients and make sure they had a good experience with you. If not, find out what they didn't like and attempt to fix the problem.

If you work hard to get new clients and big catering jobs, your efforts will start to pay off. Even if you don't get a particular job, the same client will often come back to have you give them a proposal for another job if you made a good initial impression. Go the extra mile for your new customers.

Print and Online Directories

Once you have a Web site and are open for business, take the time to make sure that you're listed in all local publications in print and on the Internet. Whether it's a list of local caterers that's listed online or a local business resources booklet distributed by the local chamber of commerce, get listed in as many resources as possible. Make sure listings are free or low-cost.

There are all sorts of directories to consider. Make sure you're listed in everything from movie-crew catering to the local yellow pages. There's a long lead time for printing new yellow pages directories, so call the local phone book companies early to get their rates. All you need is a listing, preferably in bold. If a small ad is affordable, buy one. If not, spend your valuable marketing dollars elsewhere.

Well-Publicized Events

Offer to cater some well-publicized charity or promotional events that attract the type of people you would like to work for. If you want to focus on wedding catering, offer to cater events where there will be a lot of twenty-somethings in attendance, like charity athletic events and dance-a-thons. If the budget is tight, offer to cut your prices and charge the labor and food costs to your marketing budget. If it's the right event and it has high visibility with lots of local media coverage and public relations, then it can give you invaluable contact with potential customers. Make sure to have your business cards available all over the event and that your business name and contact information is included on all press releases and printed materials.

Telephone

It's easy to get lists of prospective clients. Get a list of local companies at your local library, chamber of commerce, or local business paper. Call the main number of each company and ask to speak to the person in charge of event planning. If there is no event planner, then ask to speak to someone who entertains clients or who arranges company parties. Make a list of decision makers at local companies. These will be excellent prospects.

Call your prospects to invite them to a special tasting. If they're too busy to come to you, offer to drop off a boxed lunch if they'll give you ten minutes of their time to meet you and talk about their event needs while they eat. For a free lunch, many people will take you up on your offer.

Networking

The more people you can meet and tell about your catering company, the more quickly your company will grow. Try to meet as many people in your target audience as possible. Ask vendors if they can refer you to some of their good clients in return for recommending them to your clients. Go to as many local meetings and events as possible. Get involved with the local chamber of commerce, and join local hospital and charity boards. People on boards entertain.

E ssential

Combine your other passions with valuable networking. If you love golf, network on the golf course. If you're a woman, join local women's networking groups. If you're a minority, join your local minority business owners association.

The more groups you belong to and the more that people in your town get to know you, the more likely it is that they're going to trust you and try out your services. You need to become a local fixture in the community.

Print at least 1,000 business cards. There are many places online today that print professional-looking business cards inexpensively. There's no need to pay a graphic designer or create a fancy logo. Use vertical layouts and different colored inks to make your business card stand out from the rest.

Touch Points

Every interaction with a customer or potential customer is a touch point. The key to a successful business is maximizing the experience that a customer has with each touch point. The first e-mail or phone conversation a customer has with you is a vital touch point, but each successive meeting shouldn't be taken for granted. Understanding this will go a long way to ensuring your success.

Food Tastings

Use food tastings as a marketing tool, not as a sales closer. People will buy your services based on you, your reputation, and your proposal. Use special group tastings as a cost-effective way to develop relationships with potential clients, deepen relationships with current customers, and test new menu ideas.

Rather than having tastings for each client after they sign their contract, organize a special tasting every season and invite good past clients along with clients whose affairs are upcoming. This way, your new clients can talk to your established, happy clients and you can save time and effort by conducting group tastings.

Remember that tastings are just that. You can serve new hors d'oeuvres, new side dishes, and desserts. Serving family style can also be appropriate. Place one full-sized completed plate of each menu item elevated at the center of the table, and offer tasting guests a small sample from another plate. Tastings are not meals. Every item from your menu shouldn't be served, nor should clients be getting substantial portions.

People really have to see images of your setups and parties, taste your food, and meet you in order to buy your services, so spend money on marketing efforts that will allow your targets to meet you, see what you do, and taste your magic.

Tastings as Free Market Research

Tastings are one of the smartest, most inexpensive ways to let clients and potential clients learn about your services with all of their senses. By tasting, smelling, seeing, and feeling what you have to offer, you're giving them the best sales tool you have. During the tastings, you have an invaluable opportunity to bond with your clients and get to know them better.

Tastings are important because they have the ability to turn past satisfied customers into lifelong loyal clients. Once you have a core group of loyal customers to come to you for all their catering needs, you'll have a sales base, which will allow you to focus on getting to the next phase of growth.

E ssential

Preprint and distribute simple surveys to your guests. Ask for suggestions and supply pens for them to write with.

By letting customers taste your new recipes and dishes, you're conducting free market research for new and updated menu items. Ask the tasters to fill out notes for what they liked and didn't like. Not only will they think that you're customizing your cooking to suit their tastes, you'll get real feedback on how they like your new dishes.

Tastings for Large Clients

If you have the chance to cater a $40,000 or larger event, invite the key decision makers for a special tasting. If you don't have a location, you can offer to bring the tasting to them. Offer to cater lunch for them one day so they can get a sense of your work.

✓Expertise

The money you spend on food tastings is a cost of doing business. Tastings are marketing expenses, along with advertising and promotion, and their costs should be credited from food and labor and charged to your marketing budget. Your marketing budget should have a separate line item for food tastings. By separating tasting expenses, you will be able to more accurately capture your true food costs and better price your menus. Your accountant will be happy you're keeping your books this way.

Up-Selling

Tastings are a great way to convince clients to spend more on their catering contracts. Once they taste your premium wines, additional courses, and special desserts from your renowned dessert buffet, they're more likely to spend on upgrades.

✓Expertise

You can charge a nominal fee for a predeposit tasting, and if the client ends up booking, he receives credit for the tasting fee. If he doesn't book, you keep the fee in exchange for your time and the cost of the food. Don't do this for every prospect because you risk spending your week cooking for people who won't end up booking with you. Use your best judgment and only do this for clients who press you for a tasting and who are genuinely serious about booking your services.

Tasting Do's and Don'ts

Here are some helpful guidelines for conducting tastings that will result in bigger contract sales.

- **Do go all out!** Use your best linen, flatware, china, and stemware. Be at the door and ready when your guests arrive. Pass them a beverage and greet them with a warm smile as soon as they enter the facility. As every marketer knows, what happens in the first fifteen seconds is what matters most. Don't make your guests wait, and have your A game ready.
- **Don't try to do a tasting while you're catering another off-premise event.** You can't serve two masters. If you do need to combine the two, conduct the tasting well before the start of the catered event.
- **Do have sufficient staff to serve the event.** As the salesperson and owner, you are the host of the event. You need to be with your prospective clients. Remember to take photos of the food so that when the event actually takes place what you served at the tasting will look like it did at the tasting, and you'll have images for your Web site and portfolio.
- **Do try to close the sale at the end of the tasting if you do not have a deposit yet.**
- **Don't serve your guests full-size portions.** Give them miniportions and provide a detailed explanation of each dish. Make sure to briefly explain why you made the dish the way you did and why it's good for an event.

- **Do offer matching wines, beers, or cocktails, if possible, with each course.** You can use this opportunity as an up-sell.
- **Don't allow the client to bring the complete bridal party or the entire management team.** This is a tasting, not a banquet! Be sure that all of the key decision makers are present; three or four people should be the maximum for each potential customer. Use your judgment if you think it's important to include one or two more for a big job.

Local Advertising

Don't spend your entire marketing and advertising budget on advertising in local newspapers and magazines. Print ads only work if you're sure your target audience is reading those publications and if you consistently advertise in those publications week after week. Marketing studies have shown that the effectiveness of the print medium relies on repetition. Readers will only start noticing your company and recognizing the name after they see it more than a dozen times. This means that you'll have to spend a lot of money to become recognized among other advertisers.

The same holds true for spending with local radio stations. Rather than paying for spots, see if you can use guerrilla tools and generate some free or low-cost publicity on the radio. Radio advertisers have to buy spots at the same times over the course of many days for listeners to notice. Also, radio isn't the best medium for conveying your catering services. Hearing is the only sense you don't use to judge food, so it follows that a hearing-exclusive medium is not the most efficient way to attract clients.

By using the inventive techniques discussed earlier in the chapter, you may not have much need to advertise through traditional media. Stick with what works for you, and you will continue to attract new clients and please your existing customers.

Chapter 14

Dealing with Clients

Catering is a service business; interacting with a variety of people is an important part of the industry. Most of the people you'll deal with will be pleasant and professional. Occasionally, you'll run into someone who's difficult, and you'll need to maintain your professionalism. This chapter discusses strategies for dealing with challenging clients and situations.

Maintaining Your Clientele

Once you establish a base of clients, you'll need to make sure that they continue to use your services. You'll have to develop additional menus and event ideas so that clients can use you repeatedly and have a different type of meal each time. Clients who use you to entertain their family, friends, or colleagues often entertain some of the same guests, so you'll want to show them that you have new things to offer in addition to their old favorites.

E ssential

Once you have a loyal client, you can slowly raise your prices, if necessary, to maintain your profit margin. Loyal customers will stay with you as long as your prices don't go up astronomically.

While some clients will call you when they need you, you'll have to work to keep in touch with your clients, making sure that they're still happy with your services and keeping your business in mind. Keep an accurate database in your computer of who hired you, the organization's name (if any), the date of the event, the type of occasion, the cost of the event, and any contact information such as phone numbers and e-mail addresses. If it was a personal occasion like a birthday or anniversary celebration, make sure to record the date on your calendar and send a card a month before the occasion congratulating them and enclose a $100 gift certificate toward your catering services for an event.

E-Mail Newsletters

Maintaining an active client list takes work. You need to be proactive. Send e-mail newsletters to your clients at least once a season telling them what new dishes and services you're offering. Include some beautiful photos from recent events and make sure to link to your Web site. Include a promotional offer if your bookings are a bit slow.

E Fact

Constant Contact (*www.constantcontact.com*) is a Web-based company that can help you manage your growing e-mail list and send e-mail newsletters. The site has customizable templates for newsletters. Prices are reasonable for small businesses, and customer service agents are available to help you get your newsletter started.

Follow Up

Make sure to follow up with every client the week after the event, even if they seemed pleased during the event. Ask them if they would have liked anything done differently, and listen to what they have to say. Don't dispute them, and don't argue with them. If they give you any specifics, write them down. If they don't give you any specifics, ask them if they'd use you again.

If they say they plan to use you again and don't mention a time frame, ask them when they think their next party might be. Ask them if they can recommend you to their friends and colleagues and if you can send them business cards to give to their friends. If they agree, make sure to follow up within a week and send business cards along with a note thanking the client for their help and a certificate for a discount off your services.

E ssential

Make sure to send clients a thank-you note or e-mail the week after their event. Tell them you enjoyed catering their event and would like feedback. Send or e-mail them a certificate that entitles them to a free dessert platter or another similar item if they use you again for another event within six months.

For clients who refer business to you, send them a thank-you note along with a jar of homemade pickles or preserves or a tin of homemade cookies or chocolates. They'll appreciate the personal touch.

If the customer doesn't think that they'll use you again, find out why. This isn't easy to do, but it's necessary. Getting a concrete reason may help you change your services to make them more accessible, but some clients may simply be unreasonable.

Tell them you'd appreciate the feedback. Listen to what they have to say and thank them for being straightforward with you. Within a few days, write the client a note and tell her you've remedied the problems and hope she'll give you another chance. Include a certificate that will give her a discount off of her next job if she books within a year.

Recommendation Letters

Sometimes you may get a thank-you note from clients when you do an outstanding job. Ask the client if you can put their note on your Web site as a testimonial. If you think you did a stellar job for a client but didn't get a thank-you note, it's okay to ask him to write you a recommendation letter. Tell him it will help you with your sales and that you appreciate how busy he is. Sometimes the client will ask you to draft the note for him, so be prepared to do that as well. Make sure to draft a note that is grounded and objective; don't gush about yourself.

Client Tasting Parties

An innovative way to keep your customers thinking about you for months is to invite them to a tasting party. Invite forty of your best clients to a cocktail hour or dessert reception and use the opportunity to test some new recipes or hors d'oeuvres on customers. Your customers will be flattered with the invitation, and hopefully you'll end up with a group of at least twenty people. You can ask clients to bring a guest they'd like to introduce to your food. If you don't have a place for guests, see if a local art gallery owner will let you have the party at her gallery.

Another way to grow your business and increase revenue is to offer a meal delivery service to your clientele. You can cook meals for clients during your slow times and deliver them on a weekly basis. You can also make cookies, brownies, sandwich platters, and other easy-to-prepare items for clients who order ahead and have them pick up the items at your kitchen or deliver the orders if they're big enough.

Turning Down Clients

Believe it or not, there are times when the best decision is to turn down business. You may not be able to envision it now, but there will be times when it's best for you and the client to decline to cater their event. The rest of this chapter outlines the situations when the right answer is to say "no" to a client.

If someone asks you to do a catering job and leaves you with a bad feeling in your gut, listen to your intuition. Here are some telltale signs of bad clients and suggestions for dealing with them.

The "Poor" Client

This is the client who can't afford to hire you because she claims she has no money in her budget. This type of client will try to take advantage of you and work hard to get you to provide catering services to her at cost or below. She might even try to leverage the fact that you're new, telling you that the job will be good for your portfolio. This is likely to be a client for a not-for-profit or private organization or someone looking to cater a private event who hasn't used a caterer before. Corporate clients will always have a budget and, for the most part, will respect your pricing structure.

If a customer approaches you for a catering proposal and has an unrealistically low budget, like $15 per person for a dinner, push back. In a polite but firm way, explain that her expectations are unreasonable. If she hasn't used a caterer before, she may very likely be unaware of the costs. Educate the client and tell her what the average price for a catered dinner costs in your area. You will have the information from your competitive survey research, so you can easily show clients where your prices fall among the competition if they ask. You shouldn't be the cheapest caterer in town and you probably won't be the most expensive one either.

E ssential

As a general rule of thumb, you should charge 10 percent more than the average prices in your area for your type of catering.

Have confidence in yourself and in your work. If your services are priced correctly, there will be clients who will pay what your services are worth. Rather than catering a full meal for a tight budget, be creative and offer alternatives to a client who truly has very little to spend if you think the job is worth doing. If the client wants to serve a full dinner, but really doesn't have the money to spend on a per-person basis, suggest that she have a breakfast or brunch event instead. Alternatively, she may be able to afford a predinner hors d'oeuvre event or a late-afternoon tea event.

Don't lower your prices just because someone pleads poverty. Being the low-cost provider is not a winning strategy for caterers. Catering is a low-margin service business. You are providing a lot of time, creativity, and labor to bring someone's vision to life. You're offering a premium product and service, not selling laundry detergent or computer chips. Don't get involved in a price war. It's better to walk away from a client who is unrealistic about her budget than to get involved in a job where you'll lose your shirt.

Fact

The average price charged by caterers in the United States for a fully catered dinner is $39 per person. The average price for a breakfast is $19. Remember that these prices will be higher in large metropolitan areas and lower in most other places.

If a client objects to the price of a certain dish, offer her less-expensive alternatives. If a client objects to you marking up table and chair rental, tell her that she's welcome to deal directly with the rental company to avoid the extra fee. Let her know that you have to be compensated for your time and effort if you're going to arrange for the rental. Suggest she take on more of the work for the event to reduce costs.

You can be flexible in order to get a contract signed, but don't give away your profitability. Offer a goodwill gesture such as serving the after-dessert truffles for free.

The Exceptions to the Rule

There are two exceptions to this rule. First, it's okay to provide catering services for a legitimate charity, a 501(c)(3). You may see some benefits from catering for a charity; it's a good way to support a cause you believe in, and it will bring you good exposure. Think carefully before you accept, and consider the pros and cons. If it's a huge job, you may have to turn a lucrative client down because you only have so much labor capacity and time for preparation. The cost of the food, and the labor associated with the job, however, is tax deductible. Make sure to record the food, labor, and associated costs in your charitable donations account, not in your regular food cost and labor accounts. Check with your accountant for the specifics.

Second, it's also all right to accept barter for part of your catering services.

If a client provides a service that could benefit your business, such as public relations, advertising sales, or transportation, then it might make sense to negotiate a deal where they pay the food costs up front in cash as a deposit and pay the balance of their fee in a bartered service. Bartered agreements need to be spelled out in writing and need to be equivalent in dollar amounts. If the balance of your fee is $1,200, then you need to receive $1,200 of a comparable service. Make sure that what you're getting in return is the current market rate and that you'll get prime goods or services. Sometimes customers try to barter away old goods, undesirable ad space, or a service they'll never get around to giving you. Make sure they agree to deliver their services according to an agreed-upon schedule. You should receive part of the barter before you finish the catering job.

The Internal Revenue Service requires that the fair market value of goods and services exchanged must be included in the income of both parties. Each party must file Form 1099-B. While there are some exceptions explained on the IRS Web site, you and your client need to record barter transactions on your books.

The Needy Client

This is the client who calls you twelve times a day to ask you what color the toothpicks are going to be and how many melon balls each person will get. He changes his mind about little details, and the sound of his voice makes your blood pressure rise sixty points. He calls you at 11 P.M. and expects you to be available seven days a week.

If you're busy, it's perfectly okay to tell this client you're booked. You can tell him you'd like to help him another time. The trick is to pick up on the type of client as quickly as possible so as to avoid committing to a job before it's too late. Look for signals in the initial contact and phone conversation that this person is going to be a lot of work. Does he need to know every detail? Can he delegate responsibility to you?

If you do want to take the job from this type of client, make sure to set the parameters clearly up front and spell them out in your contract/proposal. State that any changes made after a certain date will cost extra. Make your business hours clear.

The Very Rich Client

Many new business owners love to get jobs from extremely wealthy clients such as movie stars, sports professionals, and corporate magnates. Unfortunately, some of these people have a tendency to pay their bills very slowly or not at all. They're used to getting things for free.

If you're going to take a job from a high-profile client, make sure you get a larger-than-normal deposit up front to cover all the food costs and collect the balance due before the event. Large caterers require full payment prior to the event date, and you shouldn't be any different. Don't be afraid to charge a slightly higher service charge for these jobs either, given the extra risk and work that is generally involved.

If a client squawks at the idea, tell her that you're a small business and can only offer such attractive prices and excellent service because you proactively manage your cash flow and get paid before the job is completed.

If a client isn't sure of what she wants, it's your job to ask questions and to assess her likes and dislikes. Does she like casual entertaining, or is she more formal? You can get many clues from seeing how clients furnish their homes, how they dress, and how they speak.

Once you know something about a client and the reason she wants to hire a caterer, you can start to suggest options. Let her know price ranges with each option, and she'll tell you right away if you're in the right ballpark. If she doesn't balk at the prices you're giving her, ask her if you're in her budget. If she says yes, you may have some room to up-sell.

If a client can't seem to make any choices, tell her that you're the professional, and ask if she can leave all the details to you. Get her to agree on a price per person, get a deposit, and make sure that your agreement clearly states that the client is letting you make the decisions for menu choices, tableware, and decorations as long as you stay within her budget.

Overbooking

One of the worst mistakes you can make is booking too many jobs at once. There are only so many hours in a day, and you'll only have access to so much kitchen space. You'll have to learn quickly how much you can accomplish in a day and how many jobs you can manage. You never want to have to call a client and tell him that you made a mistake and can't do the job that you've promised. That's close to professional suicide.

On the other hand, working around the clock trying to do four jobs at once is killing yourself too, only slower. It'll be impossible for you to supervise the necessary level of detail if you have too many jobs going on at once and don't have a high-caliber professional staff to help you. The quality of the jobs will suffer, and that will reflect poorly on you. Until you expand your business and are large enough to hire full-time professional managers and chefs, don't risk taking on too many jobs at once. In the catering business, your reputation depends on doing jobs consistently well. You're only as good as the last job you did, and if it ends up being a disaster no one benefits except your competition.

Never agree to an event before carefully looking at your calendar. Tell clients that you'll check your bookings and will get back to them the next day if you're busy preparing for another event.

Repeat Clients

If a former client asks you for a favor, you'll probably feel compelled to accommodate her, especially if you did a big job for her before and she was pleasant to deal with. Be careful not to fall into the "yes" trap and accept every job that comes your way.

You may relish the opportunity to work with a former client, but be truthful with yourself and your client if you are already booked for the same day or are overwhelmed with upcoming jobs. Your client will appreciate your honesty and will respect you even more if you tell her that you'd like nothing more than to help her, but that you're already booked and you wouldn't be able to do your best work if you said yes. Recommend her to someone else that you think will do a good job, and she'll know to ask you earlier next time around.

There's always a risk that you can lose a client to a competitor when you recommend a different caterer, but that chance is smaller than wrecking the relationship yourself by accepting a job you can't do well. Most often, the client won't like the competition and will prefer the personal service you provided. She'll come back to you with even greater appreciation and will spread the word about the service you provide and your professional manner.

Holiday Time

The catering business, like the candy business and the floral business, is highly seasonal. People tend to celebrate and have parties during certain times of the year. November and December are prime catering times, as are the summer months and late spring and early fall. There's a slight pickup toward the end of January if you cater Super Bowl parties and a blip in February if you specialize in catering romantic dinners for Valentine's Day, but the rest of the winter is usually pretty quiet. Of course, this will vary depending on where you live and what kind of cultural calendar your community follows.

Mid-November through December is one of the busiest times in the catering business. Unlike wedding season, which stretches from April to October, the holiday season is compacted into six weeks. Chances are that once you're up and running and people know about your services, you'll get more holiday requests for business than you can manage.

While you'll want to do as many jobs as you possibly can during this short period, be careful about promising too much to too many people. It takes time and experience to reach maximum efficiency and learn how many jobs you can handle. For holiday jobs, plan menus so that you can do as much as possible ahead of time, freezing stocks, pie shells, soups, and sauces.

The key to managing a busy holiday season is to start booking holiday jobs early. This will allow you to plan ahead. Offer clients an incentive to book their events with you by the end of September if possible, or by mid-October at the latest. If clients book their events with you early and give you their deposits, offer them free pies for dessert, free quiches for appetizers, or anything else that you can make ahead and have in your freezer.

 Fact

Record the food and labor costs of the complimentary items in your promotions budget, not in your regular food costings budget.

It's well worth the labor time and cost of the ingredients to provide an incentive for clients to book early. Much of catering involves planning and logistics. If you know what you need to prepare and when, you can group jobs together and prepare dishes more efficiently.

If you have four holiday jobs within two days, for example, make sure your holiday menus are streamlined. Remove labor-intensive and exotic dishes that aren't your best sellers. Most caterers, restaurants, and bakeries offer special holiday menus instead of their year-round menus. The sheer volume of orders dictates that special requests not be allowed and complicated multistep dishes be temporarily removed from the menu.

Make sure your holiday menu includes plenty of roasted and braised vegetables and meats. Mashed vegetables like potatoes and turnips and purees of carrots, squash, broccoli, and cauliflower are easy to make, especially in bulk. When planning for the holidays, double-check that you have enough large baking and roasting pans and mixing bowls to handle the quantities of food you'll be preparing. The last thing you want to do is realize on November 20 that you need a twenty-quart mixing bowl and there isn't one within 100 miles.

Expertise

Apply a bulk cooking method to your holiday orders. Rather than buying for one job at a time, you'll need to order for a week's worth of jobs and prep the orders dish by dish rather than job by job.

Protecting Your Reputation

One of the worst things you can do is to get involved in a catering event that could damage your reputation. If you're asked to cater an affair for an organization or person embroiled in controversy, consider the nature of the controversy. If you believe in the cause or support the person, take the job as long as you get paid up front. If the client has legal or financial problems, it would probably behoove you to turn down the job. As mentioned earlier, research the organizations that you're going to donate your services to or barter for if you're not familiar with what they do.

If you're uncomfortable catering for a client for any reason, let him know you're fully booked, recommend another caterer to him, and leave it at that.

Dealing with Difficult Clients

The key to dealing with difficult clients is preventing problems from escalating. Defuse or solve problems as soon as they arise so they don't turn into major crises. Learn to recognize the warning signs of a difficult client as soon as they appear, so you can deal with them at the outset.

Some clients may start out behaving like difficult lions, but you can turn them into lambs if you know how to deal with them. Recognize what the client needs and how she wants to be treated and act accordingly. Some clients need to feel that they're the most important client you have, whether their job is worth $1,000 or $50,000. These clients need to have their calls returned within the hour if at all humanly possible.

Since you never know how a client will influence your business in the future, aim to treat each client as if she's the most important client you have. This strategy will help you grow and become successful. Sometimes it's the small, difficult clients who turn out to be your most loyal ones and the ones who refer you the most. These clients often have influential friends and relatives who also need caterers.

The best way to deal with demanding clients is to take several deep breaths and smile before you say or do anything. Ask yourself whether the client is being reasonable or ridiculous. If you realize that the client is being reasonable, then accommodate her. However, if the client is being totally unreasonable, and it means the difference between running a profitable or unprofitable job, it may make sense to walk away. Refund the deposit and tell the client that you're not the right caterer for the job. Apologize and walk away gracefully. Better to cut your losses before the job than have a bigger problem later on.

✔ Expertise

Dean Martinus, president of Great Performances Caterers in New York City, got a call asking if he could cater an event for the president of Malaysia and one hundred other people the next day. He accepted and managed to do the event on incredibly short notice. How? Being a large caterer in Manhattan, he had access to his vendors, so he was able to quickly find out what could be delivered the next day. Then with his staff he was able to put together a menu that could be prepped and served in addition to the jobs the company already had booked.

Inebriated or Violent Guests

If your client or his guests are drinking too much at the event, offer them fresh coffee and plenty of water and club soda instead of more alcohol. Let the host or cohost know that some of the guests look like they've had enough. In some states, party hosts will be held legally liable for drunken guests who get into an accident after they leave the party, so check with your lawyer and insurance agent and make sure that you're protected as best as possible.

If a client or a guest becomes violent, try your best to calm him down and call for help immediately. Don't try to engage the guest yourself.

Sick or Injured Guests

If someone becomes violently ill at a party, try to help the guest and call for help immediately. Ask someone to call 911. It's better to be safe than sorry. When things quiet down a bit and the situation is under control, make sure to get her name and contact information from the host or a friend. This is essential in cases where the illness is caused by food poisoning or the guest tries to blame her illness on you.

Expertise

According to emergency response experts, the first response to an accident is the most important. First aid given at the scene can improve the victim's chances of survival and a good recovery.

As a caterer, you should know basic first aid and you should be trained in adult CPR and rescue breathing. Keep your certification up-to-date. Courses are taught regularly by the American Red Cross and at local community centers and schools.

If a person faints, apply moist towels to her face and neck. Position her on her back and elevate her feet. Don't slap or shake her, and don't try to give the person anything to drink, even water, until she is fully conscious.

Alert

According to the Heimlich Institute, the Heimlich maneuver can help asthma sufferers in addition to those choking or drowning. During acute asthma attacks, the maneuver expels trapped air and mucus plugs, enabling sufferers to resume normal breathing and replenish their oxygen supply.

If someone is choking, apply the Heimlich maneuver to dislodge the object. If you're not familiar with how to administer the maneuver, you can learn to do it by taking a first aid course. You can also order instructional DVDs and wallet cards from the Heimlich Institute.

Chapter 15

Considerations as You Grow

You may not be able to envision it now, but before you know it you'll have to think about how to grow your business and get to the next level in terms of size, revenue, and staffing. Growing your business involves acquiring and using some different skills and techniques. Knowing when it's time to expand your business, how to do it, and how to get the word out are discussed in this chapter.

Signs of Growing Pains

You'll know you're experiencing growing pains when you get calls to cater events and you have to turn them down because you're spread too thin and you just can't be in two places at once. While growing pains can be difficult, they're a great sign that you're ready to go to the next level as a business owner and entrepreneur. Other signs of growing pains are:

- You're exhausted from working too much. You're catering five or more events in one week.
- You need to hire someone at a higher level than a server or prep help.
- You need to buy a new, dedicated delivery vehicle.
- Your weekly food orders are two to three times larger than they used to be.
- Paperwork is bogging you down. You have so many proposals to get out, so many bills to pay, and so many invoices to prepare.
- You need a larger line of credit from your bank.

- At least half of your business is coming from referral calls and repeat business.
- You need to install an extra phone line.

These factors indicate that you've been successful in your primary goal: starting a thriving catering business. One of the first considerations in making your business even larger is increasing your marketing and promotion budget by at least 10 percent. Take your marketing and promotion plan to the next level to continue building your brand. Sponsor a local cooking competition for kids, raising money for their school. You'll be doing something very worthwhile and hopefully generating good public relations at the same time. Print a color brochure if you haven't already. Rent a booth at a couple of appropriate trade shows in your region to promote your services and raise awareness of your name.

In order to continue your success, attracting new clients is only one of many priorities. You need to consider how to expand your business without compromising on any of the personalized service or quality dishes that have boosted your reputation.

Hiring Help

As your business grows, you'll have to hire part-time and full-time staff to help you. You'll probably need a sous chef in the kitchen, an administrative assistant to help you with paperwork, and possibly a sales manager to help you sell your services. One of the keys to successful recruiting is to always be on the lookout for people who would be a good fit in your business. Whether it's meeting a bright waiter at a restaurant or finding a helpful sales associate at a department store, if you like his smile, his attitude, and his ability to think on his feet, then ask him if he'd like to work part-time as an event server.

Most event servers work on-call, meaning you call them when you need them. Call to book your best servers as far in advance as possible to make sure they're available. Many excellent serving staff work for a few different caterers or agencies, so if you find a few people who do an excellent job, offer them a higher wage than their other gigs to ensure that you'll be first on their list.

Recruiting

If you avoid union staff or staffing agencies, you'll save money and hopefully find people who are motivated to work for you by their desire to learn the business. Anyone who wants a career in events management should work in catering for a while to understand the demands of the business. New graduates or even students are good part-time hires.

Teaching food-service management at a continuing education program, culinary school, or hospitality management program will give you a steady stream of eager workers. Even volunteering to speak at career nights or being a guest speaker in a class will get you in front of many eager students. Let them know you're hiring, and give out plenty of business cards.

Here's a sample ad for catering staff that you may wish to use when advertising online or in print. Include your contact information and raise the starting hourly wage if you're located in a large urban area:

Wanted! Part-Time Help.
Do you like people and like to see others smile?
If so, join our team. We'll train you and
show you that work can be fun.
We work in a fast-paced, exciting environment.
Starting salary $8/hr.
Visit our Web site at *www.yourbusinessnamehere.com.*
E-mail your resume or call our office.

Advertise "opportunity meetings" where you ask candidates to show up for a meeting to learn about working for you. Offer free beverages and snacks. At the beginning of the meeting, talk about how tough catering is and emphasize that only the energetic and quick-thinking candidates will be able to handle the job. Discuss the challenges of working under strict timetables with few breaks. Then ask the attendees to take a five-minute break for drinks and snacks. The people who aren't afraid of hard work and who aren't looking for glamour will return, and they will most likely be good hires.

E ssential

If you've found a couple of efficient prep cooks, offer them a raise and a chance to learn other aspects of the business to keep them. A fast and reliable prep cook will keep your labor costs down and will be an invaluable resource to your business.

During the second part of the meeting, market your catering firm as a great place to work, where employees are paid and treated fairly. If you underpay and overwork your staff, the word will get out and it will be more difficult for you to find and train good staff.

Working with Staffing Agencies

Lots of catering firms use staffing agencies with varying results. Some caterers love them and others consider them a useful resource in a pinch. Much depends on the agency, as well as on the market for temporary staff in your area.

If you need to hire many servers for a very large event, you may have to contact several agencies. If you do use an agency, especially for the first time, to hire a number of workers, make sure a manager from the agency comes to your event to see that the staffers show up and do a good job. Also, negotiate with the agency so that they don't get their final payment until the event is completed. If their workers don't do a good job executing the event, you will have leverage when you complain to them.

Finding High-Quality Staffers

Along with a great smile, look for three main qualities in staffers:

- The ability to think quickly in tough situations
- The ability to act quickly in tough situations
- Positive attitude

Catering is all about thinking on your feet and reacting as soon as new obstacles are thrown in your path. Smart people can figure out how to react, and quick people can get the job done, resolving a problem before the client knows there ever was one. Someone who moves like molasses won't be able to keep up with the fast pace of an event.

A positive attitude is important in an industry like catering. Look for people who look at the glass as being half full. People with a "can't do" attitude will only bring down the rest of your team.

Unlike a traditional business interview where you sit down with a candidate and ask her a series of questions, an interview for a catering job should involve the candidate walking around and interacting with other people, if possible. The best way to facilitate this is to invite the candidate to your facility, offer her a beverage, introduce her to your other staff and watch how she moves, walks, talks, and interacts. Take her on a tour of your facility, and intentionally drop something on the floor to see if she'll pick it up. Inject some humor into your conversation to see how the candidate reacts.

E Alert

When hiring people, look for candidates who are resourceful and flexible problem solvers. These types of people will be easy to train and will be able to fill a variety of functions.

Ask the candidate how she would respond to specific real-life catering situations, such as a delay in serving the dessert, a leak in the roof directly over the buffet table, and being understaffed when a dozen extra guests show up to an event. Her answers will show her creativity, resourcefulness, common sense, and willingness to take the initiative and solve problems.

Evaluate how pleasant, confident, energetic, and personable the candidate is. Finally, ask yourself whether you would like to work with her. If a candidate passes the interview test, give her a chance to work for you. Hire her to work an event. If she doesn't do a good job, simply don't ask her back again.

Other Ways to Recruit Staff

The best sources of staff are referrals from existing staff members. Let your regular staff know when you need additional help. Pay them a cash bounty if one of their referrals works out and stays with you for a certain period of time. Remember the "buddy system" from grade school? You can apply the same principle to catering. It's intimidating for a new staffer to show up at a catered event. Promise your existing staffers that they will be able to work with their referrals.

Caterers who pay wages that are a little bit better than the competition and treat their staff at least as well as their clients seem to have less turnover and fewer staff shortages. Those who yell at their staffers and pay less always seem to need staff.

Sharing staff with a few other professional caterers can also be a good source of extra personnel. Collaborate with other caterers you like, and they'll return the favor. Also, new caterers love to learn from the pros. You were a new caterer not long ago, so don't hesitate to ask those caterers who are just starting out to work for you. Be a mentor, and you'll get a great worker. Think creatively for other staffing sources. Consider your vendor representatives. One Florida caterer uses his U.S. Foodservice salesperson as a chef in his kitchen at larger events.

 Fact

Be sure to have a place on your catering Web site where job candidates can apply online. This reduces the chance of applications getting lost, and potential candidates will be more likely to apply for a job if they can apply from the comfort of their own living room.

Training Your Staff

Give your senior staffers more per hour than first-timers to encourage them to help you train the new staffers. You must make a commitment to train new staff and invest time, effort, and money. Untrained staffers leave because they feel you didn't care enough about them, and high turnover will waste even more of your resources. Nothing makes a catering company run smoothly more than trained and motivated staff.

You need to have a scheduled training session along with on-the-job training. Use videos, live demonstrations, and role-playing. All staff must be trained in the Heimlich maneuver and in responsible alcohol serving. Teach new staff how to lift a tray and pour wine, water, and coffee. Show them how to carve, open a wine bottle, and fold a napkin. Create contests where the winners receive free movie tickets or a gift certificate to a local coffee shop or ice cream parlor.

Motivating Staff and Minimizing Turnover

Motivation, of course, starts with fair pay, fair benefits, a well-
organized workplace, and open lines of communication. You should
always treat your staff members at least as well as you treat your clients. Put yourself in your staff members' shoes. Reward them quickly
and promptly. A little cash goes a long way toward motivating a
staffer who just went beyond the call of duty to make a guest happy.

Quick and fair discipline is mandatory. Rapid correction of poor
behavior is a must. You must be prepared to fire people when they
show no improvement. Terminating or not calling back poor per-
formers goes a long way toward retaining your best workers, since
good people want to work with firms that have high standards.

There are several things you can do as a business owner to create
a positive and stable work environment. Hire enough staff. While catering staff need to work hard, avoid being understaffed. Your staff will
feel like you are taking advantage of them if you consistently expect
them to do more than their job. Make sure you work harder than every
other staffer. Always give a staffer who earns it a raise or a promotion.

E Alert

Allow your staff to solve problems for you. Empower them to make some decisions so that they can keep guests happy. Happy guests make a happy host, and it allows you to focus on the big picture and not on minute details.

Create the Right Structure

In larger catering businesses, there's a classic struggle between the kitchen and the sales staff. Some catering businesses are sales driven, and the sales team dictates to the kitchen what goes on the menu and what they should cook and serve. Other catering firms are kitchen-driven, where the kitchen tells the sales staff what to sell.

A well-functioning catering organization works best when the kitchen, sales, and marketing work together as one team to reach a common goal. Cooperation won't happen any other way, no matter how much you try to instill it. If you reward your cooking staff for hitting a food-cost goal, your sales staff for hitting a certain dollar amount of sales, and the marketing team for hitting a certain increase in sales, then the groups will not work together as a team.

Instead, pick one goal; for example, sales figures. Come up with a plan of action yourself, and get input from the kitchen, sales, and marketing to implement it. Even though the kitchen does not work directly with sales, your kitchen staff will see that there are measures they can take on their own to help meet your vision.

Moving into Your Own Commercial Space

If you're renting time in a commercial kitchen in the beginning, you'll probably need your own dedicated space once you've built up a customer base. Buying or renting your own commercial space can be daunting.

If you're planning to lease a commercial kitchen space, make sure you discuss the terms of the lease in detail with the landlord or the broker. Work with an attorney who knows commercial real estate and foodservice businesses. She will know what to look for in the fine print and find problems before you sign anything.

There are a few different types of commercial leases. In a net lease, the tenant pays monthly rent, which includes the additional costs of taxes, maintenance, and insurance. A net net lease, or a double net lease, means that the tenant will pay rent and will cover all costs except structural repair. A triple net lease holds the tenant responsible for paying monthly rent plus all additional expenses including structural repair, except possibly roof repair.

You may need to make modifications to the space to get it up to code to meet current state regulations if the building hasn't been well maintained or hasn't been used recently as a commercial kitchen. Do all your research on zoning laws and regulations in your area and hire a local construction consultant who knows his way through all the red tape. Your commercial kitchen will need to have the correct fire and smoke alarms, ventilation and plumbing systems, and lighting, and may need to comply with other regulations to pass inspection and be licensed.

☀ Alert

Whether you're offered a net lease or a triple net lease, everything is a matter of negotiation. You and your attorney must read the fine print. Every lease is different, and it is up to you to contest any provisions in the lease with which you disagree.

Find out about past tenants and why they left. Ask neighboring businesses, the local police precinct, and the local chamber of commerce about the landlord and the condition of the space. You need to know about any potential problems before you sign a lease.

Buying or Leasing a Vehicle

You'll eventually need your own vehicle to transport prepped food and other supplies to clients and other off-premise locations. A spacious car can be used for business purposes.

Check with your accountant about tax credits for hybrid vehicles and call your state's motor vehicle department about getting commercial plates for your vehicle. Consult with your insurance agent about insuring your vehicle. When your business really grows, you may want to think about buying a refrigerated truck, or a specially outfitted truck designed for catering.

E ssential

To promote your brand, order custom decals with your business name, logo, and phone number, and put them on your vehicle on both sides. You can design your own and order decals online or find a local business who can help you in the yellow pages.

If your concept involves the incorporation of a vehicle, then you'll have to rework your business plan to include the price of the vehicle and its refurbishing and outfitting. Just like renting a commercial space, carefully look over a purchase or leasing agreement and read the fine print.

Chapter 16

Partnering to Grow Your Business

There are various ways to partner with others to grow your business, allowing you to do things you couldn't do on your own. From forging marketing partnerships to making business partners, combining with the assets and skills of others makes sense for businesses of all sizes. Whether you're trying to partner with a local photographer, florist, or high-end retailer, make sure you're comfortable working with that person. Use your gut instinct. If you think the person is not going to be an honest or sincere partner, find someone else to work with.

Promotional Partners

Caterers need marketing savvy and creativity. They must be able to think outside the box to address their customers' needs. Partnering with other businesses is one way to help customers find what they need, and it's a smart way to promote your own business. By using guerrilla marketing tools and techniques, coupled with the partnering ideas outlined here, you'll have a leg up on your competition.

No matter how established you are, how big you are, or how well known you are, partnering with other businesses and other brands can help your business grow more quickly and to greater levels than going it alone. *Fortune* 500 companies routinely partner with other firms. For example, Duncan Hines uses Hershey's brand chocolate in its cake mixes, and Delta Air Lines is the presenting sponsor of *Wintuk*, Cirque du Soleil's new upcoming show at the Theater at Madison Square Garden. Cross-promotion builds brands in creative and cost-effective ways.

Companies across all industries are partnering like never before. They are learning the advantages of partnering with companies who attract the same customers. Managing partner relationships is becoming increasingly important to fulfill all customer needs.

Advertising is expensive, and customers are bombarded with thousands of messages a day on the television, radio, computer, store shelves, and billboards. Anything you can do to step away from the fray and find innovative ways to promote your business will be valuable. Seek out partners you like. Look for people you respect and whose business sense you admire. Approach people who work hard like you and who also have growing businesses. Ideal partners are those that deal with your target customers.

Tasting Partners

Even if you don't have your own facility, you still need to do tastings for important prospective clients, first-time clients who have signed contracts with you, and loyal customers who've given you referrals and repeat business. Tastings provide a perfect opportunity to partner with other local businesses. Everyone wins—you get a unique setting for your tasting, your partner gets increased visibility for his business, and your clients get an unforgettable experience.

What You Should Look For

You need to secure a nice, quiet location where you can serve your clients and discuss the food and your services with them. Ideally, the location should have some type of kitchen or kitchenette, so you can finish your food and reheat items if necessary. If you can't get a location with a kitchen, bring a hotplate with you if you really need one, but try to plan your menu accordingly so it won't be necessary.

E ssential

Approach small local hotels, bed and breakfasts, art galleries, beautifully merchandised retail stores, and any other venue that might be a pretty setting for a tasting. Be creative. A sit-down tasting isn't always necessary. A stand-up buffet might be all you need. Look for a place that will provide a quiet, private environment. As long as the venue doesn't have its own catering service and will allow you to bring in your food and guests, almost any type of space will do. Consider approaching these possible venues:

- Local museums
- Private clubs
- Day spas
- High-end furniture show rooms
- Artisanal chocolate stores
- Upscale wine stores
- Home furnishing stores

Try to partner with small independent venues. See if you can be the exclusive or preferred caterer for them. Upscale retailers often conduct special VIP events in their stores and need a caterer to provide hors d'oeuvres and other tidbits for their customers. You might be able to develop a symbiotic relationship with the venue, so that you both benefit and provide each other with additional business.

If you have to go a step further to convince the manager, you can even offer a catered cold lunch or continental breakfast for a group of a dozen or so people at the venue. You may even get your partner as a client.

Mutual Benefits

Many other small business owners will welcome the opportunity to preview their products and services to your customers if you position your request properly. Approach the owner of an art gallery, for example, and tell her what you're doing. Explain that she can welcome the group and describe her gallery's current art exhibition while the guests arrive. A small boutique hotel might have a lovely room for your group of eight to twelve people. Invite the manager to greet your guests and tell them about the hotel's rooms and services. High-end retail stores often welcome the opportunity to introduce people to their product lines in a relaxed manner while the potential customers are sipping wine and enjoying hors d'oeuvres.

Guarantee the venue owner that you'll clean up and leave the place cleaner than when you arrived. Explain the benefits of bringing in a new customer base for them. Remind them that this is a great promotional opportunity that they can take advantage of by offering discounts to your guests and keeping the cash registers open during your tasting event.

E ssential

Call a local music academy or college to find a promising music student who can play the violin or piano during part of your tasting. It will add ambience and class to almost any venue. The cost of hiring a student to play for an hour will be worthwhile. If you allow the student to pass out his card to your guests, you might be able to negotiate a discounted rate with him.

Make sure to explain the interactive tasting experience to your customers when you invite them to the event. Tell them it's an exclusive type of tasting where they can taste your food and learn about art, or see the fall's new fashion collection, depending on where you're going to hold your event.

Vendor Partners

You may start to notice the same faces taking pictures, setting up flowers, and tending the bar. Establish a network with these vendors; you work with the same clients, and you can bring each other business.

Networking

You can invite other event vendors to your tastings as a promotional tie-in. Both of you will make valuable contacts. If you know a photographer who works at some of the events you cater, invite her to your tasting. She'll appreciate the invitation and the opportunity to meet your clients. Have her take pictures of your food at the tasting, so that you have professional quality pictures for your portfolio and Web site. She can also take pictures of your guests and send them with her card afterward. If your clients need an event photographer and haven't hired one yet, your colleague might get some new business.

Do the same thing for a musician who works at the same events you do. Ask the musician to play at your tasting for a half hour or so. The music will relax your clients and might provide the musician with new business. If you need to rent linens, glasses, or other tabletop items for your tasting, invite your local rental vendor to come to your tasting. In return for some great food and a chance to show off his new products to some upscale customers, ask the vendor to provide his services to you at no charge.

 Fact

Listening to soothing music relaxes customers and allows them to enjoy and digest their meal more easily. They're more likely to close a catering deal if you provide them with a relaxing, stress-free environment.

Ask a local florist to provide a table arrangement gratis for your tasting. Invite her to the tasting, and let her bring her business cards. Your clients might hire her for their events. Some other vendors to contact for possible partnerships may include:

- Musicians and DJ's
- Photographers
- Videographers
- Makeup artists
- Florists
- Furniture rental companies
- Ice sculpture companies
- Specialty food vendors like crepe makers, popcorn cart vendors, etc.
- Lighting specialists
- Tent and restroom rental companies
- Limousine and coach rental companies
- Jewelers
- Stationers who do custom invitations

Food Vendors

To save on the ingredient costs for your tastings, partner with some of your specialty food vendors. If the guy who sells you grass-fed beef is willing to provide samples of his new dry-aged product, then develop a tasting menu that features his beef. If your local grower is willing to provide heirloom tomatoes and fresh dill in return for promoting her farm and her homemade pickles and jams, then feature her vegetables and herbs in your tasting dishes. You can even have your vendor come to the food tasting as a special perk for her.

You'll need serving help at your tastings to allow you the time to talk to your guests. Find low-cost serving help by partnering with the career office at a local school. Offer to provide a training internship for students, and teach your interns kitchen and serving skills in return for helping you serve at your tastings, complete your paperwork, and prep ingredients for your jobs. If you can meet the school's internship requirements, the student will get credit for working with you and you'll get a worker for a very reasonable cost, maybe even for free.

Partnering with Wedding Vendors

If you're interested in booking catering jobs for wedding receptions and prewedding festivities, use your creativity to partner with other wedding vendors to publicize your business.

Meet with the owners of the top limousine companies in the area. Propose a cross-promotional program, which can benefit your company and theirs. Negotiate a deal—you'll recommend their services to your clients, and in return they will promote your services in their cars and customer mailings and to their larger corporate and private clients. People who use car services to get to and from the airport and to go home after working late nights tend to be the same people who host events and need caterers for their business and social parties.

E ssential

Bridal expos are a great opportunity to gain exposure and network with other vendors. Expos can attract thousands of potential customers and hundreds of vendors. Check local events calendars for events near you, and contact the expo's planners to see if you can register as an exhibitor.

Even though you never work directly with them, travel agencies are another partnering target. Since many upscale clients and wedding couples book honeymoons through a travel agent, inviting travel agents to a special tasting in return for promoting your services to their clients makes sense. Travel agents work on commission, so you can offer them 5 percent of a catering contract if their lead results in new business for you.

The travel agent–client relationship is a special one. Clients tend to work with the same travel agents for years, and travel agents spend a lot of time working with each individual client. A good travel agent gets to know her clients. She'll be a valuable source of referrals and can also let you know who to invite to a special tasting. Since travel agents spend a lot of time working with their clients and tend to work with them over and over again, they get to know their customers pretty well. A good travel agent will know who to recommend your services to and who's worthwhile for you to invite to a special tasting.

☀ Alert

You must have a signed, written agreement with anyone who sells your services for commission. Draft a simple agreement that spells out what the rate will be, when they'll get paid, if they're allowed to sell a competing catering service, and what defines a qualified sale.

Local hairdressers are also worth networking and partnering with. Hairdressers have a captive audience, and they also tend to know a lot about their clients. They know who in the family is getting married, graduating, or having a baby. Most hairdressers have an extremely loyal clientele who listen to what their hairdresser has to say. Many people go to the same hair stylist for years at a time, often traveling to get a haircut if they move out of town. Hairdressers become part of a trusted network, so if Mrs. Smith's hairdresser recommends you to cater her daughter's wedding next May, then Mrs. Smith will be receptive to meeting with you.

Hairdressers work for tips, so offer them a flat fee if their referral ends up getting you a contract. You, in turn, can offer to promote their services to your clients. Bridal parties and guests of honor often need a hairstylist who is willing to come to the home or event venue early to help with day-of-event styling.

Local jewelers who specialize in engagement rings can be excellent partners because couples buy the ring before they start planning wedding details. Get to know the area jewelers and offer them a commission if they recommend your catering services to engaged couples. You can help the jewelers by recommending their shops to your clients. You might also be able to hold a special tasting at the jewelry store, allowing the jeweler to showcase his special line of rings and bracelets to your customers.

E ssential

If the event and wedding planners you approach are skeptical about using a relatively new vendor, arrange a special tasting for them. The time and effort you spend winning them over will be worthwhile. Referrals from this group are invaluable.

Stores that sell bridal gowns, bridal accessories, and dresses for mothers of the bridal party can also be helpful promotional partners. Any bride who's bought a gown gets to know her salesperson pretty well after going for a few fittings. Offer the salespeople a commission if their recommendation turns into new business for you.

Partnering with Event Planners

There are always more prospective clients than you'll have time to e-mail, call, or meet. Partnering with professional event planners is an efficient way to make your services known to more potential clients. Event planners always need great, reliable caterers to work with, and most will be glad to know about you. Offer them a commission or a minimum flat fee if they provide a lead that results in a catering contract for you.

Public Relations Partners

One way to generate local buzz is to partner with local media outlets. Whether it's a local newspaper, magazine, radio, or television station, they all need to keep their readers buying and tuned in. Newspapers and radio stations run contests throughout the year to keep their readers and listeners loyal.

When you offer to provide your services for free, make sure the total number of guests you'll be serving and the total monetary value of your services is within reason. You don't want to be stuck providing 100 people with a free steak and lobster dinner.

Suggest a contest where you'll cater a wedding for a local couple that's chosen by the readers of a local newspaper. This is a good way for the newspaper to create some positive publicity and goodwill. In return, you'll negotiate for the newspaper to cover the wedding and promote your services in a series of articles about the wedding.

Attracting Partners

As you approach more people for cross-promotions, word will spread, and savvy business owners will start to approach you to make deals. As you build a cadre of satisfied customers, you'll earn a reputation as an honest, hardworking small business owner who's easily approachable. Here's a list of other ways to attract promotional partners:

- **Grow your business.** People like to work with growing businesses. The more clients you get, the more you'll attract partners.
- **Generate buzz.** The more people hear good things about you and your business, the more they'll want to be associated with you.
- **Promote your unique concept.** The more interesting your concept and the more differentiated it is from other catering operations, the more people will want to work with you.
- **Be easy to work with.** The easier you are to work with, the more partners you'll have. Listen carefully, compromise, and honor your deadlines. Deliver top quality services, and people will line up to be your partner.

Whenever you're approached by a potential partner, listen to what the person has to say. Give her five minutes, because you'd want her to do the same for you. If you're not sure about what she's offering, ask her to send you a summary of her proposal. If she's serious, you'll receive a followup within a week. If she's a bit shady, she won't put the details down in writing and you won't hear from her again.

Negotiating with Partners

Successful negotiations always give a similar amount to each party and are conducted in a nonconfrontational, objective tone. If one party profits a lot more than the other, the relationship is doomed to fail. Make sure you are negotiating in good faith with the person sitting on the other side of the table. If you're not sure that your negotiating partner is who he says he is or has the authority he claims, make a few phone calls. If he's legitimate, he won't mind. In fact, he'll respect the homework you're doing.

Keep the Negotiations Simple

If the negotiations are getting too complicated, then something is wrong. The best deals are often done with a handshake and a simple written agreement. Too many stipulations are generally a sign that something isn't quite right.

 Fact

Before you enter into negotiations, research your potential business partner thoroughly. Think about the questions you want to ask and the answers you want to hear. Know what you want to get out of the negotiations and what you will settle for in the end.

View negotiating as a collaborative process that solves a problem for both parties. Try to stay objective and keep emotions out of the process. Put yourself in your partner's shoes and try to understand where she's coming from. Ask if she has any concerns about your suggestions. Make sure you listen carefully to what your negotiating partner is saying. When negotiating, timing matters. Make sure your partner isn't tired or preoccupied. It's best to negotiate when both parties are relaxed. Explain what you need and why. Think about several options that would satisfy your needs. Do not argue or try to prove your negotiating partner wrong.

If you're not adept at negotiating, pick up a book on the subject and practice a negotiation with a friend. Make the practice negotiation as real as possible.

Adding a Business Partner

At a certain point in the evolution of your business, you might want to seek out a business partner. Gaining a business partner is a more formal arrangement than having a promotional partner. There are many reasons to merge with a business partner.

Business partners can provide complementary skills and resources. If you realize that your business growth is limited because you don't have the contacts you need to get contracts with major companies and private organizations, joining forces with someone who's worked with these major clients and is excellent at sales makes sense. Since you're a small company and can't afford to pay a new sales director much of a salary, you'll need to offer a sweetened commission rate of at least 7 percent. You might even have to make him a partner in the business, giving him some stock and making him a part owner.

E ssential

Realizing that you're overwhelmed and can't possibly manage your entire thriving business is another reason to bring in a partner. Perhaps you know someone who could handle all the office operations for you and let you focus on your kitchen talent. Bringing her in as a partner rather than an employee might be the best thing for the business.

Remember, a partner will have different motivation than even the best and most loyal hourly or salaried employee. You'll be able to attract a more experienced and higher-skilled person if you make her a partner.

⚡ Alert

Fifty-fifty partnerships don't work. Someone needs to be the tie-breaker, and you started the business. Make sure you retain majority control with any partner and keep at least 51 percent of the voting rights.

Partnering with someone who has better cash flow, is more established, and can provide much needed resources is also justification for forming a business partnership. Bringing in a business partner with a different business model can strengthen your business. By partnering with a less seasonal business, you can ensure a more stable cash flow, which will allow you to maintain year-round sales staff. In this way, you'll have a better, more loyal staff and will be able to handle more clients and larger jobs.

Joining a More Established Business

Joining with a more established business will give you added clout with banks and other institutions if you need to take out a loan to buy additional equipment. Consider joining forces with an established wedding cake business, catering equipment manufacturer, or food trucking fleet. By doing this, you won't have to outsource as much.

Marketing your business will be easier if you partner with an existing, established popular brand. Rather than starting from scratch, potential customers will already recognize and trust the name of your partner, making the decision easier for them to try your services.

If you're just not making enough to stay in business, it may make more sense to partner with a slightly bigger caterer than to close up shop. You'll have to give up some of the ownership of your company, but you'll gain catering referrals and the use of other equipment and resources.

How to Choose a Partner

Be creative when considering potential partners. The most important thing about a business partner is that you trust him and that you work well together. Spend time getting to know your prospective partner and make sure that your personalities and work styles are compatible. Make sure you learn about each other during stressful days as well as more normal days. You might be able to work with someone when there's no deadline looming, but he might turn into Mr. Hyde when an event is only hours away.

Networking for a Partner

Networking is essential for finding the right business partners. Start by asking your lawyer, accountant, and other advisory professionals who they know. Meet with anyone they suggest who's willing to sit down with you. If they're not the right partners, then maybe they can introduce you to someone who is. Ask everyone you know, from your vendors to your clients. Eventually you'll meet the right person.

E ssential

Wealthy, happy clients are a great networking resource. Tell them you want to expand your business and ask if they know anyone who might be able to advise you. They might offer to help you themselves or provide valuable advice, especially if they're a lawyer, an accountant, finance expert, or consultant.

Some of the promotional partners mentioned earlier in the chapter can also make good business partners. A successful owner of a food importing company might be interested in investing in your company if you're willing to develop menus that showcase her products. An established local restaurateur may be interested in having you take over his catering operations if they're distracting him from his main business of serving his restaurant customers.

Fact

Check *www.nvca.org*, the National Venture Capital Association's Web site, to research venture capitalists who invest in food businesses. Enter local and state-sponsored entrepreneurship contests with cash prizes for winners. Present at venture capital fairs or forums. Check with the area SBA office or the nearest SBDC at a university.

Venture capitalists and private equity professionals are a possible source of business partners. These are investment professionals who specialize in investing in smaller, growth-oriented companies. Some venture capitalists and private equity specialists work at independent firms, and most investment banks have venture capital and private equity groups. If you know anyone in investment banking, try to network with them.

Venture Capitalists and Angel Investors

For venture capital and private placement, you'll need a good catering concept that can be duplicated or franchised, and you'll need to show that you're growing profitably. Venture capitalists will infuse your company with cash, but they will take a piece of the business and become owners with you.

Angel investors are another possible group. Angels are private investors who wish to support entrepreneurs. They may be experienced, retired professionals with money to invest, while others might be successful entrepreneurs who like to support other enterprising people. It's not easy to find an angel who will give you $50,000–100,000 for your company, but there are ways to try to find them. There are formal networks of angels across the country. While you're networking, ask if anyone belongs to an angel network or knows an angel. The Internet is a good place to start researching angel networks in your area. A couple of angel groups who will consider non-high-tech businesses are listed in Appendix A.

Becoming a Full-Service Event Company

Partnering with other successful entrepreneurs will allow you to create a virtual full-service event planning agency. With promotional, public relations, and business partners, you'll be able to offer every possible event-related resource to your clients in one place: your own. You'll be invaluable to your clients not only as a skilled caterer but also as an important information resource. The more you can offer your clients in an easy, efficient manner through high-quality partnerships, the more valuable you'll be.

Chapter 17

Catering Challenges and Equipment Recommendations

The catering industry is exciting, and it allows you to express your creativity in cooking, food presentation, and marketing. Having your own catering business allows you to be your own boss and serve people with your own menus, ideas, and creations. The industry also presents unique challenges. You'll need to overcome hurdles like buying the right equipment to hiring good kitchen and serving staff. This chapter provides some practical advice about what particular challenges will face you in the industry.

Equipping Your Business

One way to blow a lot of money out of your start-up budget is to buy too much equipment. The best plan of action is to buy little by little, and only add expensive pieces of equipment after you have a demand for them. For example, wait to buy a commercial-sized mixer until you have so much business that you know you'd need to use it every day.

Expertise

"After you buy your basics, buy equipment as you need it," advises Stephan Baroni, managing director of Hudson Yards Catering. Rent equipment when you need it, and don't waste money on equipment that you won't use often enough to justify the cost.

Catering equipment can be broken down into five main sectors: cooking equipment, food handling equipment, food preparation equipment, refrigeration equipment, and miscellaneous catering equipment. These products are used to store, prepare, cook, display, and serve food and to wash food, utensils, and crockery.

E ssential

Make sure to budget for each type of equipment that you know you'll need in your business plan. Price key items by checking restaurant supply sites online. Remember that the cheapest option is not always the best. Take into account brand quality and other factors.

Buying new equipment sometimes depends on the local laws in your area and whether there have been any changes or upgrades in food handling and food preparation laws. Other laws that can affect equipment purchases are ventilation and fire safety legislation. Check with your local building codes and zoning office or consult with a local professional to find out what changes, if any, have been made recently regulating the design, use, and sanitation handling for food businesses in your area.

Rising energy costs account for an increasing share of caterers' overhead, so many new catering products incorporate energy-saving features. In the past, catering equipment was built mainly for cooking performance, but today it is designed for improved energy efficiency as well. Consider energy-efficient equipment when buying new machinery.

Used Equipment

Why buy brand-new equipment when used equipment in good condition will work just as well? It makes sense to save money by purchasing some gently used materials. Stainless steel work tables, baking trays, sauté pans, and other items are fine when bought used. You can buy stainless steel tables at going-out-of-business sales and at restaurant supply auctions in your area. Some kitchen supply houses sell used supplies in addition to new equipment.

It's worthwhile to check your local paper's classified ads and any local restaurant or business trade papers for sales of used equipment. Also check *www.craigslist.com* and *www.ebay.com*. Call your local chamber of commerce and other business organizations to find out if they know of any food businesses that are selling equipment or going out of business. You can also ask your banker and attorney if they know of any businesses trying to sell off equipment.

New Equipment

If you need to buy a commercial stove to outfit a kitchen, it's worth buying a new one. Stoves have a limited useful life, and if a stove has been in a restaurant or other high-volume commercial kitchen for any length of time, it already has a lot of wear and tear. Your stove will be one of the most important pieces of equipment you use. Older stoves may not be able to keep a constant temperature, and thermostats on stoves do tend to become inaccurate as they age.

E Alert

You won't want to burn six dozen cookies or overcook an expensive veal roast, so make sure your oven is reliable. Always keep a thermometer in the oven to measure the current temperature. You can find a good oven thermometer in any kitchen supply store.

You'll also need a dependable refrigerator and freezer. If you buy them used, make sure you have the condensers, refrigerant, and electrical connections checked out carefully. Don't buy the units unless the seller plugs the unit in and demonstrates that it can keep a constant cool temperature for at least thirty-six consecutive hours.

Make sure to get parts and service warranties for any new equipment you buy. Also, ask local food professionals for repair service recommendations and keep the numbers handy in the kitchen. The last thing you want to be searching for is a repairperson if your freezer fails a week before Thanksgiving.

It's worth it to invest in brand-new cutting boards. You must have a separate cutting board for meats and fish and another for fruits and vegetables. If you're working with stinky cheeses and spices, have a third cutting board for these items.

Catering Equipment Shopping List

There are certain multipurpose products on the market that virtually every caterer knows and loves.

Bus Pans

Everyone in the food business relies on these heavy plastic receptacles to collect dirty dishes. They are cheap, strong, and incredibly versatile. They can be used to organize materials, carry things, and mix and store very large batches of food. Bus pans cost approximately $5–$10 each and last forever.

 Fact

Bus pans come in a few different colors, but black and gray are the most common. You don't want to draw attention to your bus pans; they aren't the most beautiful pieces of equipment. Their sheer utility is what makes them obligatory serving tools for every caterer.

Label your bus pans. Keep new, clean ones for mixing food. Use older bus pans to carry supplies and to collect trash from guests. Staff can collect trash and used plates from guests and put them in bus pans placed discreetly behind the bar or in other out-of-the-way places.

Hotel Pans

Hotel pans, especially disposable aluminum half hotel pans with lids, are indispensable kitchen tools.

They stack well, especially if they are full of frozen food and are staggered. You can buy perforated hotel pans for foods that need to be kept cool; simply place them in a larger hotel pan filled with ice. At a cost of about $1 each, hotel pans will be your best friend.

✓Expertise

Hotel pans are a "gift from God for caterers," say Philadelphia food professionals Robert Weinberg and Eric Matzke. They are the perfect size for ovens and freezers, as well as for commercial equipment. They can be used to mix, cook, cool, reheat, and serve food.

Chafing Dishes

Chafing dishes tend to look institutional, but they're still the best way to keep food hot during meal service. Chafing dishes come in a variety of styles and finishes. Some are designed for fancier dining rooms, while others are meant for cafeterias. Consequently, the cost of reusable chafing pans varies greatly depending on how delicate they are.

It's critical to fill the chafers with warm or hot water or it will take forever to heat the water using the Sterno flame, which is only designed to keep the water warm. The same rule applies to food; it's got to be hot to start with or the chafers will never get it up to temperature.

Disposable chafer pans come in sets with half hotel pans, the pans for heating water underneath, and a rack that holds everything plus some utensils and some Sterno. A disposable set will run around $20.

Many of today's high-end caterers have stopped using chafers and elegantly plate food in the kitchen and have staff serve guests off of platters. Discuss the use of chafing dishes with your host. Some expect that you'll use a couple of chafing dishes, while others will demand that they not be used.

Insulated Camcarriers

Camcarriers made by Cambro Manufacturing are portable plastic boxes made to fit hotel pans and keep them hot for hours. This is a great alternative to an extra oven. Many caterers will cook or reheat food in smaller batches in their oven and then place the hot food in hotel pans into the Camcarrier to keep the food hot until it is needed. These carriers aren't cheap, but you can purchase them from almost any food service supply company.

Fact

Camcarriers are designed to transport food and keep it hot enough to stay out of the "danger zone" (40–140ºF), at which dangerous bacteria can grow. Their sturdy construction allows them to retain constant temperatures for hours so your food won't cool down.

Camcarriers are a lifesaver if you're catering in a space that's far away from the kitchen. Keep the carriers stocked with hot food in your prep or staging area, and you'll have enough hot food for your guests all night long.

Stockpots and Bowls

Buy at least one extra-large stockpot and a couple of big stainless steel bowls. You can use the stockpot for everything from the mundane (cooking vast quantities of pasta) to the less routine (boiling whole chickens). Huge stainless bowls are great for mixing large batches of wet or dry ingredients and beating or whipping batters or eggs. Since they are nonreactive, you can use them for almost everything.

Portable Propane Cooking Burners

Every caterer and personal chef should have at least one portable table-top burner that runs on propane. These units come in handy for cooking demonstrations and omelet or other sauté stations at events. They can also be used to cook food if you're somewhere without electricity. These units will last on a single propane cartridge for approximately forty-five minutes of continual use or for several hours of intermittent use.

Plastic Containers

Invest in some clear, covered, plastic containers that can hold items you need as you take them with you from job to job. Have one container for dry grocery items like baking powder, flour, spices, and rice. Designate another container for utensils like tongs, spatulas, mixing spoons, and measuring cups. A third container can hold flavor extracts, olive oil, and other wet ingredients. Rubbermaid sells strong all-purpose containers, and they're widely available at stores like Wal-Mart and Target.

Glassware, Plates, and Silverware

Outsource special requests from clients like patterned dinnerware or colored glassware. However, rather than renting and re-renting the same glassware, dishes, and flatware over and over again, it may make sense for you to purchase a basic set of each, store it, and charge your clients a rental fee. Since you'll be providing the same services as a rental company, you should charge your clients the same fee a rental company would for buying, storing, and washing the tableware.

E ssential

Inexpensive but adequate-quality dishes, flatware, and glassware can be purchased at stores like Ikea and Target and from restaurant suppliers. If your average party size is 50–100 people, buy enough for 110 place settings to allow for breakage and items discarded by mistake.

Buy solid white dinner plates, bowls, and dessert/bread and butter plates. Choose machine-washable china that will not scratch or chip easily. Buy water glasses and wine glasses in a traditional stem shape. Riedel sells classic stemware for wine and wine tastings. Similar but less expensive glasses can be found at Crate and Barrel stores and online at Overstock.com, as well as from food-service suppliers.

Purchase flatware with a simple, classic design that is easy for both men and women to hold. If your hands are rather small, have a burly friend of yours test several different patterns. The same goes if you have large hands; invite a petite friend to try out your top flatware choices. Make sure the flatware won't easily bend. It doesn't make sense to eat great food with cheap silverware.

Personal Chef Equipment Shopping List

Personal chefs require different equipment than caterers. Since personal or private chefs typically use in-home noncommercial-grade equipment, smaller sized equipment suitable for cooking for two, four, or six people makes a better choice.

E ssential

Personal chefs can set themselves apart from the competition much like caterers by offering specialized menus for clients. Decide whether you want to add a personalized touch to your business with your equipment, particularly if you specialize in the creation of a specific type of food, such as sushi.

If you cook in a client's home, you may be able to use their cookware. When you have your initial client meeting, take a full inventory of the pots, pans, casseroles, knives, gadgets, and measuring utensils. Some clients will have beautiful fully outfitted kitchens, and you'll only have to bring your recipes, the groceries, and storage containers. Other clients will be poorly equipped, and it will be worth your while to bring your own sauté pans, stockpots, and casserole dishes with you to ensure that the food cooks evenly and that you have the right equipment.

Since personal chefs have to transport equipment, select pieces that have multiple uses. Pie pans, for example, make great breading plates and cooking pans. Bus pans and hotel pans, as mentioned above, have dozens of uses. Additional staples for every personal chef include the following:

- **A wheeled cart** for transporting pots and pans and heavy groceries.
- **Knives.** Every professional chef needs her own knife set. Whether it's the same one you got in cooking school or a newer set, it's always better to use your own knives. You'll know how sharp they are and you'll be used to the handgrips.
- **A large, dependable food processor.** They're great for chopping and mincing just about everything.
- **Cooking utensils.** Always carry several pairs of tongs for sautéing and grilling. Carry a meat thermometer and a deep-fat thermometer. Also travel with a ladle, large stirring spoons, a spatula, and a large slotted spoon for draining.
- **Clean dishtowels, paper towels, potholders, and clean sponges.**
- **Staples** like seasoning salt, salt and pepper grinders, baking powder, extra-virgin olive oil, fresh parsley, and thickeners like cornstarch.

☼ Alert

If you're used to cooking on thick stainless steel or anodized aluminum, for example, bring your own cookware. Your pots will be well seasoned, and you'll know what to expect from them. By using your own cookware, you'll have more to carry, but you won't be in danger of scratching or burning your clients' expensive cookware.

Even if you're cooking in a commercial kitchen and delivering your meals, you'll need to use regular home-sized pots and pans to cook most meals, since every client will have his own preference. Large, commercial-sized pots can be used to cook large amounts of rice, green beans, and other basic dishes for larger numbers of clients at one time.

Buy commercial-grade thermal storage bags or containers for transporting groceries in warm weather. You can buy foil-lined collapsible bags, or the larger Camcarriers mentioned above. You'll need a good supply of plastic or foil containers with lids for storing meals in the client's refrigerator or freezer. Restaurant supply companies carry these food-storage items and sell each size by the case. You can check styles, sizes, and prices at *www.webstaurantstore.com*.

Catering Challenges

Every business faces specific challenges inherent in its particular industry. Some businesses face stiff price competition, others have to constantly change their business model. Catering presents unique challenges, most stemming from the fact that there are many uncontrollable factors business owners must deal with.

Constant Change

From fluctuating guest counts and seating changes to weather delays, nothing in catering is static. These changes can seem daunting for an inexperienced caterer, but it's part of the business.

✓Expertise

"I've often said that the *c* in catering stands for changes, because up until the event starts, we're constantly dealing with last minute changes," says Stephan Baroni, managing director of Hudson Yards Catering. This is the nature of the business, and caterers set themselves up for success.

All caterers face the same challenges. The only difference is that the more experience you have, the better equipped you are to face the challenges head-on. The more challenges you face, the easier they become to meet. With experience, you also can avoid some of the biggest obstacles with careful planning and execution.

Hiring and Retaining Staff

Like restaurateurs, the biggest challenge you'll face is hiring good kitchen help and service staff. Hiring and keeping staff is difficult, given the wages you can afford to pay and the seasonal nature of the work. Much of the country is experiencing relatively low unemployment rates, and many young people are seeking more technical jobs, so the labor pool for catering help is tight.

Look to hire staff from different places. Young aspiring actors, singers, and dancers often work catering shifts to pay the bills. Place ads and put up notices at performing arts schools and coffee houses where artists hang out. Post ads for part-time help at women's organizations and community centers. Keep an open mind. A retired fifty- or sixty-year-old who's in shape and likes to work may be a good addition to your team. Also look for student interns. Call the employment offices of local high schools, cooking schools, and colleges and let them know that you'll mentor interns. Some students might be able to stay on part-time after their internship is over.

Trying to Control the Uncontrollable

In catering, you have to deal with many factors that are completely out of your control as a business operator. You need to be flexible and conquer the urge to manage every detail around you. Catering simply isn't a profession where you can be a control freak and survive with your sanity (and your business) intact. There are a number of X factors you'll have to account for in every job, and no two jobs will have the same combination of unknowns.

You're dealing with a live product, namely your food and servers. While you can control them to the best of your ability, you cannot prevent all accidents from happening. Somebody will drop a box of eggs, and a case of wine will get jostled too much when it goes over a pothole in a street. You have to be prepared to repair broken items and allow for some breakage or lost product.

Part of being an excellent caterer is being able to think on your feet and come up with quick contingency plans. If you drop a platter of hors d'oeuvres, then figure out how to come up with a quick alternative.

✓Expertise

"Often we are catering events in locations such as cultural institutions or offices, which really aren't designed for entertaining. It is our job to figure out how it can happen and happen well. Sometimes we are at the mercy of space limitations and find our kitchen quite a distance from the guests, and keeping food hot, for example, while it 'travels' the distance can be a challenge," explains Stephan Baroni, managing director of Hudson Yards Catering.

Food Safety

Keeping food safe and maintaining it at the right temperatures is a challenge. The key to keeping food safe is constantly monitoring it and properly training and supervising your staff. Food safety starts when you get the ingredients in your hands. The ingredients must be quickly refrigerated or frozen. The process continues when you defrost foods and start to cook refrigerated ingredients.

Hot foods must be cooled quickly and stored properly if they're not being consumed right away. A good tip for quickly cooling food that must be refrigerated is to pour the contents onto a frozen sheet pan, thus spreading it out onto a larger surface area. Once the food is at room temperature, you can pack it and refrigerate it. Nothing should go into the freezer until it has been in the refrigerator for at least a day.

The best way to get staff to follow safe food-handling procedures is to set a good example. Anytime a chef enters a kitchen, she should immediately go to the sink and wash her hands thoroughly with soap and water and dry them on a clean towel.

Sanitation and disposal offers its own challenges to caterers. Sometimes caterers have to serve large numbers of guests in a short period of time in a hot outdoor or indoor space. Large quantities of refuse are generated, and it must be kept away from perishable foods that guests will consume. Unlike restaurants and other food retailers who have on-site refrigerated rooms to store garbage, off-site caterers don't usually have that kind of facility available to them.

Event Logistics

Caterers must anticipate the flow of guests and prevent human log-jams. Experience dictates that the bar and the food are in completely different areas of a room, or in different rooms. An inexperienced host might want the bar and the food near each other, thinking that it's convenient for guests. In reality, it's a disaster waiting to happen. Lines for each meld together, and neither moves efficiently.

E Alert

If you set up a buffet, make sure that people can help themselves from both sides of the table. The buffet line will move faster, and people will be able to serve themselves more efficiently. This drastically reduces the amount of time the last tables have to sit with empty stomachs.

Estimating the quantity of food needed for a particular job is a big challenge, since every crowd is different. The amount of food people will eat varies with the time of day and even the temperature of the event space. If the event is outdoors on a very hot day, for example, people will tend to eat less and drink a lot more. Light, cool foods like cold soups and salads will be consumed before hot foods.

Even the menu choices will dictate how much to make. You might need to make more of a lighter food, like a seared tuna Caesar salad, for example, than barbecue pulled pork sandwiches. People never eat as much cold food as hot food. Even though you should usually offer some cold salad, whether it be a mixed green salad, tabbouleh, or pasta salad, allocate a relatively smaller portion per guest compared to a hot side dish.

E ssential

If you are serving passed hors d'oeuvres or a plated meal, discuss the guest-to-server ratio with your client. Having the correct number of servers is crucial to ensuring that all guests are served in a timely manner.

Estimating alcohol amounts is just as difficult as the food. Negotiate with the liquor vendor to be able to return any unchilled and unopened wine, beer, and liquor bottles. Always buy more ice than you think you'll need. It's cheap and will be sorely missed if you run out, especially during warm-weather events.

Keep guests out of the kitchen. Discuss with your client ahead of time how important it is to keep the cooking area clear of guests so that no accidents occur and you and the staff can work efficiently.

Challenges for Personal Chefs

While personal chefs are spared from some of the specific challenges of trying to serve many people efficiently in a space that's often not designed for such a purpose, there are some particular challenges that they must face.

Many people don't realize how lonely being a personal chef can be. Since you generally won't see your clients except during the initial meeting, you'll be driving, shopping, and cooking on your own most of the day. Some chefs love the quiet and independence, while others need the noise and hustle and bustle of a restaurant or large commercial catering kitchen.

You will have to live without the immediate gratification of watching guests devour your creations. In most cases, you'll have to wait for feedback from the client, or a call booking another cook date.

Chapter 18

Useful Catering Tips

The preceding chapters have taken you step by step through the various disciplines needed to start a catering business. What follows is specific advice from successful, experienced caterers. There's no replacing experience as the best way to learn catering. While reading and research helps, nothing beats on-the-job learning. Here are the best tips and lessons learned from some of the country's leading caterers. Reading this chapter will save you a lot of time, money, and effort.

Lessons Learned

From catering thousands of events, the pros have assembled a list of valuable lessons, which would take you years to learn. Here's an abbreviated education.

Always Confirm

This may seem silly to even mention. You might think that someone who gave you a large deposit and who is planning a party doesn't need to be reminded. Experience tells a different story. Make sure that you have an e-mail address and multiple phone numbers for each client. It is also helpful to have a contact number for a friend or family member. Make sure to call the client a few days before the party to get the final guest count, and call the client the day before to confirm. Talk to the client; don't just leave a message.

There have been occasions when caterers have appeared at the designated house at the designated time only to find the client away and no one at home. Events fall through for a number of reasons, and sudden illnesses or crises do happen.

Don't Put Too Much Weight on Any One Surface

Don't let the words "the table *seemed* steady" be the last words you say to a client as you attempt to explain why half the buffet just hit the floor and three of the guests are sitting on their rear ends covered in shrimp salad. No matter how stable a surface seems, make sure to double-check the braces, screws, and other fittings each time you set it up.

☀ Alert

Carry duct tape or electrical tape with you, so that you can tape down any free-floating electrical cords that may get stepped on or tripped over. Bring a basic tool kit with screwdrivers, a drill, a hammer, and pliers with you to every job.

If you think you're putting too much weight on a table or piece of furniture, you probably are. Distribute the weight evenly and make sure that everything is out of range of jumping cats, dogs, and children.

Equipment Setup

No matter how harried you are, make sure that you do a final inspection of everything before guests are allowed to serve themselves or walk into an area you were working in. Use this checklist:

— Are coffee urns or slow cookers placed safely? Can anyone knock them over when they pass by? Are the cords safely stowed and taped up, so that no one can trip over them or pull them by accident?

— Are all floor surfaces wiped dry?

— Are all area rugs and small carpets taped down?

— Are there designated places for people to put down their used plates and cups, or will they be stacked up on expensive furniture?

- Are all knives and dangerous equipment washed and stored?
- Inspect all plated food and platters for stray hairs or foreign objects.
- Inspect all green salads for sand and blackened edges.
- In hot weather, make sure all perishable food is at the correct temperature and hasn't spoiled.

Plan for the Worst

The best caterers don't even flinch when the client tells them the stove just broke or twelve extra people are coming for dinner. Always have a backup plan. Carry charcoal and a grill as backup if you're cooking at the client's. Carry extra Sterno brand fuel. Always bring flashlights, batteries, candles, candleholders, and matches in case the electricity goes off in the middle of a party.

Essential

Have a clear plastic portable container just for emergencies. Make sure it contains an up-to-date first aid kit, masking tape, electrical tape, sponges, and anything else you can think of that would be helpful in an emergency.

Always bring more food than you need in case you have to stretch a meal or dish. Bring extra cut vegetables and stocks to stretch a soup. Bring additional supplies of rice and pasta. While you might run out of an expensive main course like lobster, filet mignon, or veal roast, make sure that you have enough side dishes to feed at least ten or twelve more people, and figure that into your cost. The added cost to the client will be minimal, and they'll be happy with leftovers. They'll never forget, though, that you ran out of food.

Count the Actual Number of Guests

To make sure that you don't have more guests than were paid for, make sure to count every guest, and count until you're sure you have the right number. Wait until everyone is seated to eat dinner. If you see an empty chair, make a mental note of it and check back in a few minutes to see if its occupant returned or if it's truly empty.

Focus on the Details

Catering is detail oriented. Make sure every detail is accounted for, and you have a plan for the event to run smoothly. Clients will notice even slight delays or missteps.

✓Expertise

"Clients will tell you the one thing you got wrong, not the 100 things you did right," says Jo Herde, director of food and beverage operations at Great Performances caterers in New York.

Catering is a labor-intensive, human business. No one has found a way to automate it or outsource it. Consequently, there is plenty of potential for errors, but there is also room to do everything right and give the client a stellar experience.

Practice What You Preach

The only way you'll have a well-trained staff is if you invest time, effort, and money into teaching them the right way to do things. However, all the training in the world is counterproductive if you don't follow your own rules.

You must be the hardest-working person on your team if you want your staff to work hard. If you want your staff to treat guests and others in a friendly, professional manner, it's up to you to set the tone.

Tips from the Pros

There are certain general rules that most caterers agree form the basis of catering protocol. The following is a compilation from professional caterers around the country who have decades of valuable experience under their belt.

Essential Rules of Catering

The first rule of catering: Never give anything away for free. If you give something away for free, clients will always expect freebies. You must train your clients to pay for your services and value your talent. You can give a discount for a charitable event, but make sure you cover all your costs and some of your time. This is your living. Other rules to keep in mind include:

- Always get a 50 percent deposit before you start working on a job.
- Quadruple your food cost to determine a base price for a client if you need to give an estimate off the top of your head.
- Always put in writing what you're going to do for a client and what the client is going to do for you. Don't rely on a verbal agreement.
- Be the most organized person on the planet.
- Be ready for unexpected things to go wrong at a moment's notice, and be able to handle it with split-second decision making.
- Hire fantastic staff that will work hard with you and not allow you to fail. They must be ready and willing to walk through fire with you.
- Have a sense of humor and use it often.
- Be ready for some intense manual labor.
- In order to protect your reputation, you have to know your limits. Saying no to something that you aren't equipped or trained to do or turning down an event on a day when you're already booked is better than doing it poorly.
- Book staff ahead; the good servers get booked early.

- Don't get into the rental business. There are enough bases to cover in the catering business without having to get involved in being a full-service rental agency. Establish a good relationship with a reputable vendor, and rely on them for your major rental needs.
- If you're in need of a commercial kitchen to work in, take a walk or ride around town and go into as many commercial kitchens as you can. If you can find a breakfast and lunch commissary that works mainly overnight and in the mornings, you might be able to use it in the afternoons and evenings for your events.

These rules will become engrained in your memory after you start catering and gain experience. For now, it's helpful to have a list to refer to.

Food Presentation Tips

Food presentation is as important as taste, texture, and smell. One way to differentiate yourself in the catering business is to excel at food presentation. This means that your plated dishes, food stations, and buffets will stand out from the rest. You're creating a whole atmosphere and experience for guests to enjoy, and presenting the food in an unforgettable way adds to the event.

E ssential

Be creative with food presentation. Gather ideas from magazines, cookbooks, and other food-merchandising displays you may see elsewhere. Keep photos and sketches in a "Food Display" notebook. Use fresh vegetables, produce, and herbs to spruce up your displays. Colored cauliflower or a display of fresh wild mushrooms can enliven a salad or soup display.

Design is a critical element in party catering. Make sure you have the right equipment for displaying your food. Many caterers add height on buffet tables by covering upside-down containers with table linens, but there are attractive, affordable accessories on the market that are specifically made for the job.

The Florida-based company Front of the House, for example, sells three attractive height-adding buffet products. The company's metal risers are manufactured with a brushed chrome finish that will complement any décor. To display the latest cutting-edge trend of small bites, you can use Front of the House's slanted bowl holder. The holder offers an alternative to flat food presentation.

Tips for Personal Chefs

Cooking for a client in their home requires different skills from cooking in a commercial kitchen. It also requires a lot of planning. The following is some very practical advice. Experienced Chicago-area personal chef Terry Riesterer (*www.paragonchef.com*), advises:

- **Don't spend a lot of money on new equipment when you start out.** If food has been your passion, then you have everything you need at home. Use your home equipment as much as possible until you get your feet well planted in your business and see what you can't do without.
- **Know that your first few cook dates are going to take you a long time to finish.** You will get faster as you gain more experience as a personal chef.
- **Wear your chef coat everywhere.** People will ask you where you work, and it's an open invitation to give your one-minute spiel on who you are and what you do. Have your business cards wherever you go, and hand them out.
- **Always promote your business, whether you're in a store, in a restaurant, in line at a movie theater, or waiting at a bus stop.** You will hear people talking, and you can look for the "in." If they're carrying groceries or talking about food, let them know that you can relieve their stress and save them time by cooking for them.

- **It takes a while before you generate enough income** to live off what you're making, so plan ahead and spend wisely.
- **Clients choose what they want to eat** 98 percent of the time, so offer them a lot of variety.
- **Join the APPCA.** The organization can help take your existing skills and shape them into a career.
- **Help other personal chefs around the country.** Exchange recipes, share pricing sheets, and network with each other. It's still a young industry, and helping others to promote it will help all personal chefs.

Know what type of pets are in the home. Ask the client before you get to the house if they have dogs, cats, birds, snakes, ferrets, pigs, or anything else. Be sure to know the size of the pets, especially if they're very big or very small and can get stepped on or easily escape from the house. Stipulate in your contract or on your pricing sheet that you are not responsible for pets. Let your client know that while you are in the house, they must be locked in a cage or room or put in a gated area outside before you arrive.

Always ask the client what kind of smoke and fire detectors they have, and have them show you where they are located and how to turn them off if needed. One caterer was flashing some steaks in a kitchen and accidentally activated one of the smoke detectors. He wasn't aware that the system was hardwired to the local fire department. When the fire chief showed up a few minutes later, no one was amused. False alarms can result in hefty tickets, so make sure you turn on fans, open windows, and avoid excess smoke.

E ssential

If you're going to be driving to many areas you're not familiar with, invest in a personal GPS navigation system for your car. It will save you valuable time. Portable systems are now available from several large electronics stores. You can get a unit for less than $500.

Always ask the client if they have an alarm system, and make sure you know how to turn it off if it is triggered by accident. Some caterers have been caught in otherwise empty houses by police showing up with guns drawn!

Personal chefs will usually have to enter homes and apartments when their owners are at work or away. Clients will leave garage door openers, alarm codes, and/or keys for you. Make sure you know how to get into the property and know how to lock or rearm the property when you leave.

Make sure you're on the security list to gain access in gated communities or apartment buildings. Let the superintendent or the local police know who you are. Give them some sandwiches or cookies when you introduce yourself; they may have client referrals.

Marketing Tips for the Personal Chef

Personal chefs, like caterers, will have to market themselves, even if they join a professional association like the American Personal and Private Chef Association, which matches clients to chefs. The most successful entrepreneurs market their business through a variety of means, so they have several ways of reaching customers.

Reserving a Domain

Many people will ask if you have a Web site. It's easy to design one and get it up and running, and it will be an invaluable marketing and sales tool. The first thing you'll need to do is find a domain, or a place for your site on the World Wide Web. The domain should match your business name exactly. A dot-com (.com) ending for a domain is the most popular. The "com" stands for "commercial," indicating a for-profit business.

After you have your domain reserved and your e-mail set up, you can build a simple Web site using specialized software like Page-Maker or the online software that companies like Network Solutions provide for their clients. You can build a standard five-page Web site in just a few hours, and you can post photos, cooking history, menus, pricing, and service information all for a couple of hundred dollars a year.

Targeting the Right Customers

Good targets for your service are working women and successful single moms. Many working moms with kids and a demanding
career would love to hire a personal chef if they could find one that
was reliable and reasonably priced. Offer to speak at local women's
groups.

Market your services to personal financial planners at local Mer-
rill Lynch and Fidelity branch offices. High-net-worth people who
use financial planners generally don't want to spend time on daily
chores like grocery shopping and meal preparation and are a great
source of potential business for personal chefs.

If you know of any local celebrities, try contacting their personal
assistants. Research the professional athletes who live in your area,
and contact them through the team's main office. If there are big
companies in your area, target the senior managers from the firm's
annual report. Call the company and ask to talk to their secretaries.
Tell them what you do and send information to them. Many people
don't use personal chefs simply because they're unaware that chefs
are locally available, easy to use, and reasonably priced.

Solicit Recommendation Letters

Ask clients for recommendation letters. If you don't yet have any
clients, see if you can find a small neighborhood event to cater, or
ask a colleague if she'll use you to cater her son's graduation party.

Even if you work at a discounted rate, it will be good experience, and you can get some solid recommendation letters for your Web site.

After you've cooked for them, ask a few clients if they'd be willing to write a letter of recommendation for you. Some people will write their own, while others will ask you to draft one for them. Ask clients who write their own to type them and print them on their letterhead, if at all possible. For clients who want you to draft a letter, e-mail it to them and ask them to sign it and print it on their letterhead. Once you have a few letters, scan them into PDF format so that you can e-mail them to prospective clients and post them on your Web site.

Chapter 19

Outsourcing

Outsourcing means hiring or subcontracting other vendors or professionals to provide certain parts of an event for you. You can outsource specific tasks or products. Outsourcing makes good sense for small and medium-sized catering businesses that can't do everything in-house because they lack the skills or resources. Through outsourcing, a business can seem bigger than it actually is and provide its clients with total event solutions. Knowing how to outsource, when to outsource, and whom to outsource to are crucial skills for any small business owner.

Why Outsource?

Some large caterers can afford to have in-house specialists for almost everything. Still, even large operations must hire outside specialists for special lighting and audiovisual needs, tent rentals, and other services.

Expertise

Barton G. in Miami has full-time floral arrangers and carpenters on staff for constructing custom food stations for clients. The company strives to deliver a total experience for clients, encompassing the food, décor, and service.

There are several reasons to outsource certain components of an event. Often, it's more efficient to outsource a complicated product or service than trying to provide it yourself. Caterers need to focus on planning menus and executing them well. You should leave areas outside your expertise to others.

Save Time

First, as you're well aware, there are only a certain number of hours in a day, and try as you might to do everything, there just isn't time. A good reason to outsource is to save time. If you just can't get something done to meet an event date, particularly during a busy party season, it makes sense to outsource certain tasks. Rather than stressing yourself and staying up all night before a big event, find a passionate, trusted vendor to create those floral arrangements or hand-dip those twelve dozen smoked salt and caramel chocolate truffles.

A supplier who specializes in floral arrangements or handmade chocolates will, most likely, be able to do a better job than you could, and your clients will be thrilled with the quality. The prices will generally be a bit higher because you're paying a middleman, but in the end, the guests will appreciate the quality and the high level of customer service.

☼ Alert

If you're booking an event during peak holiday time, plan to outsource the components that are the most time-consuming and reflect the higher prices in your proposal pricing. Plan ahead and have the prices for your trusted outsourcing vendors handy. If you think there might be a price increase before the actual event, protect yourself and add 10 percent to the outsourced prices.

Outsource Specialized Skills

Second, you'll want to outsource the aspects of the job you simply don't have the skills to perform yourself. There's no shame here. No one person has the skills to complete every piece of a complex event efficiently. Dozens of skilled professionals are required to set up most elaborate charity, corporate, and private events. Even if you're a talented chef, providing elaborate gum paste decorations on a cake may be beyond your ability if you haven't trained extensively as a pastry chef and aren't adept at working with this medium.

Virtual Full-Service Company

You'll want to outsource when you start your business so that you appear to be a full-service caterer to your clients. Outsourcing allows even the smallest of businesses the ability to offer a wide range of services without taking on extra overhead like additional personnel, equipment, and inventory. If a client needs a caterer who does ice sculptures but you've never carved more than your initials in a tree, then you'll need to know about ice sculpture vendors in your area and their prices and turnaround times.

E ssential

It is customary to mark up any outsourced product or service at least 10–15 percent, since you're providing a one-stop catering service to your client and saving them the time and effort of finding the specialty vendor. In effect, you're operating as an event organizer or as an event coordinator, and you should be compensated for the service.

Save Money

Finally, sometimes it may actually be cheaper to outsource something than to do it yourself. Unless you put yourself through school making balloon sculptures for kids at parties, it's well worth the money to outsource balloon arrangements to a professional who's adept at handling and sourcing special shapes, sizes, and colors. Anything that is outside your particular skill set should be delegated to someone who has those skills. It's a waste of your valuable time trying to master something you're new at.

When to Outsource

If you lack expertise in a certain area or don't have the staff or time to fill a certain request, it's time to outsource. Sometimes you might find yourself too busy to provide a client with hand-decorated cookies, so you might have to find a cookie specialist in your area. If you're not adept at making wedding cakes, which is really a pastry specialty that requires specific skills and techniques, then outsource the cake's production and delivery to someone who creates wedding cakes on a weekly basis.

If you're "in the weeds" and are so busy with bookings that you don't have time to bake the pies or make the chocolate truffles for an event, then call some trusted suppliers and have them do the pies and chocolates for you, to take some of the pressure off of you. Working yourself too hard and getting run down will only cause more problems in the end.

Remember you should outsource things that you can't do easily yourself or when you get a special request for something you don't usually do. You need to know at the beginning of the job what you will outsource and what you will do yourself in order to figure out the right prices to charge your client. What will be outsourced should be made clear to the client. To prevent any misunderstanding, you should let them know what items will be handled by a vendor other than yourself.

What to Outsource

Almost everything except the basic food for an event can be outsourced. Compile a comprehensive list of vendors you can use for subcontracting arrangements. This will make you look better to potential clients. Make sure your list is complete and contains only top-quality vendors. It's a good idea to have at least two vendors for each category, so that you have a backup.

Event Planning

If a client wants you to design the décor for an event and handle details such as booking the entertainment, ordering personalized gifts, making the place cards, and keeping track of responses, you can either refer the client to an event planner or you can work with the event planner yourself and create a virtual partnership agreement.

If you create a relationship with an efficient and reliable event planner, you can create a virtual full-service event agency, capable of handling all aspects of an event. You and the event planner can refer work to each other and pay each other a commission based on the total cost of the party. By creating this kind of value-added partnership, you'll further differentiate yourself from other caterers who can only provide food. Creating this type of relationship requires time and effort. Finding the right event planner is difficult; make sure you can work with them before you form a partnership. In the meantime, find a reliable event planner you can either outsource to or refer the client to. Start by asking friends and acquaintances if they've used an event planner for any recent weddings or big fundraisers. Also see if there's a chapter of ISES (the International Special Events Society) in your area. They're headquartered in Chicago, but have chapters around the country; see *www.ises.com*. You can find a CSEP (Certified Special Events Professional) in your area by searching on their site.

Wedding Cakes and Specialty Baked Goods

Wedding cakes are very time-intensive and require special pastry skills to assemble and decorate. These specialty cakes take dozens of hours to complete. Leave it to a specialist unless you're adept at it yourself. According to WeddingChannel.com, the average cost of a wedding cake is around $500. Find a local wedding cake specialist and get their pricing and lead times. Get some photographs of their cake styles to show to your clients and mark up the cost of the cake 10–15 percent.

E ssential

Since you're saving the baker the time and effort of the sale, see if they'll give you a discount.

You'll also want to outsource specialty cakes that require hours of decorating. Get to know cake decorators in your area who can create confections that look like everything from designer shoes to Scottish castles.

Specially shaped hand-iced cookies are very labor intensive and require a lot of artistic skill. These cookies can be easily shipped cross-country, so definitely outsource these from pros.

Chocolate

Fresh, handmade chocolates made with high-quality chocolate couverture taste exponentially better than manufactured chocolates filled with preservatives. A talented chocolatier who properly tempers the chocolate can make shiny, beautiful, delicious little gems. If you're not skilled working with chocolate, outsource to a professional.

Bread and Rolls

Except for easy-to-bake crescent rolls and biscuits, leave the bread and rolls to the professionals. Baking large amounts of fresh, delicious bread that has a hearth-baked crust on the outside and is soft and moist on the inside isn't easy to do. Bread is a living, breathing thing, and you must carefully control the kitchen temperature when baking it. When you don't have a lot of time to let bread rise naturally, you must do a lot of time-intensive kneading.

E Fact

Read local magazines to keep up on new vendors in your area. Visit new bakeries, meet new event planners, and keep track of businesses that move or close.

Bread artisans do nothing else but bake bread. Bread should be eaten the same day it is baked, so get to know the best bread baker in your area. Bagels and bialys should also be purchased from the pros.

Ice Sculptures

Ice sculptures must be outsourced unless you're trained as a sculptor, feel comfortable working with a melting medium, and are good with a chainsaw! Professional ice sculptures and drink luges require specialized transport and display lighting to look their finest.

Floral Arrangements

Floral arranging is both an art and a skill, and if you're not trained to do it, hire a professional. There are all types of floral arranging, from modern to traditional to Asian to aquatic. Florists use special supplies to build and hold floral arrangements together, and they use many tricks of the trade to keep flowers in place and looking their freshest for an event. Florists are also experts at making wedding bouquets, boutonnières, wristlets, wreaths, corsages, and other specialty flower decorations. Another reason to outsource floral arrangements is that floral designers have the best sources for fresh and exotic flowers. There are thousands of high-quality floral designers around the country. Check your local listings and get to know a couple of reliable and creative designers.

Linen Rental

According to Catersource, almost all caterers they surveyed offered linen rental. It makes sense for most caterers to buy a set of white tablecloths to cover buffet tables. Renting the same tablecloths over and over will waste time and money. If you can't launder the linens yourself, take them to a laundry and dry cleaner. Charge your client for the linen rental. Depending on the types of events you cater most often, you may also want to invest in a dozen or so round, white linen tablecloths.

Still, linen vendors should be near the top of your outsourcing list. You won't be able to accommodate all of your clients' requests for different linens. Find at least two linen rental vendors in your area and check the quality of their rentals and their prices. Make sure they deliver tablecloths, napkins, and other items that are in good condition and not stained or stitched up.

Liquor and Wine

If you don't have a liquor license, you'll have to outsource all beer, wine, and liquor procurement to an outside vendor. Check with your insurance broker and your attorney to find out the rules regarding mixing and serving alcoholic drinks in your state. In most cases, you'll be allowed to help serve the beverages if you and your staff are certified in responsible alcohol serving.

Find a couple of liquor distributors and wholesalers in your area, since prices can vary widely. Shop around. One supplier may have great domestic beer prices, while another may specialize in

French and Italian wines. You'll need different types of alcohol to pair with different types of foods for various events. Get to know a local wine expert who can help you create wonderful food and wine pairings.

Specialty Foods

From supplying crepe and omelet makers to cotton candy vendors and Italian ice carts, check your local listings to find specialty food vendors in your area who can come to your event and serve their delicious treats.

Additional Vendors

It's helpful to have a current list of vendors in your area who tackle different aspects of event planning, even if they don't provide services you could use for outsourcing work. You can use these contacts to offer joint promotions to clients, and you can recommend these vendors to clients.

Tents/Dance Floors

Large event tents require special equipment to erect, and you will need to find a reputable vendor for this service. Be particularly careful when hiring a tent vendor and don't shop for tent rental just on price. Nothing can ruin an event like a moldy, smelly, leaky, or faulty tent. Make sure a representative from the company will be on-site during setup and during the event in case anything goes wrong.

E ssential

You should keep a copy of a current certificate of insurance for all outside vendors you use in case anything happens and you have to contact your insurance company.

Furniture and Prop Rental

Most events will require table and chair rental. Find a reliable furniture rental company. Today, many event designers incorporate couches, beanbag chairs, beds, settees, and other props into the event's design. Many bar and bat mitzvahs and sweet-sixteen parties feature special lounge areas and use comfortable furniture. There are furniture rental companies that specialize in providing furniture for upscale events, stage productions, and trade shows.

Portable Restrooms

Renting a port-o-potty will not suffice for the vast majority of events. Such utilitarian lavatories are only suitable for construction sites and large outdoor concerts. If you're catering an outdoor event without available on-site restrooms, advise your client to rent a trailer with restrooms.

E Alert

Renting an upscale portable restroom can be expensive, and many have to be reserved far in advance. Neglecting to arrange for a facility can be a very costly mistake.

It makes no sense to spend thousands of dollars on catering, tent rental, music, and liquor and not provide guests with clean, comfortable restrooms. Skimping on providing appropriate facilities can ruin an entire party.

Entertainment

Whether it's a classical quartet, a ten-piece jazz band, or a comedian, clients will ask you where they can find entertainment. Get to know some of the local bands and agents who book local talent. Speaker's bureaus provide entertainers, and local music schools can provide both amateur and professional musicians.

Photography and Videography

Nowadays clients want their events photographed and filmed. Photographers vary in quality and professionalism. Some get in the way and make guests pose all night. Others are like stealth fighters and go largely undetected, taking terrific candid shots. Get to know some photographers and videographers in your area whose style you like. See some of their work and get their pricing.

Invitations

Get to know a couple of high-quality local stationery suppliers who do custom engraving and printing jobs. Make sure that they have a variety of sample books from different vendors reflecting all types of invitations from formal to contemporary.

Premiums

For customized T-shirts, napkins, beach balls, pens, picture frames, bags, and umbrellas, you can use an online premium company. Suggest appropriately themed customized gifts for your clients. For example, if you're catering a lavish picnic, suggest that the host create custom cushions, cup holders, picnic baskets, or umbrellas for each guest. Negotiate with the premium vendor to get a referral fee for orders you send their way.

Transportation or Valet Parking

Sometimes a client will need to transport their guests to an off-premise event at a garden, museum, or park. Get to know a couple of local limousine, van, and bus companies that cater to corporate and upscale clients. If you live in an area where water taxis or old trolleys are used for transportation, keep their information on file.

E ssential

When renting transportation, always rent a vehicle that is easy for the guests to step into. If there are women in high heels, make sure you rent a limousine or bus that has steps that can be lowered. Don't make women in short skirts and high heels climb into a van or other awkward vehicle.

Get to know a few qualified, insured, bonded, mature valet services. Having a car damaged by a parking attendant is a terrible way to end an evening, so your clients will be grateful if you're able to recommend a dependable valet service.

Balloons

Renting a helium tank and blowing up the balloons yourself is not the way to go. Balloon artists are efficient at what they do, and they know how to arrange balloons without popping them. Whether it's someone to entertain guests with balloon sculpting or creating a large balloon arch or special centerpieces for tables, hire a local balloon expert.

Lighting/Audiovisual Rentals

Corporate clients will almost always require a special audiovisual setup if their event includes any type of meeting, brainstorming, or award ceremony. Among the most common needs are microphones, PC or LCD projectors, screens, speakers, podiums, and special lighting. Some of these resources may be available at the event site. If not, keep a list of local vendors who rent such equipment.

 Fact

If you can't find a local vendor, Audio Visual One rents equipment and does conference and meeting setups across the country. Leave the electronics setup to a specialist so you can concentrate on timing each course around the day's speakers or the night's entertainment. Check out their Web site at *www.audiovisualone.com*.

Find a local company that specializes in event and meeting setups. They'll be able to provide lapel microphones, laser pointers, and everything else that speakers need. Meet with the company and get their pricing information. Discuss referring business to each other and giving each other a finder's fee or commission.

Whom to Outsource To

From the client's perspective, outsourcing should appear seamless. The client won't care what you made and what was outsourced, as long as everything is top quality.

Your reputation is at stake every time you use someone else to supply something for one of your events. Never outsource to anyone unless you've met them, interviewed them, tried their products, and checked their references. Since you're hiring the outside vendor, it's your responsibility to make sure that the supplier is up to your high standards.

Alert

Outsourced vendors must be re-evaluated at least once a year. What was once the best florist in town may now have new, inexperienced management. Don't allow outside suppliers to rest on their laurels. You can't, and neither should they.

Network

The best way to find excellent vendors to outsource to is to get referrals and to network. Ask other caterers you respect who they use to make gorgeous wedding cakes and custom ice sculptures. Ask local event planners and small local hotel catering managers for recommendations. Spend a couple of hours each week looking at local florists, bakeries, and chocolatiers. Visit the shops, see whose work you like, and keep notes about their products and services. If you find someone you really like, talk to her about partnering. Sooner or later, a client will ask you for a source, and you'll be ready with the answer.

Create an outsourcing notebook. Start with a blank loose-leaf notebook or binder and add a divider for each type of vendor from balloons to wedding cake suppliers. Take this book with you when you visit local vendors. Make notes about the business. Describe the style of cakes or floral arrangements they specialize in, take photos if at all possible, and paste them in the notebook. Insert price sheets, ordering information, and any notes about the owner or the products they make.

E ssential

Bizbash is a good resource for planning parties and events in the New York, Miami, and Southern California areas. Their trade shows are a great opportunity to meet dozens of potential suppliers and virtual partners in one day. Take a look at their Web site at ✐*www .bizbash.com.*

Outsourcing can be a valuable venture for you, your clients, and your fellow vendors. You will be able to guarantee your clients a high level of service, and you will bring new business to other vendors. As you gain more experience in catering, you will gain more business contacts and become more familiar with what to outsource, when to outsource it, and whom to outsource it to.

Chapter 20

New Trends
in Catering

The catering business is always changing and evolving, borrowing trends from the restaurant and entertainment industries and from popular culture. With such a competitive industry, you'll need to stay on top of what's new and exciting and get rid of what's old and passé. Change is one of the elements that makes the catering industry so interesting. Adapting to new trends will allow you to offer new products and services, differentiate yourself, and help keep you in high demand.

Caterers as Entertainers

Rather than merely preparing and serving food, caterers are now considered part of the entertainment. The role of the caterer has evolved from behind-the-scenes hired help to integral member of the main act, entertaining guests. Clients now look to caterers to provide excitement for their friends and family. Whether it's cooking right in front of clients as part of a chef's demonstration, providing a guided food tasting, or creating exciting food and beverage stations, catering is no longer a business of silent service.

Many of today's celebrity chefs are entering the catering business, and chefs who start in the catering industry end up opening their own restaurants.

Cooking classes have become so mainstream that cooking parties for guests are a twenty-first century form of entertainment. Instead of having a caterer fully prepare a meal for twenty people, guests now help chop, mince, and sauté. You as the caterer still plan the menu, buy the ingredients, and prepare the meal, but you make part of it in front of guests. Partygoers experience some hands-on fun, learn about preparing new recipes, and bond with each other as they don aprons and help prepare the ingredients they're about to eat. You and your staff finish the meal, serve it, and do all the cleanup.

Today, your role as caterer has expanded to include providing the headline entertainment. Your appearance, technique, and presentation skills are vitally important. As the entertainment, you can add "Interactive Cooking Parties and Chef Demonstrations" to the services you offer. You'll need to tailor menus to cooking parties, creating dishes that are fun and easy for amateurs to prepare without getting too messy. You can also offer special chef demonstrations, which highlight your specific skills. From preparing flambés to decorating cupcakes, the possibilities are endless.

E Alert

When designing interactive meals and demonstrations, make safety your number-one consideration. Make sure guests are wearing closed-toe shoes if they're working in the kitchen. Give guests easy tasks like whisking ingredients together and piping ingredients into molds.

Cooking classes and demonstrations can be marketed for all types of occasions, from children's parties with cookie decorating to bridal showers and cupcake decorating to couples dinner parties. Make sure you offer gift certificates and cooking party certificates for clients to buy as gifts for friends and family on your Web site and mention them when you're doing an on-site party.

Food Trends

From utilizing different ingredients to entertaining guests, the food you serve is more important than ever. People want to be entertained as they sample new and different dishes. Guests want to learn, see, hear, and smell how foods are made.

E ssential

The caterer can add excitement to his events by cooking simple but tasty dishes in front of diners. From simply grilling thin slices of meat for Mexican appetizers or mini tuna burgers for exotic sliders, finishing a dish, decorating, or even chopping in front of diners involves the guests and creates an air of entertainment.

Hand-rolling sushi and sushi stations are so popular because people love to watch the sushi artisans at work, plus they know the food they're about to eat is fresh and healthy. Serving freshly grilled and barbecued items is also very popular at catered events around the country.

New Cuts and Types of Meat

Restaurants and catering chefs are experimenting with under-utilized cuts of meats. Many of these cuts are flavorful and less expensive than traditional cuts like sirloin and filet mignon. With proper cooking and the use of delicious marinades, serving these cuts will reduce your food costs while keeping your guests happy. Flat iron steak is only around $5 per pound versus more than $6 per pound for sirloin steak. Skirt steak and boneless beef short ribs are also flavorful and great for more casual events.

On the high end, chefs and caterers are experimenting with Kobe (or Waygu) beef, which can cost $30 a pound for some cuts. Kobe beef comes from Waygu cows in Japan. The animals are fed beer and massaged, and the marbled meat is known for its rich flavor and tenderness. Some caterers are grilling Kobe beef burgers and buying Kobe beef hotdogs for their guests. Other caterers are buying grass-fed meat direct from the ranch.

Smaller Is Bigger

As guests want to taste the best that the caterer has to offer, they want tastings rather than one big portion of an entrée. Tasting dishes are in. Tastings are easily handed out to guests in square shot glasses on trays. Everything from shucked oysters with a spicy Tabasco chipotle sauce to sips of fresh, minty mojitos cocktails can be served to guests this way.

✓Expertise

Abigail Kirsch in New York features tasting dishes on her menu. There are several smaller tastes of different things composed on a plate. Creamed spinach, for example, is placed in a small, ceramic, white oval dish on the plate, rather than letting a creamy dish run all over the plate.

Call them bocaditos (little bites) or antojitos (little whimsies), Mexican appetizers are mainstream now. Freshly made taquitos, empanadas, rolled tortillas, and quesadillas are convenient finger foods, and they can be made with flavors from around the globe. Quickly searing thinly sliced meats over grills and serving them with chilies and grilled onions on soft tortillas will entertain guests, fill the event space with delicious aromas, and satisfy hungry clients while keeping your food costs low.

Innovative Food Stations

Newer types of stations are in vogue. Barbecue is in fashion across the country, and depending on your location, you can give it a special twist.

✓Expertise

With the increasing popularity of ethnic cuisine, particularly Latin cuisine, elaborate iced guacamole stations are appearing at events in major urban areas. At least three different types of guacamole are served in bowls on a station filled with crushed ice. The guacamoles should be served in mild, medium, and hot varieties. You can serve traditional guacamole; guacamole made with fresh mango, pineapple, and chipotle chili; and hot guacamole made with black beans, fresh lime juice, and habanero chili. Tier an assortment of colorful tortilla chips above to create a dramatic, colorful effect. Salsa, shredded roast duck, and other accoutrements can be served at the station as well. Tortilla cups, which can hold dips and avoid drips, are available for purchase from foodservice companies. You can jazz up the station by serving mojitos out of a large, clear glass spigot jar into shot glasses.

The guacamole station allows you to entertain and wow clients by having a staff member hand-grind fresh cilantro leaves in a traditional lava dish with a mortar, or *en molcajete* in Spanish. Servers can peel avocados and slice them in front of guests and add fresh chopped tomatoes, onions, and salt for superfresh guacamole.

Mashed potato bars are also in vogue. They're relatively inexpensive, easy to prepare, and are on trend with the popularity of comfort food and retro foods. You can use everything from fresh chives and artisanal bacon bits to farmstead cheddar cheese crumbles and homemade venison chili.

✓Expertise

Bill Hansen offers his guests a variety of different types of upscale mashed potatoes from sweet and red bliss to Yukon gold. He includes an assortment of fresh fixings to add to the mashed potatoes.

Baking potatoes and "all-purpose" potatoes like Yukon Gold, Peruvian Blue, Superior, Kennebec, and Katahdin have the best kind of starches for making mashed potatoes, so that you end up with smooth and creamy rather than lumpy results. New potatoes are just that—immature, small potatoes of a particular variety.

Innovative Cocktail Stations

Cocktails are in, and caterers are using fresh ingredients and artisanal methods to create festive, colorful, and delicious cocktails. From fresh, minty mojitos and martinis with fresh fruit purees to sweet, decadent chocktails, caterers are reinventing the mixed drink. With so many shapes and colors of glassware to choose from, serving beautiful cocktails has become easier. To please the nondrinkers and designated drivers among your guests, offer virgin and regular varieties of cocktails.

✓Expertise

Barton G., a Florida-based caterer that pushes the envelope, has pioneered the Nitro Bar. It's part of the cutting-edge molecular mixology movement, an offshoot of the better-known trend of molecular gastronomy. Nitrogen tanks are used to immediately freeze alcohol, which only freezes at very cold temperatures. Guests are wowed by the visuals—lots of "smoke" and instantly frozen alcohol.

Cocktails are a great way to personalize an event. If you are an experienced mixologist, you can create your own concoction and dedicate it to the wedding couple or the hosts of the party.

Vegan and Vegetarian Catering

Vegan and vegetarian catering is no longer just an exception. Approximately 5–7 percent of Americans label themselves as vegetarians, and this segment of the population is growing in both size and in sophistication. No longer is it acceptable for caterers to expect vegetarian guests to eat the salad and side dishes served with the regular meal.

 Fact

Vegans exclude all animal products and by-products from their diets, including eggs and butter. *Vegetarian* is a relatively loose term, but it generally refers to people who eliminate meat from their diets but may consume dairy and/or eggs.

Caterers now prepare separate, tasty dishes for vegetarian guests. The good news is that with the rise in availability and popularity of locally grown and heirloom vegetables, creating exceptional vegetarian entrées is easier than ever before. With fresh vegetables, all the chef has to do is highlight their natural flavor. Cooking with fresh tofu; hearty grains like quinoa, spelt, and barley; and a variety of beans makes some delicious meals. Use spices and recipe ideas from Indian and East Asian cookbooks, as these cuisines have wonderful ways of using vegetables.

Of course, *vegetarian* means different things to different people. Some people actually call themselves vegetarians and eat fish or poultry. Some don't eat red meat, while some are strict vegetarians and abstain from all animal flesh. As a caterer, you must talk with your host and find out what exactly they mean when requesting "vegetarian" meals. The guacamole, lettuce, and mashed potato stations mentioned above are great for vegetarian parties, too.

Food Safety and Health Trends

The caterer is an entrusted educator, food supplier and preparer, server, and entertainer, and there's a lot of responsibility that goes along with the job. With timely concerns about trans fats and their negative effects on health, clients will look to you to use healthy fats and avoid trans fats totally.

Trans fats are hydrogenated fats, fats that have been altered by the manufacturing process. Trans fats were created in the 1950s to extend the shelf life of food products and add texture to some products. Now that the dangerous health effects of trans fats are better understood, and we know that they adversely affect heart health, there's no reason to use them.

E ssential

Scientific studies show that eating saturated fat, trans fat, and foods high in cholesterol raises low-density lipoprotein (LDL), or bad cholesterol levels, which increases the risk of coronary heart disease (CHD). According to the National Heart, Lung, and Blood Institute of the National Institutes of Health, more than 12.5 million Americans have CHD, and more than 500,000 die each year.

There are plenty of safe, healthy alternatives to trans fats. Even Crisco oil has been reformulated to remove the trans fats. All you need to do is talk to your suppliers and make sure the oils and any processed ingredients you buy are trans fat free. Check the ingredient listing of any bread, pastry shells, tortillas, and other premade items you might use to make sure that partially hydrogenated oil isn't listed. If you have recipes calling for hydrogenated oils, you'll need to test them with nonhydrogenated oils because the flavor profiles will change slightly and the texture may be different. Experiment with several different alternatives until you get the taste and texture exactly right.

Another serious public health concern is E. coli and the danger it poses in fresh vegetables like bagged spinach. Harmful bacteria that may be in the soil or water where produce grows may come in contact with the fruits and vegetables and contaminate them. Fresh produce may also become contaminated after it is harvested, such as during preparation or storage.

☀ E ☀ Alert

E. coli causes diarrhea, often with bloody stools. Although most healthy adults can completely recover from these bacteria in about a week, some people can develop a form of kidney failure called HUS. HUS is most likely to occur in young children and the elderly. This condition can lead to serious kidney damage and even death.

Eating contaminated produce (or fruit and vegetable juices made from contaminated produce) can lead to food-borne illness, which can cause serious—and sometimes fatal—infections. Properly storing, cleaning, and cooking raw vegetables, meats, and fish is crucial for any caterer, as is knowing how to avoid cross-contamination.

Properly storing and maintaining the temperature of perishables not only affects the quality but the safety as well. Strawberries, lettuce, herbs, and mushrooms, in particular, must be continually kept at a temperature of 40°F or below. Fresh-squeezed juices from fruits and vegetables must be handled properly, as cross-contamination with peels and rinds may occur with improper handling.

Dessert Trends

Just as guests want savory foods for their appetizer and entrée, they want many tasty sweet confections for dessert instead of having one large piece of cake. Luckily, there is no limit to the inventive ways you can create and serve delectable desserts.

✓Expertise

Abigail Kirsch's trademark is her pick-up sweets—bite-sized brownies, cheesecakes, and other pastries available in eight different varieties. They're easy for guests to pick up and eat with their fingers while they're dancing or standing and conversing.

Cake Trends

More and more wedding cakes are departing from the traditional. Traditional white frosting pales in comparison to modern chocolate. Colorful designs that accent the wedding's color scheme are a popular choice for cake decorations.

✓Expertise

Jeffrey Stillwell of Abigail Kirsch says the bestselling wedding cake at the trendy Lighthouse at Chelsea Piers is carrot cake with a cream cheese icing. Nontraditional cake options and specially designed cakes are becoming more and more prevalent in the wedding industry.

Tiered, individually decorated cupcakes represent a trend that has being going on for quite a while. Separate dessert tables with a multitude of options allow guests to choose what they'd like to have for dessert instead of limiting them to one slice of cake.

Chocolate Fountains

Towering chocolate fountains spilling warm liquid chocolate are still popular. Varying sizes and heights of machines are available to rent or purchase from companies around the country. These machines attract attention, and guests love them. The fountains serve as a perfect centerpiece for any dessert buffet, and are cost-effective and easy for a caterer to use. You just have to add chocolate and a little bit of oil to the fountain. All you need to do is prep fresh fruit slices, marshmallows, and other goodies on long sticks, and the guests do the rest. Use your imagination for what would taste fun and delicious dipped in chocolate.

Serving Trends

Serving tastings of soups and other nonsolid foods in individual Chinese spoons is popular, and some caterers are going so far as to create edible spoons, mostly out of flour or wonton skins, to serve these foods. While this requires more kitchen labor, it's something that can really impress guests.

Caterers on both coasts are using foams of savory solutions to decorate and complete dishes. ISI Foods North America (*www.isinorthamerica.com/foodservice*) works with chefs around the country to create new kitchen tools for chefs to create beautiful and artistic effects. Their whipping tools are used to create Parmesan, basil, lobster, and other savory foams that put a delicious finishing touch on crab cakes, mashed potatoes, or fish dishes.

✓Expertise

Bill Hansen, a popular Florida caterer, offers his very own version of a surf and turf option by serving mahi mahi and beef tenderloin on the same plate. He has received overwhelmingly positive reactions from his happy guests.

Inspired by guests who order an entrée but never remember what they asked for, some caterers have switched strategies and are serving dual entrées. This saves time, speeds up the meal service, and offers guests variety.

Catering Display and Equipment Trends

High-end caterers are now building custom-built stations to display food at sites and in clients' homes. If you're adept at building things out of wood and plastic, offering this service is a way for you to differentiate yourself and offer this special high-margin service to clients.

Grills and Roasts

The Evo Grill is a round, flat-topped grill that comes in consumer and professional models. Caterers across the country use these grills to create excitement for their clients. You can cook a lot of food quickly right in front of guests, attracting a lot of attention. Tabletop and floor models are available.

Also popular are large roasting boxes for pigs, turkeys, lamb, brisket, and more. LaCaja China grills are large wooden boxes mounted on wheeled carts that come in various sizes, with grills on top. Prices range from around $200 to $300 per unit.

Tents

Entertainment tents have come a long way. No longer are tents the indoor party's poor cousin. Technological innovation in frames and fabrics has given today's party tents new features. Clear tents allow stargazing, and tents that don't require any interior support poles clear up the interior. Outdoor parties have come a long way.

✓Expertise

Barton G. creates elaborate custom-built stations and tents for golf events with *Fortune* 500 corporate sponsors. Barton G. has designed events for clients as varied as Turner Sports, T-Mobile, Neiman Marcus, and Gap.

Some party planners even create separate spaces within tents to create clublike atmospheres with separate seating areas, dance floors, and lounge areas. Carpeting, fresh flowers, and special lighting and audiovisual systems are also available for tent parties.

Portable Restrooms

Along with the evolution in high-end tents for outdoor entertaining have come upgrades in portable restrooms. Being able to provide your client and his guests suitable restroom facilities for an elegant party is important. The answer is fancy bathrooms in trailers that can easily hook up to home electricity and outdoor hoses. Many of these trailers are designed for use at outdoor corporate events, outdoor pro sporting events, or on movie sets, and are now increasingly being rented for private parties and weddings. These trailers aren't always easy to find, and prices can be in the thousands of dollars for an evening. But if the client is throwing an extravagant party, making sure his guests have a comfortable place to freshen up is a necessity.

This part of the rental industry is growing. You may even want to partner with a company that specializes in building or renting such trailers and high-end tents. Since these trailers are in short supply, investing in buying or building one in your area may make sense and help to keep you in demand.

Insulated Bags

For delivering food without the mess of ice or dry ice, try transporting perishables in disposable plastic, insulated, snap-handle bags. These bags keep food hot or cold from kitchen to catering halls or event sites for up to three hours. They cost less than $3 apiece, can be reused, and hold up to thirty pounds. With triple-wall construction, these bags also can be imprinted with your firm's name and logo. Food trays, box lunches, chafing pans, cans, and bottles will slide right into these insulated containers, and the snap-handle makes it easy to carry things.

New Trends in the Wedding Business

There are an average of 2.4 million weddings performed in the United States annually. The U.S. wedding business is estimated at more than $70 billion in sales a year. Not all of that is catering, but a large portion of it is. As a caterer, you'll probably be involved in wedding catering at one time or another.

Commitment Ceremonies

Imagine a whole new segment of customers in the profitable wedding industry. Gay marriage celebrations are a profitable, growing segment of the business. While gay marriage isn't legal everywhere, commitment ceremonies and celebrations are on the rise, and the gay community is looking for vendors who will cater events with understanding and respect.

According to the U.S. Census Bureau's 2000 Census, there are approximately 600,000 homosexual couples living together, and commitment ceremonies are likely to represent a growing segment of the catering wedding business.

Brides and Grooms as Hosts

As couples marry in their thirties and beyond, many are finding that they have more money to spend on a wedding than their parents did. Caterers used to deal with the parents of the bride, who traditionally financed the nuptials, but more frequently the brides and grooms themselves are taking charge of the wedding budget and their catering options.

✓Expertise

Jeffrey Stillwell, catering director for Abigail Kirsch at the Lighthouse at Chelsea Piers, says between a third and a half of weddings are now being paid for by the couple. Consequently, brides and grooms are requesting specific dishes, themes, and details, since they're footing the bill.

You'll need to be up on trends for the thirty-something crowd, understand pop culture, and be able to relate well to Generation X, those champions of PDAs and e-mail. Most of them are not old enough to remember the 1969 moon landing, and they believe anything is technologically possible. They're concerned about what they eat and where it's from. It's the caterer's job to satisfy clients' wishes and stay up-to-date on trends.

Appendix A

Resources and Suggested Reading

SUGGESTED READING

CATERING

Hansen, Bill, and Chris Thomas. *Off-Premise Catering Management*. 2nd ed. Hoboken, NJ: John Wiley & Sons, 2005.

MARKETING

Antion, Tom. *The Ultimate Guide to Electronic Marketing for Small Business: Low-Cost/High-Return Tools and Techniques That Really Work*. Hoboken, NJ: John Wiley & Sons, 2005.

Bradburn, Norman M., Seymour Sudman, and Brian Wansink. *Asking Questions: The Definitive Guide to Questionnaire Design—For Market Research, Political Polls, and Social and Health Questionnaires*. San Francisco: Jossey-Bass, 2004.

Levinson, Jay Conrad. *Guerrilla Marketing: Secrets for Making Big Profits from Your Small Business*. 4th ed. Boston: Houghton Mifflin, 2007.

McQuarrie, Edward. *The Market Research Toolbox: A Concise Guide for Beginners*. 2nd ed. Thousand Oaks, CA: Sage Publications, 2006.

NEGOTIATION

Cohen, Herb. *You Can Negotiate Anything*. New ed. New York: Citadel, 2000.

Shapiro, Ronald M., and Mark A. Jankowski. *The Power of Nice: How to Negotiate So Everyone Wins—Especially You!* Rev. ed. New York: John Wiley & Sons, 2001.

CUSTOMER LOYALTY

Denove, Chris, and James Power. *Satisfaction: How Every Great Company Listens to the Voice of the Customer*. New York: Penguin, 2006.

FOOD REFERENCE

Herbst, Sharon Tyler. *The Food Lover's Companion*. 3rd ed. New York: Barron's, 2001.

Mariani, John. *The Dictionary of Italian Food and Drink*. New York: Broadway Books, 1998.

Mariani, John. *The Dictionary of American Food and Drink*. New York: Hearst Books, 1994.

GENERAL

Bartlett, John, and Justin Kaplan (editor). *Bartlett's Familiar Quotations*. 17th ed. Boston: Little, Brown & Company, 2002.

CATERING PROFESSIONAL ASSOCIATIONS

National Association of Catering Executives
✍ *www.nace.net*

International Caterers Association
Washington, DC
(888) 604-5844
✍ *www.icacater.org*

American Association of Personal and Private Chefs
www.personalchef.com

United States Personal Chef Association
www.uspca.com

TRAINING FOR CATERING STAFF

USAWAITER.COM
www.usawaiter.com

HotelTraining.com
www.hoteltraining.com

EQUIPMENT RENTALS

PROPANE BURNER RENTALS AND OTHER EQUIPMENT RENTALS

Encore Party Rentals
www.encorepartyrentals.com

GRILLS AND ROASTING BOXES

Evo Grills
www.evo-web.com

LaCaja China
www.lacajachina.com

HIGH-END TENTS

Snyder Event Rentals, South Carolina
www.snydereventrentals.com

Classic Tents, Torrance, California
www.classictents.com

Starr Tents, Mt. Vernon, NY
www.starrtent.com

HIGH-END RESTROOM RENTALS

All Time Favorites
www.alltimefavorites.com

Mr. John
www.mrjohn.com

Black Tie Event Services, Chicago
Andy Gump Inc., Santa Clarita, CA

PORTABLE REFRIGERATED TRAILER RENTAL

Cook & Chill
www.cooknchill.com/trailers.htm

CHOCOLATE FOUNTAINS

Sephra Chocolate Fountains
www.sephrafountains.com

RENTAL FURNITURE AND PROPS

Props for Today
www.propsfortoday.com

FormDecor
Los Angeles and New York
www.formdecor.com

ICE SCULPTURES

Ice Sculpture Designs
(866) 877-3360
www.icesculpturedesigns.com

National Ice Carving Association
www.nica.org

PROFESSIONAL REFERRALS

WEB DESIGNERS FOR SMALL BUSINESS

Get Webbed, Inc.
President Bruno Dosso
www.getwebbed.net

CATERING LAWYER

Stephen Barth
Conrad N. Hilton College of Hotel
& Restaurant Management
University of Houston
(713) 963-8800
SBarth@HospitalityLawyer.com
www.HospitalityLawyer.com

BUSINESS PLAN WRITER AND CONSULTANT

Eric Gelb, MBA, CPA
✐ www.PublishingGold.com

INSURANCE

RC Knox Insurance Agency
Hartford, CT
(800) 742-2765 (Stacie or Janet)

PERSONAL FINANCIAL PLANNER

Kathy Sarmiento
Caterers Financial Network
ksarmi@bellsouth.net.
✐ www.leadingcaterers.com/
introducingkathysarmiento.asp

PROFESSIONAL ORGANIZATION TOOLS

Franklin Covey
✐ www.franklincovey.com

CATERING SOFTWARE

CaterEase
✐ www.caterease.com

CaterEdge
✐ www.cateredgesoftware.com

Synergy
✐ www.synergy-intl.com

CATERING RESOURCE WEB SITE

✐ www.bizbash.com

FOOD SAFETY

U.S. Food and Drug Administration
✐ www.fda.gov

SOURCES FOR OUTSOURCING FOOD

EDIBLE PHOTOS

Icing Images
✐ www.icingimages.com/
systems.php?link=1

SPECIALTY CAKES

Cake Divas
9626 Venice Blvd.
Culver City, CA 90232
(310) 287-2609
✐ www.cakedivas.com

Ron Ben-Israel Cakes
42 Greene St.
New York, NY 10013
(212) 625-3369
✐ www.weddingcakes.com

Cakes 'N Shapes by Edie
466 West 51st St.
New York, NY 10019
✐ www.boey.com/cakesnshapes

SPECIALTY COOKIES

Eleni's
4725 34th St
Long Island City, NY 11101
(212) 255-7990
✐ www.elenis.com

ARTISAN BREAD AND ROLLS

Sullivan Street Bakery
New York City
✐ www.sullivanstreetbakery.com

ARTISAN TEA

Serendipitea
✐ www.serendipitea.com

ARTISAN CHOCOLATIERS

Chocolate Celeste
2506 University Ave. West
St. Paul, MN 55114
(651) 664-3823
✐ www.chocolateceleste.com

Kee's Chocolates
80 Thompson St.
New York, NY 10012
(212) 334-3284
✐ www.keeschocolates.com

Lillie Belle Farms
Jacksonville, OR
Patti Phillips-Kahn
(541) 899-0115
www.lilliebellefarms.com

Jin Patisserie
Kristy Choo
Venice, CA

L.A. Burdick Chocolate
Michael Krug and Larry Burdick
Walpole, NH
Christopher Elbow
Kansas City, MO

Garrison Confections
Drew Shotts
Providence, RI
Michael Reccuitti
California

CATERING SUPPLIES

REUSABLE INSULATED BAGS

Your Bag Lady
www.yourbaglady.com

CUSTOM LABELS

iPrint
www.iprint.com

CUSTOM-PRINTED SHIRTS AND OTHER PREMIUMS

Custom Ink
www.customink.com

GLASSWARE

Riedel Crystal
http://riedel.com/website/English

DISPOSABLE FOOD CONTAINERS FOR MEAL STORAGE

Web Restaurant Store
www.webstaurantstore.com

POSSIBLE SOURCES OF FUNDING

Vermont Investors Forum
Curt Carter
Department of Economic
    Development
National Life Building, Drawer 20
Montpelier, VT 05620
(802) 828-5233
curt@thinkvermont.com ·

Arizona Angels
Greg Cobb, Managing Director
7000 E. Shea Blvd, # F1840
Scottsdale, AZ 85254-5261
(480) 922-1455
gcobb@arizonaangels.com

Gathering of Angels
Tarby Bryant
#4 Hawthorne Circle
Santa Fe, NM 87506
(505) 982-3050
tbryant@nm.net

United States Small Business Administration
www.sba.gov/sbdc

California—San Diego SBDC
Debbie P. Trujillo, Regional Director
Southwestern Commu-
    nity College District
900 Otey Lakes Road
Chula Vista, CA 91910
Phone: (619) 482-6388
Fax: (619) 482-6402
dtrujillo@swc.cc.ca.us
www.sbditc.org

California—Los Angeles Region SBDC
Sheneui Sloan, Interim Lead
    Center Director
Long Beach Commu-
    nity College District
3950 Paramount Boulevard, Ste. 101
Lakewood, CA 90712
Phone: (562) 938-5004
Fax: (562) 938-5030
ssloan@lbcc.edu
www.lasbdcnet.org

Illinois SBDC

Mark Petrilli, State Director
Department of Commerce and
  Economic Opportunity
620 E. Adams, S-4
Springfield, IL 62701
Phone: (217) 524-5700
Fax: (217) 524-0171

mpatrilli@ildceo.net
www.ilsbdc.biz

Massachusetts SBDC

Georgianna Parkin, State Director
University of Massachusetts
School of Management, Room 205
Amherst, MA 01003-4935
Phone: (413) 545-6301
Fax: (413) 545-1273

gep@msbdc.umass.edu
http://msbdc.som.umass.edu

Minnesota SBDC

Michael Myhre, State Director
Minnesota Small Business
  Development Center
First National Bank Building
332 Minnesota Street, Ste. E200
St. Paul, MN 55101-1351
Phone: (651) 297-5773
Fax: (651) 296-5287

michael.myhre@state.mn.us
www.mnsbdc.com

New Jersey SBDC

Brenda Hopper, State Director
Rutgers University
49 Bleeker Street
Newark, NJ 07102-1993
Phone: (973) 353-5950
Fax: (973) 353-1110

bhopper@njsbdc.com
www.njsbdc.com/home

Pennsylvania SBDC

Gregory Higgins, State Director
University of Pennsylvania
The Wharton School
3733 Spruce Street
Philadelphia, PA 19104-6374
Phone: (215) 898-1219
Fax: (215) 573-2135

ghiggins@wharton.upenn.edu
http://pasbdc.org

Texas-Houston SBDC

Mike Young, Executive Director
University of Houston
2302 Fannin, Suite 200
Houston, TX 77002
Phone: (713) 752-8425
Fax: (713) 756-1500

fyoung@uh.edu
http://sbdcnetwork.uh.edu

Glossary

Artisanal
Made by hand, referring to items such as cheeses and chocolates.

Bartering
The exchange of goods or services without exchanging money. An example of bartering is a plumber doing repair work for a dentist in exchange for dental services.

C Corporation
A business partnership that adheres to Subchapter C of Chapter 1 of the IRS Tax Code. There is no limit to the number of investors a C corporation may have; many large businesses are C corporations.

Catering
The term *catering* means "to provide food and service for." For our purposes, catering is the business of people who work in licensed commercial kitchens, who are properly insured, and who are trained and skilled in preparing and serving a variety of foods to groups of guests.

Certified Public Accountant (CPA)
An accountant who has passed a regulated exam and meets the requirements of her state.

Chafing Dish
A vessel commonly used for buffets to hold food and keep it warm.

Cook Date
A date that a personal chef arranges with her client to go to the client's home to cook. Often the client will be out, so the personal chef will have a code to bypass an alarm in order to enter the residence.

Costing
The assigning of a price to each service offered. In catering, this usually includes the costs of food, labor, and overhead, plus a markup. Gratuity is sometimes also taken into account.

Demographics
The measurable physical characteristics of a population, such as age, sex, marital status, family size, education, income, and religion.

Differentiation
A marketing term used to describe the distinguishing of one business from another in terms of specialty or niche within a field.

Farmstead Cheese
Cheese that is produced at a dairy using milk from the dairy.

Focus Group

A small group of potential customers brought together to discuss a new product or service for the purpose of gathering an unscientific sampling of feedback and opinions about the product or service before it is launched.

Glycemic Index

A dietary index used to rank carbohydrate-based foods. The glycemic index predicts the rate at which the ingested food will increase blood sugar levels.

Gum Paste

A substance that contains gums and sugar or glucose that is pliable and slow to dry, thus making it a good medium to work with in forming edible decorations.

Hazardous Foods

Foods that require special attention because of the danger of causing illness if improperly handled.

Limited Liability Company (LLC)

A business entity that is allowed the liability protection of a corporation and the tax benefits of sole proprietorship.

Line Cook

In the hierarchy of the traditional commercial kitchen, line cooks work under the sous chef to turn out meals.

Marketing

Advertising or promoting any product or service that's to be sold in a market situation, that is with buyers and sellers operating under the forces of supply and demand.

Outsourcing

Hiring or subcontracting of other vendors or professionals to provide products or services for an event.

Overhead

Fixed business costs associated with running a business, such as expenditures for rent, utilities, equipment, and insurance.

Pareve

A kosher term referring to food that contains no meat or dairy ingredients and so may be served with either meat or dairy dishes.

Positioning

A marketing term used to describe the process of advertising a business relative to its competition.

Prepping

Washing, cleaning, gutting, cutting, peeling, and chopping ingredients before they're ready to be used in a recipe or served to a guest.

Price Sensitivity

The extent to which price is an important criterion in your customer's decision-making process.

Primary Research

The direct collection of data. The researcher designs the research method, carries out the research, and analyzes the data.

Qualitative Data
Data that cannot be measured in numbers. Examples include interviews and written surveys.

Quantitative Data
Data that can be counted or measured in numbers. Examples include sales figures and number of employees

S Corporation
A business partnership set up under Subchapter S of Chapter 1 of the IRS Tax Code. S corporations may have a limited number of investors, and so they are most commonly small businesses.

Secondary Research
Data collected from outside or previously existing sources.

Service Charge
An additional cost tacked on to a bill to cover gratuity or other expenses.

Soft Costs
Variable costs, which include supervising, staff tips, and profit.

Sole Proprietorship
An extremely flexible business structure with a single person as its head. The single owner is not confined by other partners but also is not shielded from potential liabilities and financial responsibilities.

Sous Chef
The next in command after the executive chef. Pronounced "sue," *sous* means "under" in French. The sous chef is in charge of all food production and oversees the cooks. The person who fills this position must be very responsible and able to delegate tasks and make quick decisions.

Subcontracting
The hiring of a third party to provide services or products for a client.

Tableware
Anything that goes on the table when setting it, including glassware, serveware, and flatware.

Tasting
A meeting with clients or prospective clients in which menu items are showcased for sampling.

Up-Sell
To upgrade or add on options that increase the value of a product or service and allow the caterer to charge a premium.

Vegan
A person who abstains from consuming or using animal products of any kind.

Vegetarian
A person who relies on a non-meat diet; the diet may or may not include animal products such as dairy and/or eggs.

Personal Chef Client Information Form (LDA Form)

Your Business Name
(555) 555-5555
www.yourbusinessname.com
Your Business Slogan

Client Name(s): _____

Date: _____

Address: _____

_____

Number of Adults: _____

Number of Children: _____

City: _____ State: _____

Zip: _____ Phone: _____

E-Mail: _____

Cell: _____

Children's Names and Ages:

_____

Pets? Names: _____

How did you hear about our business?

_____

_____

Special requirements for your meals

❏ Low Fat ❏ No Fat ❏ Vegan ❏ Vegetarian
❏ Low Carb ❏ Diabetic ❏ Sugar Sub. ❏ Lactose Intolerant
❏ Light Salt ❏ No Salt ❏ Organic ❏ Wheat Free
                                    ❏ None

Comments: _____

_____

Special medical concerns : _____

❏ Weight ❏ Recent ❏ Chemo ❏ High ❏ Diabetic
Loss Surgery ❏ Cardiac Cholesterol ❏ None
❏ High Blood ❏ Food Condition
Pressure Allergy

Comments: _____

_____

Food sensitivities or specific allergies: _____

_____

❏ Vinegar ❏ Nuts ❏ Alcohol ❏ None
❏ Garlic ❏ Onions ❏ Bell ❏ Shellfish
❏ Nuts ❏ Other Peppers ❏ Mushrooms

Comments: _____

_____

Special medical concerns: _____

Global Cuisines You Enjoy

❏ Mexican ❏ Asian ❏ Thai ❏ Middle ❏ Italian
❏ French ❏ Greek ❏ German Eastern ❏ Other

Comments: _____

_____

How would you like your food to be spiced?

❑ Wave the bottle over the dish and call it spicy   ❑ Make it mild   ❑ Burn, baby, burn!

As a main dish, would you enjoy

Soup

❑ Yes   ❑ No   ❑ Hot   ❑ Cold

Comments:_____

_____

Salad

❑ Yes   ❑ No   ❑ Hot   ❑ Cold

Comments:_____

_____

Pasta

❑ Yes   ❑ No   ❑ Hot   ❑ Cold

Comments:_____

_____

How often per month do you eat in a restaurant?

_____

_____

Where do you go?

_____

_____

How often per month do you eat takeout or delivery?

_____

_____

Where is it from?

_____

_____

Beef   ❏ Never   ❏ Once in a while   ❏ A lot

             ❏ Ground   ❏ Steaks   ❏ Roast   ❏ Ribs

             ❏ Tenderloin ❏ Fillet

*Comments:*_____

_____

Pork   ❏ Never   ❏ Once in a while   ❏ A lot

             ❏ Ground   ❏ Chops   ❏ Roast   ❏ Ribs

             ❏ Tenderloin ❏ Fillet

Comments: _____

_____

Chicken ❏ Never   ❏ Once in a while   ❏ A lot

             ❏ Dk. Meat   ❏ Wt. Meat   ❏ Both (dark and
                                          white meat)

             ❏ Skin   ❏ No skin   ❏ Ground

Comments: _____

_____

Turkey   ❑ Never   ❑ Once in a while   ❑ A lot

             ❑ Dk. Meat   ❑ Wt. Meat   ❑ Both (dark and white meat)

             ❑ Skin   ❑ No skin   ❑ Ground

Comments: _____

_____

Seafood/ Fresh Fish   ❑ Never   ❑ Once in a while   ❑ A lot

             ❑ Lobster   ❑ Crab   ❑ Oysters   ❑ Scallops

             ❑ Shrimp   ❑ Tuna   ❑ Clams   ❑ Catfish

             ❑ Haddock   ❑ Shark   ❑ Salmon   ❑ Orange roughy

             ❑ Flounder   ❑ Perch   ❑ Trout

Comments: _____

_____

Vegetarian   ❑ Beans   ❑ Nuts   ❑ Grains

             ❑ Bulgur   ❑ Cheeses   ❑ Tofu

Comments: _____

_____

General questions about your likes and dislikes, meal packaging, etc.

Do you like to eat fresh breads or rolls with your meals?
❑ Yes
❑ No

If so, what are your favorites?

_____

_____

_____

_____

Do you like tossed salads with your meals?
❑ Yes
❑ No

Favorite Greens:

_____

Do you like cherry/grape tomatoes?
❑ Yes
❑ No

Are there any fruits or vegetables you dislike?
❑ Yes
❑ No

Comments: _____

_____

Are there foods/spices that people eat and you can't figure out why?
❑ Yes
❑ No

Comments: _____

_____

May I cook with wine and/or liquors? (or any other alcoholic
substances, i.e., extracts)
❑ Yes
❑ No

Comments: _____

_____

Would you like meals prepared for you to cook on the grill?
❑ Yes
❑ No

Comments: _____

_____

List any favorite recipes that you no longer choose to prepare yourself that I can prepare for you:

_____

_____

_____

Is any member of your household on a weight-loss program?
❏ Yes
❏ No

Comments: _____

_____

Would you like portion control?
❏ Yes
❏ No

Do you like your containers to be:
❏ Microwaveable
❏ Oven safe

If you were walking the "Green Mile," what would be your last meal?

_____

_____

_____

_____

_____

_____

_____

_____

_____

If I'm cooking in your home, please note any security arrangements necessary for me to be able to enter your home:

_____

_____

Any other comments or concerns:

_____
_____
_____
_____
_____
_____
_____
_____
_____
_____
_____
_____
_____
_____
_____
_____
_____
_____
_____
_____
_____
_____
_____
_____
_____

(555) 555-5555   **Your Business Name**

www.yourbusinessname.com

Index

The Everything® Career Guide Series

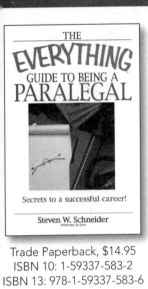

Trade Paperback, $14.95
ISBN 10: 1-59337-583-2
ISBN 13: 978-1-59337-583-6

THE
EVERYTHING
GUIDE TO BEING A
REAL ESTATE
AGENT

Secrets to a successful career!

Shahri Masters
Author of The Everything® Homeselling Book, 2nd Edition

Trade Paperback, $14.95
ISBN 10: 1-59337-432-1
ISBN 13: 978-1-59337-432-7

Trade Paperback, $14.95
ISBN 10: 1-59869-227-5
ISBN 13: 978-1-59869-227-3

THE
EVERYTHING
GUIDE TO BEING A
SALES REP

Winning secrets to a successful–
and profitable–career!

Ruth Klein

Trade Paperback, $14.95
ISBN 10: 1-59337-657-X
ISBN 13: 978-1-59337-657-4

Trade Paperback, $14.95
ISBN 10: 1-59869-417-0
ISBN 13: 978-1-59869-417-8

Helpful handbooks written by experts.

THE
EVERYTHING
GUIDE TO CAREERS IN
HEALTH CARE

Find the job that's right for you

Kathy Quan, R.N., B.S.N., P.H.N.

Trade Paperback, $14.95
ISBN 10: 1-59337-725-8
ISBN 13: 978-1-59337-725-0

THE
EVERYTHING
GUIDE TO
CAREERS IN
LAW ENFORCEMENT

A complete handbook to
an exciting and rewarding life
of service

Paul D. Bagley

Trade Paperback, $14.95
ISBN 10: 1-59869-077-9
ISBN 13: 978-1-59869-077-4

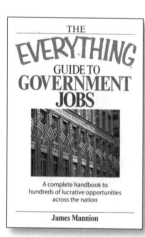

THE
EVERYTHING
GUIDE TO
GOVERNMENT
JOBS

A complete handbook to
hundreds of lucrative opportunities
across the nation

James Mannion

Trade Paperback, $14.95
ISBN 10: 1-59869-078-7
ISBN 13: 978-1-59869-078-1

THE
EVERYTHING
GUIDE TO STARTING
AND RUNNING A
CATERING
BUSINESS

Insider's advice on turning
your talent into a lucrative career

Joyce Weinberg

Trade Paperback, $14.95
ISBN 10: 1-59869-384-0
ISBN 13: 978-1-59869-384-3

THE
EVERYTHING
GUIDE TO STARTING
AND RUNNING A
RESTAURANT

Secrets to a successful business!

Ronald Lee, Restaurateur

Trade Paperback, $14.95
ISBN 10: 1-59337-433-X
ISBN 13: 978-1-59337-433-4

Everything® and everything.com® are registered trademarks of F+W Publications, Inc.
Available wherever books are sold.
Or call us at 1-800-258-0929 or visit *www.adamsmedia.com.*